SIGNWORK

SIGNWORK
A CRAFTSMAN'S MANUAL

Bill Stewart

GRANADA
London Toronto Sydney New York

Granada Technical Books
Granada Publishing Limited
8 Grafton Street, London W1X 3LA

First published in Great Britain by
Granada Publishing 1984

British Library Cataloguing in Publication Data
Stewart, Bill
Signwork.
1. Signs and signboards
I. Title
659.13'42   HF5841

ISBN 0-246-12195-5

Printed and bound in Great Britain by
Richard Clay (The Chaucer Press) Ltd, Bungay, Suffolk

Contents

Preface

In 1874, James Callingham, in the preface to his book, *Sign Writing and Glass Embossing*, expressed considerable concern that the word signwriter seemed to have disappeared from the English language. Not only was it missing from lists of trades, it was omitted from contemporary dictionaries. Sometime between that date and the 1950s the word was re-established, but was in danger of falling into disuse again about 100 years after Mr Callingham showed his original concern. This was due largely to the mass use of illuminated signs, particularly the development of plastics as a sign material during the 1960s. During this apparent revolution the hand produced one off sign did not disappear, it just became less obvious in the jungle of cut and moulded plastics. As the 1980s dawned and the popularity of plastic signs receded the skilled craftsman was 'rediscovered'. An ever increasing number of people began to appreciate the versatility of the signwriter and glass decorator and the individuality they could bring to even the most simple sign.

The revolution was not limited to the type of signs being produced, but affected the type of people who were preparing them. It was traditional in many parts of the country for signwriting to be carried out by painters and decorators. Any writings on the skills associated with painted signs were generally found in books on painting and decorating. Very few works were published in the first part of this century which dealt exclusively with signwork. As the emphasis on the work of the painter changed, signwriting became a very peripheral skill, and any new writings tended to omit references to signwork until it became an undocumented skill. By the same token it was dropped from examination syllabuses and in the 1970s it was being taught in very few places and no book had been published on it for over twenty years.

Now is the renaissance of the craftsman. Because the 'dark ages' tended to suppress craftsmanship there are few people available with the skill and training to pass on the essential knowledge to the increasing number of potential sign craftsmen. It is the purpose of this book to document the skills of the signmaker, namely signwriting, glass decorating and small run screen printing in order to supplement the knowledge of the teachers and to offer a training manual to the trainees. Not only does it instruct on drawing letters and producing signs, it offers advice on the materials from which signs can be made, how they may be fixed and how much they may cost. In addition it briefly describes a few other methods by which signs can be hand made. The advice is aimed primarily at the one man firm or the very small business – the backbone of the small production sign industry. But if the larger sign producers wish to develop hand skill processes, then this book will serve them as effectively.

The book should be of value to the young trainee who is able to attend a college or training centre as part of an apprenticeship. It should be of even greater value to the person who is determined to follow a creative and satisfying pursuit like signmaking and who does not have an opportunity to use a college because of age, geography or lack of local facilities. Although a practical approach is maintained throughout the book it is not intended only for prospective professional signmakers. Those people who wish to produce signs or use the signmakers techniques merely as a leisure pursuit will find the book helpful and sympathetic.

As a back up to the claim for a renaissance in hand skill signmaking a City and Guilds certificate is now available for the first time. The book follows a parallel course to that of the syllabus produced by Hammersmith and West London College which is the basis of CGLI 593 Signwork.

Acknowledgements

Whatever success this book may have will be due largely to F.C. Horstmann and C.P. Thompson, two teachers who instilled in me a deep appreciation of lettering and craftsmanship during my formative years. During this period they produced a large number of examples of lettering as part of their teaching which I have adopted blatantly for many of the illustrations in this book.

Since those early days everyone with whom I have worked, talked or taught about lettering has contributed to the contents of this book and to these people I am sincerely grateful.

Throughout the year that the book was being researched and written I consulted a number of people in order to guarantee accuracy and the documentation of current practice. Not all of them can be named but all of them have contributed and to them I offer my thanks. There are a few people I wish to pick out for mention because of their special contribution.

Maurice Burton whose enthusiasm and wide knowledge of the sign business has been invaluable, not only currently but over a number of years. Raf Staiano, a signwriter of exceptional talent, whose Roman alphabet I have used. James Clark and Eaton who showed me generous hospitality and help, and particularly Mike Snow and John Bonney whose contribution to the glass decoration section has been unique. Also John Holland of Pemberton Signs who added his expertise to my glass knowledge. Bill Lane of Aerosigns Ltd who put me right about banners. Tom Handley of British Airways who allowed me to see a jumbo jet being liveried. Len Gibbons who gave me his time, shared his expertise and read some of the manuscript. The kind people of Wolstenholme Bronze Powders, The Lettering Centre, Nero Signs, Hartington Publicity, E.T. Marlers, E. Ploton Sundries, A.S. Handovers, Signs and Components, Winsor and Newton, Rawlplug and Spraylat for their interest and assistance. And to my good friends who work under the title of Padim Technical Authors for their practical help and their permission to use some of their illustrations from *Painting and Decorating Information Manual*.

A special thank you must be expressed to Mary Thorold who typed the entire manuscript. Not only is she the best typist in West London, she must now be the best signwriter as well.

The final and most vital appreciation is due to my friend of many years, Harry Hooper, whose exceptional talent with lettering and signwriting is clearly displayed in the mass of illustrations he has prepared for the book. Without his generous contribution this book would have been a shadow of its present form.

One
Letters

Development of the Alphabet

Our alphabet took many thousands of years to develop. This development was concentrated in the Mediterranean area, with the Romans putting the finishing touches to it and spreading it throughout Europe. In 2000 years we have not changed the shape of the twenty-three letters which the Romans originally used, although we have added a further three characters to enable us to express our language a little better.

During the 2000 years of its existence, and particularly in the past 100 years, the alphabet characters have been used in a variety of different styles. The signwriter and the calligrapher have played their part in the stylising of the letters, allowing the brush and the pen to vary the shapes without destroying their identity. The printer also influenced the changing styles by introducing a more staid and mechanical aspect to the letters. With the great boom in advertising during the twentieth century and the rapidly growing commercial need to identify a product or a company in an immediately recognisable graphic form, the variations of the twenty-six characters of our alphabet have become limitless. The modern signmaker can be asked to produce a sign in any one of hundreds of different styles of published alphabets.

Faced with this colossal range of alphabet styles the trainee signmaker has great difficulty in knowing where to start studying letter shapes in order to be able to set them out for reproduction by signwriting, printing or cutting. One solution is to return to the source. To study the original letter forms used by the Romans and develop an appreciation of why letters have taken a certain shape and how the shape of one letter can be related to the shape of another.

Legibility and Good Looks

Most people reading a sign see it in two ways. One, as an easily understood text. Two, as a pleasant, good looking arrangement of acceptable letter shapes. The first is functional, the second aesthetic. All signs should satisfy these two needs if they are to achieve their purpose, e.g. to be read.

Letters can be shaped in many ways yet retain their identity. But although certain shapes are immediately recognisable by a majority of people, there are certain shapes which most people will prefer. If letter shapes do not please the eye of the reader they may be rejected and the sign has not achieved its objective.

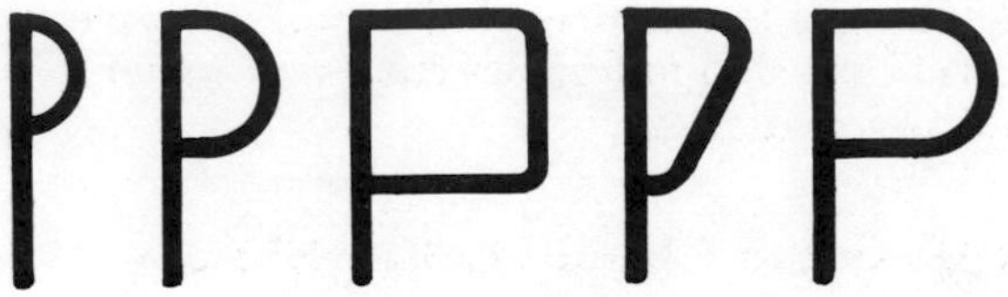

PPPPP

Fig. 1.1   Letter P in many styles

Figure 1.1 shows the letter P in many styles, which are readily identified by the majority of people. If those people were asked to select the one which they prefer, the largest number of votes would be cast for the second letter. The reason for this is that the curved shape is most clearly based on the circle, and that the top shape takes up an apparent half of the upright.

RSTUVW

RSTUVW

RSTUVW

Fig. 1.2   Comparison of letters of different styles, similar width, and those based on the circle

This aesthetic feeling can be taken one step further. Figure 1.2 shows six consecutive letters of the alphabet drawn in three different ways. All the letters are easily recognisable but the third line is the one preferred by the majority of people. The first is a hotchpotch of styles selected from six different alphabets. In the second one all the letters are drawn to exactly the same width. In the third one all the letters are related to the circle or occupy an area similar to the circle. These illustrate that letters not only have an accepted basic shape but need to be related by a similar bond to other letters in the same alphabet.

Studies of the many Roman inscriptions, which are still available throughout Europe, have shown that the circle was a vital element in the construction of the letters and provided the link between all the letters.

The student of lettering will find it invaluable to be able to draw letters in their original, or classic, form. The knowledge and appreciation absorbed during this exercise will be applied to the reproduction of all other styles of lettering and make that signmaker a more versatile and discriminating craftsman.

Methods of Drawing Classic Letter Shapes

There have been many published methods by which letters can be drawn in their correct classic proportions. The three most common ones have used as their bases the point, the square and the circle.

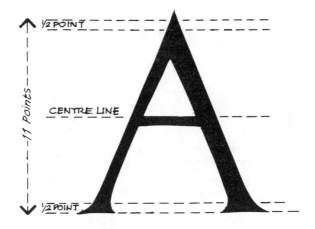

Fig. 1.3   The point system of letter proportions

Point system
This was devised by Edward Sanderson in the 1920s. The point refers to the thickness of the stroke of the letter, or the thickest stroke if they do vary. Every letter then is given a point rating and this multiplied by the point determines how wide the letter will be. For example, the Classic Roman A is 9 points and the P 5½. Therefore if the thick stroke is 10 mm, the A will be 90 mm wide and the P 55 mm. The width does not include the serifs which project a further one point. (See fig. 1.3.) The system has been adapted to cover both Roman and block capital and lower case alphabets. It can prove difficult to use because every letter must be learnt as a number and exercises in its use become more a mathematical problem than a drawing project.

Square system
Many published books on lettering have shown the classic alphabet constructed in squares or parts of squares. The 0 is a full square, the H four-fifths of a square, the E half a square, and so on. Some books show each letter drawn in a squared grid of 100 squares. (See fig. 1.4.) The method is restricting because no letter is a square, therefore this artificial basic shape is not related to the letters. Also its use invariably reduces setting out to a mathematical problem.

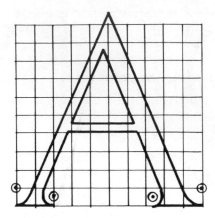

Fig. 1.4   The square system of letter proportions

OHV system
This method uses the circle as its basis therefore is immediately related to the basic shape which many people require in a letter. It requires no remembering of numbers to determine letter widths, being based more on drawing shapes than arithmetic. It can prove easier to apply to setting out letters for students than the previously described methods. Because it requires the setter-out to make judgements and comparisons it has a more lasting effect in training the eye to register good shapes.

OHV System

The system is based on the premise that all curved letters are circles or parts of circles, and that the H takes up the same area as a circle but is not the same width.

Fig. 1.5.1 shows the letter 0 as a circle, with an upright drawn either side forming a square and diagonals through it. When upright lines are drawn through the points where the diagonals cross the circle as in fig. 1.5.2 a rectangle is formed which is approximately equal in area to the circle. This is the proportion of the H. Fig. 1.5.3 shows two angled lines from the bottom centre of the circle, through the same point where the circle and H cross and on to the top line. This represents the proportion of the letter V.

It is from this simple device that the proportion of most letters of the alphabet can be found. Apart from the three letters already defined the letters C and D can be seen, see figs. 1.5.4 and 1.5.7. It is the D shape which is also the basis of the B, P, R and S. Each of these four letters contains a shape or shapes which are the proportion of the D. The S is two D shapes, the top one backwards and the lower one forwards, see fig. 1.6.

Table 1.1 shows the related proportion of each letter to the OHV. Drawing to these instructions produces a skeleton letter shape to

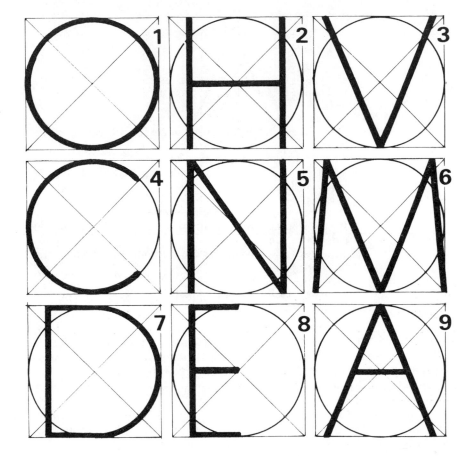

Fig. 1.5 The OHV system of letter proportions

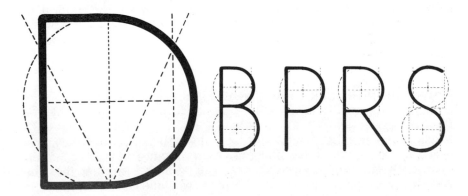

Fig. 1.6 The D as a basis for other letters

Table 1.1   Alphabet related to OHV.

A	V reversed
B	Two Ds
C	O stopped by right hand stroke of H
D	O stopped by left hand stroke of H
E F L	½ H
G	C with ½ stroke of H
J	Straight stroke with ⅓ curve of circle with radius of ⅓ height
K	Two strokes meeting at 45°
M	V with two sloping strokes widening to O width at base
H N T U X Y Z	Width of H
OQ	Width of O
P	D shape taking up ½ height of letter
R	P with sloping stroke issuing from inner angle to just outside curve limit
S	Two D shapes, top one back to front and lower one in right position
V	V
W	Two Vs crossing or two Vs of 40°

which can be added the thickness or thicknesses to produce Block (sans serif) or Roman capital letters. The thicknesses are sometimes added either side of the skeleton, and sometimes inside.

The method by which each letter can be constructed to draw the classic block alphabet is described below. The block alphabet is a convenient one for the student to start with because it can be constructed almost entirely with drawing instruments. By drawing each letter in this way the trainee will learn the true shapes and will be able to identify the particular characteristics and problems peculiar to some of the letters. In the early days of training for signwriting full size lettering layouts will be necessary to work from to gain confidence as well as to learn shapes. For screen printing and most glass work a full size drawing is usually required at all times and on many occasions it is necessary to draw the letters when some form of enlarging equipment is not available. When these letter shapes and proportions are established in the seeing sense there will be no need to use the laborious methods described.

Constructing Block (Sans Serif) Capital Letters

Preparation
Having decided what height the lettering will be (see Layout) it is necessary to draw two parallel lines that distance apart and within them draw the OHV device shown in fig. 1.5.1. Assuming that the lettering will be a light style (see Letter Forms) measure one tenth the height of the lettering and mark it on a piece of paper about 50 × 20 mm. Exactly central between these two points place another mark, see

fig. 1.7. This will be used to mark the weight or thickness of every lettering stroke. A marker of this sort is more accurate to use than a ruler because after a period the eye may miscount the units on the ruler resulting in errors.

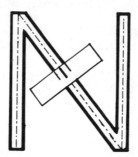

Fig. 1.7   Marker for letter weight

A set square is required for drawing lines particularly vertical ones, a pair of dividers for use in taking off measurements from the OHV device, and a compass for drawing curves.

A   Fig. 1.8: open compass or dividers to half the width of the V and mark this distance at the bottom and either side of a vertical line. Join these two points to the top of the line forming an inverted V. Place the centre line of the marker at right angles to the top of the left hand line and mark off the half of the thickness either side. Repeat the process at the base of the stroke, and at the top and bottom of the right hand line. Join these points up and an upside down V will be drawn. The cross bar must be positioned so that it looks equal distance from the top and bottom. Rarely does a measured centre look right. Draw two lines in the selected position the exact distance of the marker apart.

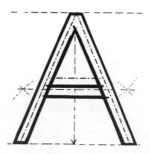

Fig. 1.8

B   Fig. 1.9: draw the upright stroke exactly measured with the marker. Mark the thickness down from the top line and up from the bottom and draw them in to form a partial E. Draw a central horizontal line. Because a B will appear to be top heavy if both curves are drawn exactly the same size it is necessary to make the top shape slightly smaller than the bottom. This can be done by placing the centre of the marker on the centre line and moving it up a fraction before marking the weight either side and drawing the centre arm. Find the centre between the two inside lines at the top, and the two inside lines at the bottom and draw the two horizontal centre lines. Open the compass to the distance between the top centre line and the underside of the top arm, which will be the radius for the top inside curve. Place the compass point in the centre of the upright stroke on the horizontal centre line and mark the radius on the centre line. This is the centre for the two lines which will form the top shape. Draw the inside one with the same radius and open up till the compass lead touches the top line of the lettering and draw in the outside curve. Repeat the process for the bottom shape. This method should produce two D shapes similar in proportion to the D on the OHV device. If it looks too wide, move the centre point fractionally to the left. If too narrow, move to the right.

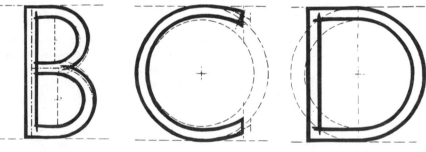

Fig. 1.9   Fig. 1.10   Fig. 1.11

C   Fig. 1.10: any letter whose curve touches either the top or bottom line must be drawn very slightly bigger so that it appears to be the same height as all other letters. Therefore, draw a circle which projects above and below the two lines fractionally and equally. Mark the weight and draw the inside shape from the same centre. Using the OHV device measure the distance between the left hand of the O and the right hand of the H and mark it from the left of the drawn O. Draw a vertical line through at the mark so forming the width of the C. Because the inside points of the C tend to be low it is sometimes necessary to slightly redraw the ends of the curves freehand to reduce this tendency.

D   Fig. 1.11: draw the skeleton D exactly as it appears in the OHV device. Measure the thickness with the marker on the inside of the straight stroke and the curve and draw the inside shape.

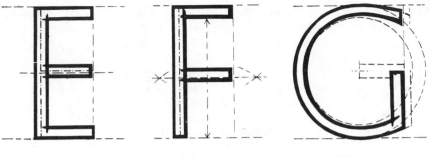

| Fig. 1.12 | Fig. 1.13 | Fig. 1.14 |

E   Fig. 1.12: draw the upright stroke using the marker to determine the thickness. Draw the top and bottom lines in the same way described for the B. Measure and draw the centre line exactly in the centre. Open the dividers to half the width of the H, place the point in the centre of the upright stroke at the top and mark off along the top line. Draw this line vertically so forming the length of each cross stroke.

F   Fig. 1.13: draw in the same way as for the E but omit the bottom arm.

G   Fig. 1.14: draw the C and add on a vertical stroke from the bottom curve up to the horizontal central line. If the letter appears to be tipping forward reduce the length of the top curve so that it stops in line about half way across the upright.

H   Fig. 1.15: draw the H skeleton exactly as it appears on the OHV device. Mark off the thickness either side of the two uprights and the central horizontal bar and join them up.

I   Fig. 1.16: this is a single stem the thickness of the marker.

J   Fig. 1.17: draw an I. Open the compass to one third the height of the letter and mark this distance above the bottom line and draw a horizontal line. Place the compass point where this line touches the left hand side of the I and mark off the distance along the line to the left. This point is the centre for the two curves, one will touch the upright stroke and the bottom line, the other will touch the inside of the upright stroke. The curve is finished vertically where it is considered to be correct.

| Fig. 1.15 | Fig. 1.16 | Fig. 1.17 |

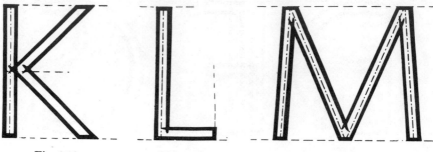

Fig. 1.18   Fig. 1.19   Fig. 1.20

K   Fig. 1.18: draw an I. With a 45° set square draw two lines to meet
      at a point in the middle of the I. Mark off the thickness at right
      angles to right of the two lines and join up. If it appears top heavy
      the centre meeting point will need to be moved up fractionally.

L   Fig. 1.19: draw in the same way as the E but omit the two top
      arms.

M   Fig. 1.20: draw the skeleton V. With the dividers mark off half the
      width of the O either side of the point of the V and draw lines from
      the marks to the top of the V forming a skeleton M. Mark off the
      thickness either side of each of the four lines holding the marker
      at right angles to the strokes. Join up the marks.

N   Fig. 1.21: draw two lines the same distance apart as the strokes of
      the H. Draw the diagonal line from top left to bottom right. Mark
      off the thickness either side of each of the three lines holding the
      marker at right angles to the strokes and join them up.

O   Fig. 1.22: draw the outside circle slightly bigger than the top and
      bottom lines. Mark off the thickness and draw the inside shape.

P   Fig. 1.23: draw an I. Measure down the thickness from the top line
      and draw the horizontal bar. Mark the centre between this line
      and the bottom line of the lettering. Place the marker centre on
      this point, move it up fractionally and mark the thickness either
      side. Draw two horizontal lines through these marks to form

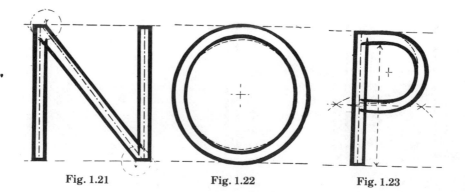

Fig. 1.21   Fig. 1.22   Fig. 1.23

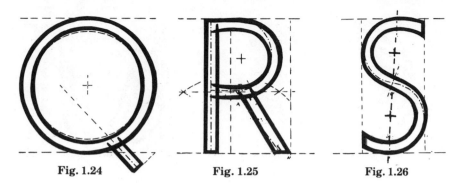

<table>
<tr><td>Fig. 1.24</td><td>Fig. 1.25</td><td>Fig. 1.26</td></tr>
</table>

centre bar. The distance between the two bars should be fractionally smaller than the distance between the bottom line and the underside of the centre bar. Find the centre and draw the curve in the same way that the B top is drawn.

Q   Fig. 1.24: draw the O and draw a short bar from any correct looking position at the bottom at about 45°.

R   Fig. 1.25: draw the P. Place a mark on the bottom line in line with the outside of the curve of the P. Draw from this point to the inside top angle of the P. Mark the thickness at right angles either side of this line and join up.

S   Fig. 1.26: like the B the S must be drawn with the top slightly smaller than the base otherwise it looks top heavy. It needs to be drawn with a slightly forward lean in order to appear upright. In keeping with other curved letters it must be drawn slightly bigger to look the same as other letters. In addition to all these problems an S drawn with instruments rarely looks correct and needs slight freehand touches to improve its appearance. Draw the centre line at a slightly forward angle. On this line and just above and below the top and bottom lines mark off the thickness. Mark off half the thickness either side of a point just above the centre of the angled line. Find the centre between the top mark and the lower mark in the middle, and between the bottom mark and the top mark in the middle, and mark them on the angled line. Place the compass point on the top mark, open it until it touches the top mark and draw a circle which should touch the lower middle mark. Draw the inside curve from the same point to touch in the inside top mark and top middle mark. Repeat the procedure at the bottom so that both circles overlap and look like an 8. Draw two uprights from the outside of the bottom curve. These mark the place where the top and bottom curves end to form the S. The letter may need to have a few freehand touches to make it look correct. The most likely place is in the length of the top and bottom ends, also their curves may need 'flattening' in the same way that the C curves are. The curve where the two circles join in the centre may need to have a hump removed.

Fig. 1.27

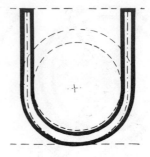

Fig. 1.28

T   Fig. 1.27: draw like Ls upside down. The width at the top of the T should be as wide as the skeleton H.

U   Fig. 1.28: draw an H without the cross bar and draw a vertical centre line between the two strokes. Open the compass to the distance between the centre line and the outside stroke and mark the distance up the centre line by putting the compass point just below the bottom line. This mark on the centre line will be the centre for the two curves forming the bottom of the U.

V   Fig. 1.29: draw in the same way as the A, reversing the shape and omitting the cross stroke.

W   Fig. 1.30: occasionally the W is shown as two Vs crossing in the centre. The most common method is to use two narrow Vs touching at the top. The best looking angle for the narrow V is 40° at the base and this can be drawn with an adjustable set square or a protractor. Draw the two Vs in skeleton form first and mark the thickness either side of the four strokes holding the marker at right angles to the stroke and join up.

XYZ   Fig. 1.31: these three letters are sometimes described by the angle of their strokes. This can be complicated to draw and as they are rarely used the simplest method is to construct them within the width of the skeleton H. In each case draw the two lines of the H

Fig. 1.29

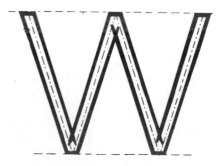

Fig. 1.30

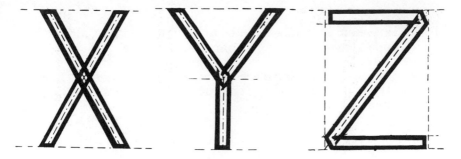

Fig. 1.31

and draw diagonals for the X, top part of the diagonals plus the lower stem for the Y, and just one diagonal for the Z. The marker is placed at right angles and half the thickness marked either side of each stroke, except the top and bottom of the Z where the thickness is placed under the top and above the bottom.

OHV and Roman caps

The skeleton form produced by the OHV provides the basis for Roman capitals as well as sans serif. After the practice of drawing and painting sans serif letters based on this construction the trainee will find it relatively easy to draw the thick and thin strokes to the same skeleton to produce similar proportioned letters in this different style. The characteristics of the Roman letter are explained in chapter 2.

OHV and variations of classic styles

If sans serif or Roman capitals are required in a condensed form, i.e. based on the ellipse or oval rather than the circle, the OHV system can be used to maintain the right proportions. The device can be set out around an ellipse which has been drawn to the shape decided for the O, see fig. 1.32.

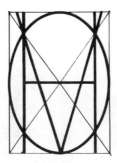

Fig. 1.32 OHV adapted for condensed letters.

Lower case

The OHV system cannot be adapted to lower case letters, although the basic shape remains the same, namely the circle. Most lower case letters contain curved shapes which can be related to the letter O. The curve of the b, c, d, e, p and q are variations of the O, see fig. 1.33. The curve of the a, f, h, i, j, l, m, n, r, t, u and y are all similar and vary only slightly from the O, see fig. 1.34.

Fig. 1.33   Lower case letters
related to the 0

Fig. 1.34   Lower case letters
of similar curve to the 0

Type faces

Types faces are so varied that it is not possible to adapt a common system for determining proportion. But certain elements which show up in the OHV system can help to study an unknown typeface so that letters can be related. For example in many of the standard Roman and sans serif faces the H, N, U and X are the same width. Although E's are generally wide in many typefaces there is a common link between O, C, G, D, P and R which is a characteristic of OHV also.

Optical Illusions

In the detailed description for constructing capital letters reference has been made to the adjustments necessary to counteract the strange way that the eye reads certain letters. Before leaving the subject of letters these illusions should be emphasised. Although these phenomena occur mostly with sans serif capital letters, they can affect the appearance of Roman letters and lower case letters.

Letters which meet the top or bottom line in a curve will appear smaller unless they are deliberately drawn bigger. This applies mainly to C, G, O, Q, S and U. See fig. 1.35.

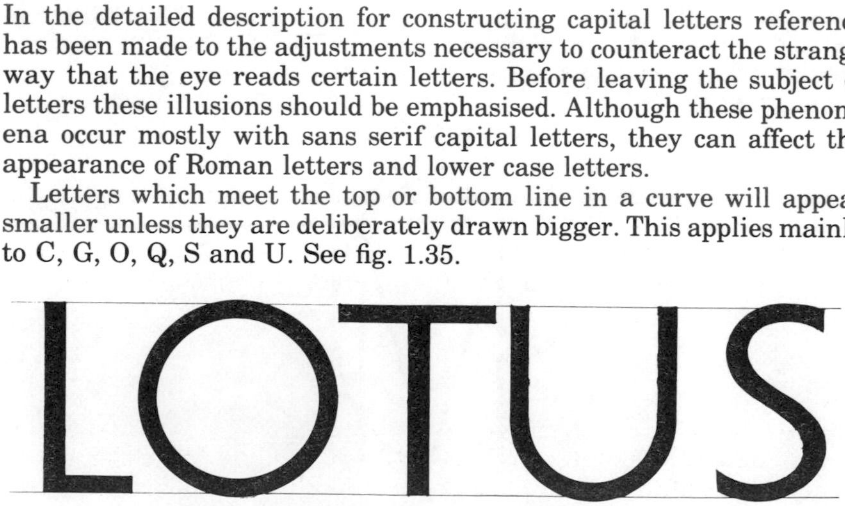

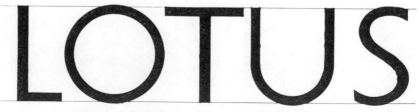

Fig. 1.35   Curved letters extend beyond the height lines

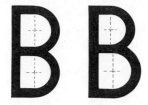 

Fig. 1.36 The B in wrong and right proportion

Fig. 1.37 Pointed letters project above height line

Letters made up of two equal parts will appear top heavy unless the bottom part is drawn fractionally bigger than the top. If the bottom looks bigger it has been over compensated. See fig. 1.36. This applies mainly to B and S. A slight variation of this rule applies when drawing the P and R. If the top curve terminates in the true centre of the letter it will appear too small. The balance is right when the space inside the curve matches the space below the curve.

Letters with points at the top or bottom should penetrate the top and bottom lines slightly so that they appear the same size. See fig. 1.37. This does not apply to the classic sans serif letters because no letter has a pointed finish. It does apply to some classic Roman letters such as A, M, N, V and W. Adjustments in the design of these letters have occurred over the years to overcome the problem. Many signwriters paint the A, M and N with serifs at the top points for example. Some typefaces, like Times Roman Bold, deliberately flatten the point to improve the appearance of these five letters. See fig. 1.38.

Fig. 1.38 Flat tops and cross over serifs used to avoid problems with pointed tops

When drawn exactly the same size some curve strokes may appear thinner than the straight strokes. An adjustment to overcome this is best carried out during signwriting because this is when it is apparent, particularly when there is a strong contrast between the colour of the lettering and the background of the sign. (See chapter 5.)

Spacing

The spacing of letters requires the same amount of care and attention that is taken to produce the letter shapes. A sign can be completely spoilt if beautifully constructed and painted letters are arranged in a haphazard way.

Fig. 1.39   Letters set by the printer

TALE

Fig. 1.40   Letters overlapped to improve spacing

There is one golden rule for good spacing. The area of the space between each letter must appear to be equal. This is visual and cannot be overcome by simple arithmetic. Except with Gothic and some of the compressed typefaces measured spaces invariably do not produce equal areas because each letter has its own characteristic and every combination sets new problems of spacing. Unfortunately there are very many poor examples of spacing, for which the printer must take much of the blame. Printing consists of laying one letter down at a time, each one being contained within a convenient area. That convenient area is probably just a fraction bigger than the extreme borders of the letter. So letters are spaced by the area of the 'thing' that contains them and not by the needs of the letter. Fig. 1.39 shows the word TALE set by the printer. The feint lines around each letter represent the space each letter requires so that it can be reproduced mechanically. These shapes are exactly the same distance apart but the letters do not look equally spaced. A person preparing a sign by hand would have overlapped the T and A and increased the space between the L and E to make the word look right, as in fig. 1.40.

The hand signmaker has considerable flexibility in the way that letters are positioned and must not be influenced by the poor arrangements which are forced on to the printer.

TOGGLE

Fig. 1.41   Spacing problems when using compressed letters

Some typefaces have been designed to overcome spacing problems. They are the compressed styles with straight sides such as Compacta and Folio Bold Condensed. But these have problems with letters such as J, L, T and X which create more space around them than the straight sided ones like B, C, D, G and O. See fig. 1.41. Gothic is another style which has fewer problems when spacing, and a method for spacing these letters is described later.

The more conventionally shaped letters, particularly the classic Roman and sans serif, need considerable care in their arrangement because they are designed as shapes to be recognised readily and not as shapes that can be spaced easily.

Tile Form and x Height

Some agencies design their letters in tile form. It is used as a reliable method of obtaining a designed alphabet or corporate image in a standard form regardless of the number of contractors who are employed to produce the signs. Local authorities, large companies and advertising agencies are common users of this system. Each letter is produced within a rectangle so designed that whatever text is prepared the spacing will remain constant. In addition to the space taken up by each letter other features are uniformed also. The x height, which is the height of the lower case letter, is fixed. All other measurements, such as stroke thickness and capital height, are related to the x height.

Rules of spacing
Every word sets a new problem so precise rules about spacing cannot be given. If the following points are considered when spacing letters problems may be minimised.

(1) Straight sided letters appearing together require more space between them than curved letters. For example in the word DOMINO (fig. 1.42) the D and the O are much closer together than the M, I and N. Inexperienced persons are very reluctant to allow sufficient space between straight letters. It is an important consideration when setting out letters in single line for direct signwriting because the stroke thickness is painted either side of a single straight line so much of the originally allowed space will be used up. Whereas round letters usually have the thickness painted inside the confines of the single line marked out and do not reduce space. Therefore on painting, straight letters get closer and round letters appear to get further apart. There are occasions when round letters, particularly double Os, need to be almost touching.
(2) Letters such as A, J, L, T and W often need to overlap the bounds of other letters. For example, in fig. 1.40 the top of the right hand stroke of the T projects well over the bottom left hand stroke of the A. Unless this is done other letters will need to be moved so far apart to match the spacing that the word will lose its cohesion and will read as single letters.

Fig. 1.42 Spacing variations for straight and round letters

(3) To ensure consistency of space between the letters of a word or line of text, the space between similar letters can be used for checking whether spacing is increasing or decreasing as the setting out progresses. For example, on a sign which states, ONLY STAFF ALLOWED BEYOND THIS POINT, certain aspects of spacing solved when drawing out the first two words can be used to help the spacing of the other words and keep a check on the amount of space being allowed, see fig. 1.43. The space between the O and N in ONLY must be the precise distance allowed between O and N in BEYOND and O and I in POINT can be used to help determine the space between the O and W in ALLOWED. The space between the two straight letters, N and L, in ONLY will be echoed in BEYOND between N and D, in THIS between H and I, and in POINT between I and N. The A and F space in STAFF will help space A and L in ALLOWED. This cross checking is necessary as well as useful for both full size drawings and direct marking out because letters can be gradually closed up or opened out without it noticing until the job is completed and viewed from a reading distance.

(4) There is an accepted distance between letters of a word but there is no way to define it. If letters are too close or too far apart they are difficult to read, and this is the only criterion for correct spacing. It is a temptation at times to spread out a word or words to fill a space or cramp letters together when space is restricted, but in both cases the right solution is to make the height of the letters bigger or smaller which will reduce or increase the amount of room available to space the text.

(5) Letter shapes should not be corrupted to make spacing look better. This is particularly so when using a typeface which has been specially commissioned by a client, because once changes are made the type is no longer accurate and may not be accepted. As in (4) the solution is to increase or decrease the height of the letters. It is not necessary to keep each letter entirely separate from its neighbours. Letters such as A, R or Y invariably produce spacing problems and quite often the problem can be minimised by making them touch the letter either side. With brush drawn letters such as the classic sans serif or Roman a greater freedom is enjoyed and letters of these styles can be linked at times to aid a layout. When carried out skilfully it is rarely noticed by the reader.

(6) Space between words should be the width of the letter O ideally. Slight variations either side of this are generally acceptable but considerable differences will affect legibility. A too small space may not be recognised at all as a void between two words. A too large space will separate words so much that the sense of the text may be affected. The suggestion in (3) regarding cross checking of spaces between words is equally as important for checking consistency of space between words. Once a space has been established between words on the first line it must be adopted for all other word spaces throughout the text.

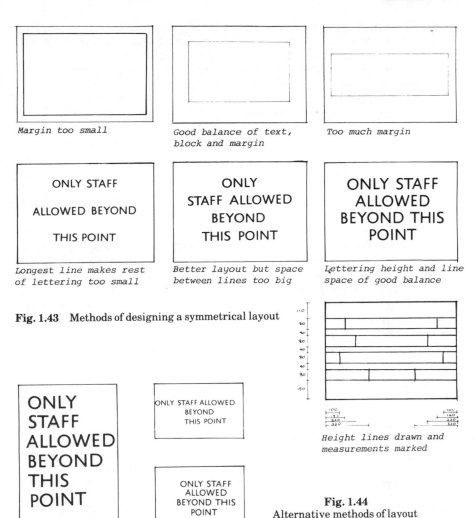

Margin too small

Good balance of text, block and margin

Too much margin

ONLY STAFF

ALLOWED BEYOND

THIS POINT

Longest line makes rest of lettering too small

ONLY
STAFF ALLOWED
BEYOND
THIS POINT

Better layout but space between lines too big

ONLY STAFF
ALLOWED
BEYOND THIS
POINT

Lettering height and line space of good balance

Fig. 1.43 Methods of designing a symmetrical layout

ONLY
STAFF
ALLOWED
BEYOND
THIS
POINT

"Poetry" layout

ONLY STAFF ALLOWED
BEYOND
THIS POINT

ONLY STAFF
ALLOWED
BEYOND THIS
POINT

Assymetrical layouts

Height lines drawn and measurements marked

Fig. 1.44
Alternative methods of layout

Method of spacing

When setting out a full size drawing a practical method of spacing is to concentrate on it after the letters have been constructed and not as a combined task. The problem of drawing the letters required should be solved first. This can be done by counting the number of each type of letter required and setting them out on a large sheet. For example for the layout shown in fig. 1.43 the letters required are: A, B, D, E, F, H, I, L, N, O, P, S, T, W and Y. These are drawn to the required height, preferably in one long line. A piece of tracing paper with the lettering height lines marked on it can be placed over the master sheet and moved backwards and forwards until the right position for each letter has been decided. For the first line the only positions which are certain are the O which must come at the beginning of the line and the second F which must come at the end. The remaining letters need to be spaced, which requires a degree of trial and error.

First lay the tracing paper over the master copy until the height lines match, then draw in the letter O with drawing instruments at the extreme left position. Move the paper along to its extreme righthand position, lay it over the drawing of the F and draw in using a set square. Then move the paper until the O on the tracing paper is next to the N on the master and with a soft pencil sketch the N. Move the paper along, judge the same distance as that between O and N, and sketch in the L. Continue in this way until the two words are complete, the O and F drawn properly and the remaining letters sketched in position. If all the letters could not be fitted into the space, it is necessary to rub out the sketched letters and re-arrange them using less space between the letters until they do fit. If too much space is left between the two F's the sketched letters will need to be spaced again allowing a fraction more space between them. When they fit it is necessary to check the spacing between individual letters.

Most errors show up immediately and can be put right by moving a letter or letters one way or the other to improve the arrangement. Others may not be so obvious and must be checked carefully at this stage because a slight error in the drawing will look considerably worse when it is painted or printed. Check three letters at a time. Cover up all letters except the O N L and critically view it to decide whether the N is exactly in the centre of the O and L. If it is not rub it out and retrace it in the right place. Then cover up the O and expose the Y and decide whether the L is central between N and Y, and adjust if necessary. Continue this process right along the line. This may be the only adjustment necessary but if many of the letters have needed to be moved the entire balance may have been disturbed and other moves may be necessary. In some circumstances it may require many changes before the spacing seems equal throughout. When the spacing is right each letter can be traced off carefully in the correct position. The process needs to be repeated for each line, using the measuring aids and checks suggested earlier.

For the trainee this process can be time consuming and laborious but the skill of producing correct letter shapes and spacing is fundamental to the signworker and it is only by application to acquiring the skill early in training that craftsmanship will be achieved.

The visual effect of letters when painted can be entirely different to that when drawn in outline. Therefore if particular problems have occurred when spacing a drawing it is a sound principle to paint in the letters before using the drawing. Rather than spoil the working drawing, if a piece of detail paper is placed over it the letters can be roughly painted in with black ink and the finished affect will be more accurately seen.

Spacing Gothic letters
Gothic lower case letters were designed to take up as little space as possible therefore they need to be kept very close. A simple method of

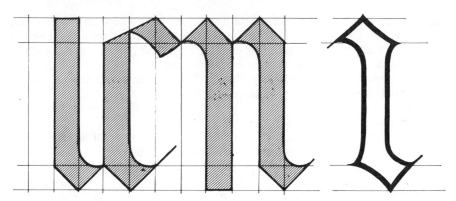

Fig. 1.45   Spacing Gothic letters

setting out and spacing these letters is shown in Fig. 1.45. Having decided what height the lettering should be, draw the height lines and divide the space into seven equal divisions. Draw a line parallel to the top height line the same one-seventh distance away, and draw a similar line above the base line. Between the height lines draw a series of vertical lines all the same one-seventh distance apart. Each vertical space represents either the letter stroke, the space in the centre of the letter, or the space between the letters. The horizontal markers indicate the point where the top and bottom 'curves' spring from and help gauge the angles of them.

Most letters can be spaced within this grid but a few require adjustment to maintain an even space. The c, r and t need to be moved closer to the letters on their right. In some cases the extreme points need to be touching. There are many versions of the Gothic alphabet and most of them can be constructed within a similar form of grid. It may be necessary to adjust the grid size if the one-seventh suggested above seems too thick or too thin.

Spacing script letters
The biggest problem with any of the script alphabets is giving them too much space. The letters must be kept close together so that they can be joined. One method of overcoming this is to set it out quickly and to write it in like handwriting. If letters are spaced individually they tend to spread out.

Once the height and the space which the letters will occupy have been fixed and marked it is necessary to draw or snap a series of lines equal distance apart at the angle which the lettering will slope. In this way a constant check can be made, throughout the drawing and painting, that all the letters are sloping at the same degree.

Layout

The arrangement of the letters or the words on the sign area is called the layout. It is a design skill which can require a special study of graphic art to achieve a high standard of competence. Most signwriters after some years' experience adopt a set of standard layouts from which they select the one that seems to suit the particular requirements of the job. Imaginative layouts are usually the work of graphic designers, then painted by the signwriter.

In the early part of learning the craft of signmaking the following points will help to develop a simple design sense.

Margins
Like a printed page the space around the lettering of a sign is as important to legibility as the words. If margins are too small the lettering overpowers the shape. Large margins make the lettering insignificant. For simple signs the generally acceptable arrangement is for the top and side margins to be about the same size. The bottom margin should be slightly bigger than the top margin. If they are made the same size the top one will appear bigger and the layout will seem to be slipping off the sign. If a border or line is to be used around the sign it is essential that margins are equal.

Line spaces
If lines of lettering are placed too close together they become difficult to read. When the lines are too far apart the unity of the text is lost and the lines are read independently and the meaning may not be clear.

Too much space often occurs when the distance between lines exceeds the height of the letters. An acceptable distance is about half the height of the letters. This is not a hard and fast rule but does offer a guide line and a check should the layout be difficult to read.

Particular care must be taken when line spacing with lower case letters. The ascenders and descenders of lower case can give a false height to the letters. Most letters come with the general height, i.e. the height of the o, but if this measurement is used for laying out and half of it allowed for line spacing there will be no room for the ascenders and descenders. If the full height, i.e. the height of the h, is used for line spacing too much space will occur because so many letters will be at the general height. The best rule is to keep the top of the full height as close as possible to the bottom line of the line above. Problems will arise when descenders and ascenders mingle but slight imaginative adjustments can usually overcome them.

Method of Layout

When drawing and spacing letters concentration is directed at individual characters. When laying out or designing the sign it is the full text which must be considered. Therefore it is sometimes easier to think of the blocks of areas taken up by the lettering rather than of the individual letters.

Fig. 1.43 shows a method of deciding the way that a sign can be arranged. Although the shape of the sign should be drawn to scale or proportion the layout sketches must be done freehand. If a ruler is used at this early stage there is a danger that lettering height will be determined too soon and the opportunity to try different designs will be lost.

Therefore by sketching blocks of lettering areas the best balanced effect can be selected. Within this selected block, the arrangement of the words can be sketched to find the one which gives the best balance between lettering height and space between lines. Finally a ruler can be used to draw lettering height lines and convert them to full size measurements.

During the last two processes when letters are being sketched care must be taken to give full width to each letter. If the classic styles of sans serif or Roman are being used the Cs, Ds and Os must be drawn as circles. An inexperienced person tends to sketch letters too narrow and the essential quality of these early sketches is that they convert reasonably accurately to full size. If these full width letters do not fit into the desired shape the height must be reduced until they do. To corrupt letter shapes at this stage to make them appear to fit will create considerable problems at the next stage when the full size drawing or marking out is carried out. It is at the final sketch stage that the spacing problems become obvious and it is easier to work out methods of overcoming them at this size and in sketch form than at full size stage.

Other Layouts

The above method describes a symmetrical layout. The areas of lettering are equal either side of a centre line. This is the most common form of layout, the one which is easier to produce a satisfactory design, and probably most acceptable for the majority of signs and clients.

There are variations of a symmetrical layout which can be applied to some jobs.

When many lines of lettering are used, it can be very time consuming to make each line equal to the vertical centre line. If the lettering is being prepared as a full size drawing the problem is not so great because the measured centre can be found after the drawing is complete and fitted to a centre line on the sign. But for direct marked signs a lot of adjustment may be necessary to fit each line symmetrically. This can be overcome by using the method adopted for setting out printed poetry and keep the left hand margin in line and let the right hand lines finish where they will.

This layout works reasonably well when considerable amount of lettering is involved.

Assymetrical layouts
These are much more difficult design forms to produce. The signs and the clients have to be chosen very carefully for such layouts. See fig. 1.44.

Designing the text
An essential quality of an information sign is that it is read easily and quickly. Generally the best signs are those which put over their message in the least number of words. Getting the text right is often an

important consideration when designing a layout.

The sign layout in fig. 1.43 states its message in the least number of words, and any person reading it should know immediately what they can do. An alternative text could be: IT IS PERMISSABLE ONLY FOR MEMBERS OF THE COMPANY STAFF TO PROCEED BEYOND THIS POINT. This contains three times as many letters therefore takes three times longer to read and is less efficient.

Circular or Elliptical Sign Layouts

For layouts which require the lines of lettering to be horizontal symmetrical layouts invariably are more acceptable on circular or elliptical signs. See fig. 1.46.

Fig. 1.46   Horizontal symmetrical layout on a circular sign

If the lettering is required to follow the shape of the sign to form a border the letters must radiate from the centre of the shape. See fig. 1.47.

Fig. 1.47   Radiating layout on a circular sign

When setting out, the centre line of each letter should radiate from the circle or ellipse centre. The strokes of the letters should be parallel to this centre line and not radiate to the centre otherwise considerable distortion will occur. Some designs do require a diminishing letter but unless this sort of distortion is particularly required it should be avoided.

The method described earlier for setting out a full size drawing can be adapted for circular and elliptical signs. The lettering can be set out within two parallel, horizontal lines, and spaced and traced off to fit within height lines drawn to match the curve of the sign.

Problems occur at the top and bottom of letters. For some styles of letters the tops and bottoms can match the curve and look acceptable. Other styles may look out of character finished in this way. The alternative is to draw a straight line at the base and top of each letter which is tangential to the curve. It may be necessary to make individual adjustments to each letter to produce an acceptable appearance.

Spacing is a problem also. The bottom of the letters will be close together but the tops will be far apart. With many letters this is acceptable because the fan shape space can be made to look even. Letters such as L and J which have a lot of space at the top look very widely spaced when radiated.

Setting Out

Methods of adopting layouts and on site methods of setting out are described in chapter 8.

Two
Lettering Forms and Styles

The signmaker will be involved in using lettering in many forms and styles. Although there are only twenty-six characters in the alphabet they can be reproduced in hundreds of ways yet still retain their legible shape and individual characteristics. Letters can be thick or thin, capital or lower case, upright or leaning, with or without serifs, simple or decorative, or many other variations. The signmaker at times may be expected to select lettering styles to suit a particular job, or use a form which will be most legible in a certain position. The signmaker will always have to interpret instructions about lettering and read and work to published material on lettering and therefore will need to know the technical language surrounding lettering.

Signwritten and printed letter forms
Lettering can be roughly divided into brush drawn letters and typefaces. The first one is the form which signwriters develop to suit their abilities and the sort of work they are commonly required to do. The style of work will usually have as its base the classic form of Trajan Roman and the sans serif style developed from it. Typefaces are styles of letters originally designed for use by printers. They were made in cast metal for easy application to the many printing methods for producing books, newspapers, posters and packaging. A vast number of alphabets have been designed over the past 100 years and many of them are still popular and in demand by designers. A signmaker could be asked to reproduce any of the published typefaces and there are numerous books which document the alphabets from which the letters can be copied.

Weight

Weight usually means the thickness of the stroke of a letter, which in turn is related to letter height. For example a heavy letter is one whose weight is about a quarter of its height, and a light letter one whose weight is about one tenth its height.

Letter Forms

Capitals or caps, majuscules, upper case
This is the original form of our alphabet, as used by the Romans. It is very widely used on signs, particularly where single or few words are

needed. Capitals are necessary for initials of names and at the beginning of a sentence. See fig. 2.1.

Lower case, or miniscules or small letters
These letters developed much later than the capitals and are the result of the original caps being written with a pen. Their use has become very popular in the second half of the twentieth century. As books and newspapers are printed in lower case, people are more used to reading this form of letter. Although they look well when used in bulk they are successfully used on road signs where they may only form single words. See fig. 2.2. Lower case letters can cause problems in layouts because of the ascenders – letters which project above the general height such as b, d, f, h, k and l – and descenders – those which project below the line such as g, j, p, q and y. See fig. 2.3. If the height of lower case letters is calculated as that of d most letters will be less than this height therefore the space between the lines may appear too big.

Fig. 2.1   Capital sans serif and Roman letters

Fig. 2.2   Lower case Roman and sans serif letters

Fig. 2.3   Lower case ascenders and descenders

Light letters

Light letters are those whose weight is about one tenth their height. They are most legible when used for small lettering, up to about 60 mm. On larger lettering they look spindly and lose clarity at a distance. Some styles of lettering are available in 'extra light'. See fig. 2.4.

Medium letters

The weight of medium letters is about one sixth their height; very commonly used for lettering, up to about one metre high. See fig. 2.4.

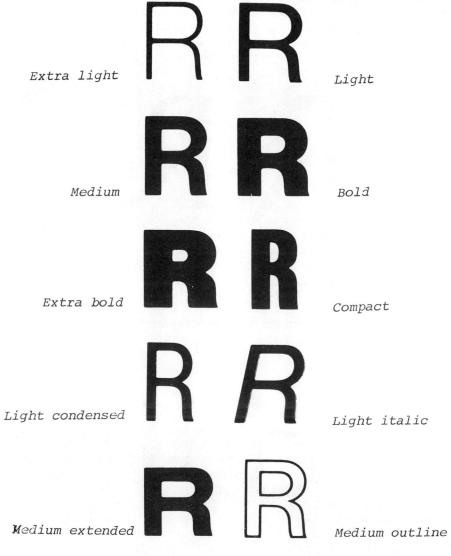

Fig. 2.4   Variation of the Helvetics typeface

Bold letters
This usually refers to letters whose weight is one quarter their height. An ideal letter for long distance viewing particularly when 2 – 3 metres high. Some styles are available in 'extra bold'. See fig 2.4.

Condensed letters
Letters which have been compressed so that they take up the minimum amount of space yet still retain their legibility. See fig. 2.4. It is a style of letter which can be used to good effect when space is restricted, but when used in bulk it is more difficult to read compared with full width letters. Effective when read foreshortened such as painted on a road, see fig. 2.5.

Fig. 2.5   Foreshortened letters painted on the road

Italic letters
Although originally used to describe a condensed sloping form of Roman lower case letters it is now a common title for any sloping letter. Usually, only light or medium forms of letters look well as italic. Books use italic to give emphasis to words and it is most effective on signs when it is restricted to this use.

When setting out or signwriting italic lettering special care must be taken to maintain a constant angle. If a number of parallel lines of the correct angle are drawn on the paper or chalked onto the sign before setting out starts they can be used to check the angle as the work progresses, see fig. 2.6.

Fig. 2.6   The use of sloping parallel lines when setting out italic

Extended letters
These take the opposite form to condensed and are pulled out to take up as much room as possible. Extended letters are particularly useful on long, narrow signs, and look best when used for large letters. See fig. 2.4.

Fig. 2.7   Alternative forms of outline

Outline
Outline letters can take one of three forms.

(1)   A constant thickness of line around and touching a letter. It accentuates a letter and can add an interesting feature to a sign. Most commonly used around gilded letters on glass. See fig. 2.7.
(2)   A similar sort of line as (1), but applied so that it is not touching the letter. Occasionally used on shop fascias to add a different quality to the letters. See fig. 2.7.
(3)   A letter formed in outline only. Some typefaces are available in this form. See fig. 2.4.

Whether the outline is painted or screen printed it can take a long time to produce and careful consideration must be given to this aspect when pricing a job that includes outlines.

When Roman letters are outlined a better effect is often achieved if the ends of the serif are blocks off square rather than running to the end of the point. See fig. 2.8.

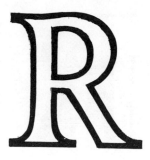

Fig. 2.8   Squared off ends of outline to serifs

Shaded
Shading is a method of making the letter appear in three dimensions.
See fig. 2.9. It has remained a reasonably popular form of lettering
since the nineteenth century. Shading is a decorative feature, it does
not improve the legibility of a sign. There are very few letters that
cannot be shaded although it invariably distracts from the basic letter
shape.

There are very many forms of shading.

(1)   Block, which shows the edge and top or bottom of what could be a
letter in relief. Usually it is set out with a 45° set square and can
be shown on the left or right of the letter. The method of setting
out is to draw a 45° line from each corner of the letter and from the
top and bottom curves. A line drawn below the letters at the
thickness the blocking is required to be will mark the angled lines
where the uprights need to be drawn. Curved letters and angled
strokes, such as on the A and N, present particular problems and
the only rule that can be applied is to adjust the curves or the
thicknesses until they look right. If the letter is to be outlined as
well this must be drawn or painted first and the 45° lines projected
from the extreme points of the outline.
(2)   Cast, is an attempt to make the letter appear projecting from the
surface and casting its shadow upon it. An effect can be produced
by drawing or painting the letters exactly the same but slightly to
one side of and below their original position.
(3)   Block and cast becomes more involved. The blocking needs to be
produced first and then the cast image set after.
(4)   Infinity block shows relief letters diminishing to a vanishing
point. Quite often the vanishing point is above and in the centre of
the letter but there are many variations where the point may be
required in any position.

Blocking and shading takes considerably longer to do than a plain
letter. Pricing for such work must be carried out with considerable
care.

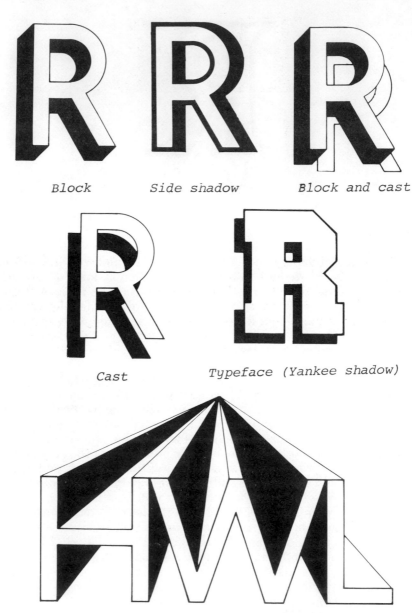

Block   Side shadow   Block and cast

Cast   Typeface (Yankee shadow)

Infinity

Fig. 2.9   Forms of shaded letters

Block or slab serif (sometimes called Egyptian)
This is a form of lettering which was introduced in the nineteenth
century and has retained its popularity ever since. Some very
interesting and attractive forms of typefaces have been produced with
slab serifs. Many styles are based on Roman by having thick and thin

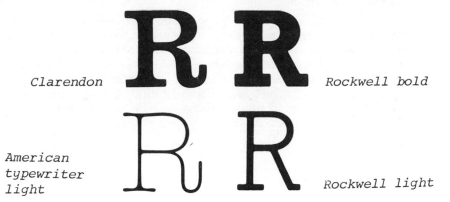

Clarendon

Rockwell bold

American
typewriter
light

Rockwell light

Fig. 2.10 Types of slab serif letters

strokes but some basic shapes do not have strokes of varying thickness. See fig. 2.10.

Clarendon and Rockwell Bold are popular examples of Roman slab serifs. American Typewriter Light and Rockwell Light use a letter stroke of constant thickness. These forms of letters look well when outlined or shaded. Slab serif letters take longer to draw and paint therefore jobs which involve their use must be carefully estimated.

Decorative
Decorative capital letters were used extensively on Medieval illuminated manuscripts and they have retained a degree of popularity ever

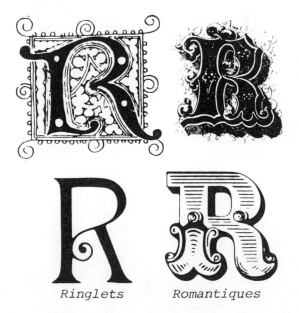

Ringlets   Romantiques

Fig. 2.11 Decorative letters as illuminated caps and modern typefaces since. It is a title which can be applied to any letter which has considerable decoration painted around or over it, or the use of natural forms twisted or arranged to depict a letter shape, or decorative features attached to a basic letter shape. Many typefaces have been introduced over the years which have the decorative appendages.

Generally, decorative letters are less legible than standard forms and should be restricted to single letters or single words. They are very expensive to produce particularly those which require many colours and blending. See fig. 2.11.

Numerals
The ten characters of 0 to 9 which are universally used throughout the world are sometimes referred to as Arabic numerals. Fortunately Roman numerals were not adopted along with their letters because they used a very complicated method of writing figures and numbers.

Arabic numerals, like letters, can be produced in a variety of forms and styles yet retain their identity. For most styles of lettering there is a matching style of numerals. On occasions, numerals in the classic Roman style are shown ascending and descending the height lines. The traditional method was to ascend the even figures, and descend the odds. See fig. 2.12.

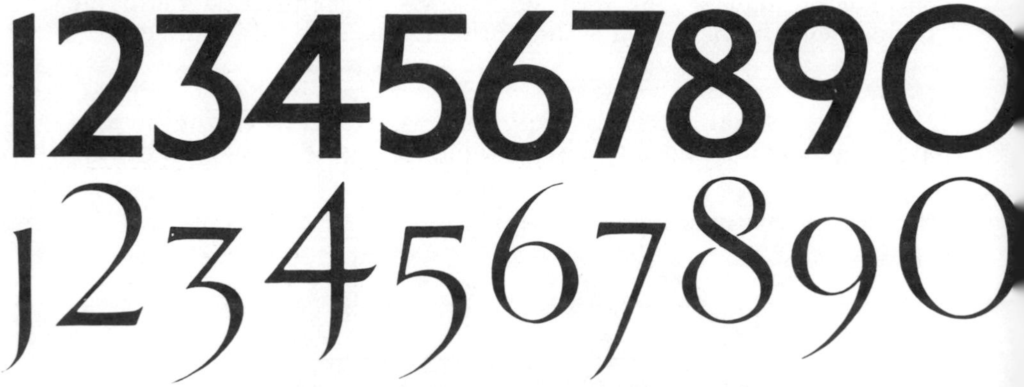

1234567890
1234567890

Fig. 2.12   Sans serif and Roman Arabic numerals

Roman numerals are still used, particularly on film credits, clock faces (fig. 2.13) and house numbers. Therefore the signmaker may need to read or interpret written Roman numerals, or to use them in a sign, which would not be possible without some knowledge of the system. Roman numerals consist of seven characters each one having a different value – see table 2.1. When arranged in a line the values are either added together or subtracted and the total is the number they depict. When the characters are in correct descending order they are added, any character out of descending order is subtracted from its right hand neighbour:

MCLX are all in correct order so are added together to make 1160. MDCDLIV are not in order, therefore the C is taken away from the value of D and the I is taken away from the value of V. The sum now is 1000 (M) + 500 (D) + 400 (D – C) + 50 (L) + 4 (V – 1) = 1954.

They can be shown in sans serif or Roman form and either joined top and bottom with a bar or not joined at all.

Fig. 2.13 Roman numerals used on a clock face

Table 2.1   Roman numeral values.

I	= one	C	= hundred
V	= five	D	= five hundred
X	= ten	M	= thousand
L	= fifty		

Fig. 2.14   Variations of the ampersand

Ampersand

The ampersand is supposedly a corruption of *et*, the French word for and. It is widely used in signwork and takes as many forms as the letters. See fig. 2.14. Occasionally the mathematical plus sign is used as an abbreviation for 'and'.

Point size

Printers refer to letter height in point sizes and occasionally it appears in instructions to sign makers. (See fig. 2.15.) It refers to the size of the block that contained the original type letter. A common rule is that 72 points are equivalent to about 25 mm. This rule cannot be applied precisely because some letters may require a bigger block size to contain them so will print smaller.

Letter Styles

Roman

A style of letter which always has both thick and thin strokes and the ends of 'straight' strokes swell out into serifs. The Romans produced all their letters in this form, most of it carved in stone, and always in capitals. The belief is that lettering was marked out for the carvers with a brush which naturally produced an up and across thin stroke and a thick down stroke. Also where the brush was placed on the surface and where it was removed at the end of the stroke a small flourish occurred. When the carver interpreted this free drawing he retained the thick and thin strokes and formalised the flourishes into gently swelling serifs.

The Romans left a great many examples of their carved letters throughout Europe but the one inscription which was considered to be the most beautiful was that on the base of Trajans Column in Rome.

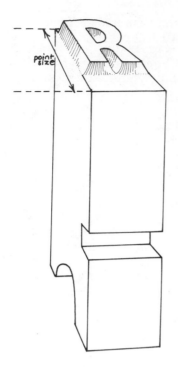

Fig. 2.15   Printers cast type showing
point size

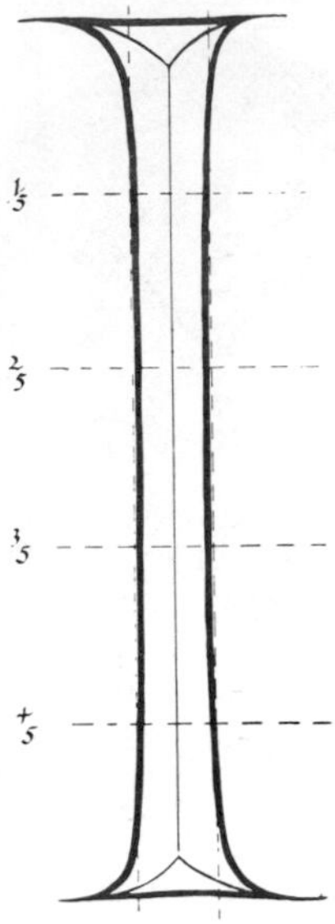

Fig. 2.17   True form of the
Trajan Roman stroke

This one has been particularly studied and many drawn and painted versions have been published and commonly called Trajan Roman. Classic and Antique Roman are two other names by which it is known. See fig. 2.16.

The true Trajan Roman has many characteristics which the student of lettering must learn before the style can be reproduced effectively and before this knowledge can be applied to learning the many other styles that have developed from the classic form.

The 'straight' stroke is not ruler drawn. It may appear straight but is very slightly curving for most of its length. The shape is a result of the natural stroke of a brush which designed it. Starting at the top in the serif with little pressure the brush is pulled into the vertical stroke with increasing pressure, and then released again into the bottom serif. Fig 2.17 shows an analysis of the Roman stroke. The illustration is not shown as a method to be copied when setting out. But if the form is kept in the mind as the letters are being painted there is a greater chance of the true shape being produced. By its nature, Trajan Roman is more effectively painted than drawn.

Serifs should end in very fine points. If the top and bottom lines of serifs are painted exactly straight they tend to look as if they are swelling or convex. To overcome this illusion the tops and bottoms should be painted slightly concaved so that they appear straight. See fig. 2.18.

ABCDEFG
HJKLMNO
PQRSTUV
WXYZ

abcdefgghij
klmnopqrstu
vwxyz

Fig. 2.16 Brush drawn Trajan Roman

Fig. 2.18   Version of serifs showing
slight concavity

Fig. 2.19   Top of Roman D extending
beyond height line

The top curve of the B, D, P and R slightly project above the line. The curve starts at the serif, rises to the maximum height of its curve above the line and then into full curve. See fig. 2.19. The bottom of the B, D and R finish on a straight line.

The tops of the A, N, M and W should finish in points. So that the lettering can be painted more quickly many signwriters put serifs on the cross over thick strokes, and the thin stroke of the M. See fig. 2.20.

Fig. 2.20   Roman A with point and crossover serif

Many type faces are based upon the classic Roman letter. In keeping with types the mechanical methods employed to produce them have resulted in the subtleties being lost. Most of them have straight sides, rarely break the height lines and have no concaved finish to the serifs.

Perpetua   *Albertus*   *Optima*

Loose new roman   *Clearface gothic*

Fig. 2.21   Roman typefaces

ABCDEFGH
IJKLMNOP
QRSTUVW
XYZ

abcdefghijkl
mnopqrstuv
wxyz

Fig. 2.22 Sans serif alphabets

R R R

Gill sans   Univers 65   Avant Garde

Fig. 2.23 Sans serif type faces

The serifs vary considerably also. Some are very subtle as in Optima, some have none as in Clearface Gothic, where others are very exaggerated as in Loose New Roman. Fig. 2.21 shows some examples of common Roman typefaces.

Block or sans serif
This is a version of the Roman letters, introduced during the nineteenth century. See fig. 2.22. The strokes are of constant thickness and finish in square ends. The characteristics of a basic sans serif alphabet is fully described in chapter 1.

   There are innumerable versions of sans serif letters available. They are probably more widely used than Roman styles. The style which most closely resembles the 'classic' form is Gill Sans, which was designed by Eric Gill who, with Edward Johnston, was responsible for the improvements in lettering standards in the first part of the twentieth century. Most sans serif styles keep within the bounds of conventional shapes, but some deviate considerably. Fig. 2.23 shows some examples of common sans serif typefaces.

Gothic or Old English
This is based on a pen drawn letter which was developed for use on medieval manuscripts. It is a very compressed style, designed to get as

Fig. 2.24   Gothic or Old English alphabets

Fig. 2.25 Gothic typefaces

much lettering as possible into a minimum of space. It produced a solid mass of lettering and for this reason is sometimes referred to as Black Lettering. See fig. 2.24.

Gothic has remained a popular style of lettering in spite of its poor legibility. In its original form it was a lower case alphabet only, the Gothic capital letters in common use now have been developed by printers and signwriters and invariably are more difficult to read than the lower case. The lower case basic form is that the stroke, space within the letter and space between letters is equal. A method of setting out Gothic letters is described in chapter 1. Typefaces based on Gothic are Old English, Fraktur and Pamela, see fig. 2.25.

Italic
A compressed, sloping, flowing form of Roman lower case. It looks at its best when produced as a light letter with the thin strokes of infinite

abcdefghijkl
mnopqrstuv
wxyz–&?!;)
ABCDEFG

Fig. 2.26 Italic alphabet

Fig. 2.27 Copperplate alphabet

width as if produced by the edge of a pen nib.

The version shown in fig. 2.26 retains the character of the pen stroke upon which the alphabet is based. Unlike Roman lower case the thick parts of the O are not in line horizontally. The weight is towards the bottom on the left side and towards the top on the right. This same character is applied to all other curved letters. A simple way of drawing the round letters is to base them on two overlapping ellipses, one upright and the other at a slight forward slope.

Script
There are two common forms of script: copperplate and brush script.

Copperplate (see fig. 2.27) is a very elegant, flowing lower case alphabet based upon the common legal handwriting of the eighteenth

Fig. 2.28   Free painted copperplate script

Flash

Gillies gothic

Fig. 2.29   Brush script typefaces

and nineteenth century. It has many of the qualities of italic, although it is generally more compressed, set at a greater slope, and has no serifs. The letters must be joined up and kept as close together as possible. A method of setting out copperplate is described in chapter 1.

Copperplate allows great scope to the skill and design sense of the signwriter. The ascenders and descenders can be flourished to form intricate scrolls or exaggerated loops, and made to link up with other letters on the same or neighbouring lines. See fig. 2.28. The capitals should only be used as initials and are often painted very freely and generally larger than the tallest of the lower case letters. There are a few typefaces based on copperplate, such as Palace and Balmoral.

Brush scripts have developed from the slick, one stroke brush letters of the ticket writers. Many signwriters perfect their own fast painted script type letter for jobs where speed is more important than style. Many typefaces are based on brush scripts, some very free such as Flash and Brush, while others are much more controlled like Gillies Gothic and Harlow, see fig. 2.29.

Selection of Letter Styles

If a signmaker is commissioned by a designer or an architect the style of lettering will usually be specified and the signmaker's task will be to reproduce that style precisely. On other occasions the client may ask for the signmaker's advice on what style to use, or the signmaker may be given a completely free hand. With the colossal choice available selecting the right style to suit the job can be a difficult task. The following suggestions may help to reduce the problems.

Built environment
Lettering is an important part of the built environment and should be in keeping with the age of the building and the style of the architecture with which it will be used.

Eighteenth century buildings were built in the classic style of the Romans and Roman letters look well in any situation on or in such buildings. Roman lettering is most suitable for many nineteenth century buildings also, but during the later part of the century architecture was heavier and a bolder type of Roman such as Clarendon, Caslon or Berling can be used effectively. Art nouveau letters such as Arnold Broklin and Desdemona suit buildings of the early part of the twentieth century, and Broadway and Gallia fit in well with 1920 and 1930 architecture. The simple and stark architecture of the late twentieth century is more happily lettered with sans serif types, see fig. 2.30.

Fig. 2.30   Sans serif lettering used on a twentieth century building

Occupations and activities

Some styles of lettering are traditionally associated with occupations and activities. Gothic is always considered to be old and used by firms who deal with things of the past, such as antique dealers and second hand dealers. Churches also are often associated with Gothic lettering. But Gothic is difficult to read and Roman has much older roots, is more legible, and generally more aesthetically pleasing.

Copperplate script is a style commonly used by firms with some sort of legal association, it is used also by firms who want to project a classy image. Florists, hair stylists and art dealers are inclined to use scripts.

Decorative styles, like Romantiques, have a strong fairground feeling particularly when brightly coloured. The same styles are used on barges and with other travelling communities, see fig. 2.31.

Fig. 2.31 Decorative lettering suitable for a fairground

Fig. 2.32 Sans serif letters used for a road sign

Attracting attention

Signs always need to be read, but some have to be read more urgently than others. Warning and instructional signs need to be produced in simple lettering styles so that nothing distracts from their text. For this reason sans serif letters are generally preferred, road and motorway signs being good examples of their use, see fig. 2.32. The typeface Helvetica is used extensively for the simple sign.

Shop fascias need to attract attention as well as to display a name or occupation therefore more attractive and decorative styles can be used.

Simplicity

The most effective signs generally are the simple ones. Simple signs do not mix many styles. If a style has been selected as the most suitable for the situation that style should be used throughout. If a lot of lettering is to be used the sign can be made more interesting and readable by using capitals and lower case of the same style, which is more aesthetically pleasing than mixing styles.

The grammatical and accepted method of producing words is either in capitals or lower case with or without an initial capital letter. Using large initial capitals with smaller capital letters for the rest of the word rarely improves the appearance of the sign.

Three
Drawing and Heraldry

A signmaker will need to do some form of drawing. The drawing may be a full size working drawing for signwriting, screen printing or glass decoration. It may be a scale sketch to help with setting out, or to indicate to a client the layout that will be produced. A signwriter working directly onto a sign will need to draw some shapes to work to. There may be a need to produce detailed, finished drawings in order to clinch a contract.

Occasionally the drawings are freehand. Often the drawing needs to be completed with drawing instruments. Always the drawing must be accurate and to achieve this certain aids are available.

Drawing Instruments

Drawing boards and T-square
These are necessary when preparing precise scale drawings, presentation drawings for clients, and to a lesser degree when setting out small, instrument drawn letters. The most common sizes of drawing boards are A1 (920 × 650 mm) and A2 (650 × 470 mm). An AO size (1270 × 920 mm) is available, but it needs so much space and is so expensive that it is unlikely that a signmaker could justify one. Boards can be simple wooden sheets with a separate T-square which slides up and down one edge, or they can have a parallel motion blade which slides up and down a wood or plastic faced board that is mounted on a simple support frame or a free standing, fully adjustable stand (see Fig. 3.8).

Any smooth, flat bench can be adapted as a drawing bench and a large T-square can be made up which can be run along one edge for drawing horizontal lines and upon which can be rested set squares for vertical and angled lines.

Set squares
Adjustable set squares are available which can be set to draw lines at any angles. They are expensive and not very convenient for carrying around. The most practical set squares are the standard 45° and the 30/60° version, fig 3.1. For setting out they should be as big as possible and no less than 300 mm on the longest edge. Smaller ones may be more useful for carrying around.

Pencils
For scale drawings and geometrical drawings an H and HB grade pencil is most convenient. For large working drawings and sketch

Fig. 3.1   Standard 45° and 60/30° set squares

layouts a softer pencil is more suitable, such as a B or 2B. The pencil needs to be kept sharp with as long a point as possible obtained with a sharp knife or pencil sharpener.

Rule
For bench work the ideal rule is 600 mm long, in transparent plastic, with a bevelled edge, and a hole in one end so that it can be hung up when not in use. For site work a folding metre rule or a 3 m steel tape are more convenient.

Scale rule
A scale rule is essential for both preparing scale drawings or sketches, and for taking measurements off a scale drawing for site marking out. The 300 mm rule is the most useful size and should be marked in the following scales: 1:1; 1:10; 1:100; 1:5; 1:50; 1:20; 1:200. See fig. 3.2.

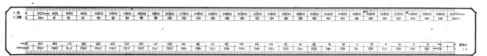

Fig. 3.2   Scale rule

Compass
Probably no other drawing instrument is available in as many qualities, patterns, sizes and variations as compasses. If the signmaker is doing a lot of setting out the ideal arrangement is to have a set of three instruments: a compass, a divider, and a spring bow compass. The compass will be used for drawing curves and bisecting, the divider for taking off and transferring measurements, and the spring bow can be set for drawing curves of equal size. When drawing is carried out only occasionally the most suitable compass is one that can be quickly converted from a lead to a point so that curves can be drawn and measurements taken quickly and accurately with the same instrument, see fig. 3.3. The compass arm needs to be at least 120 mm for full size drawings and 300 mm for site drawings.

Beam compasses, see fig. 3.4, are very useful instruments for drawing large curves. Some compasses can be fitted with an extension

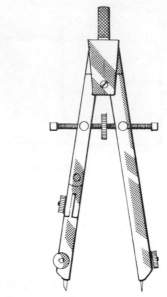

Fig. 3.3 Compass

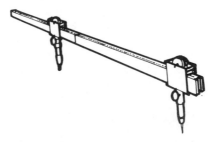

Fig. 3.4 Beam compass

arm to reach radii of about 160 mm, but a beam compass can reach over 500 mm.

A spring bow compass that can be fitted with a cutting blade is very useful when cutting stencils for screen printing and lead foil when glass decorating.

Protractor
Although they have a limited use protractors are inexpensive and are worth having available particularly when setting out polygons and some letters.

French curves
These are carefully designed shapes which contain a series of different radius curves which can be adapted to draw most shapes. They can be adapted for drawing lettering, but they are most useful for drawing heraldic shapes, or logos, or decorative features on script lettering. See fig. 3.5.

Fig. 3.5   A French curve

Flexi-curve
A thick, square sectioned, plastic covered soft wire which can be bent
to any shape and around which a line can be drawn. It is not as
adaptable as a French curve, but can be more useful for large setting
out.

Templates
These are thin plastic discs or plates from which geometrical shapes
have been cut. A great variety of shapes are available. Those which
contain circles are the most useful for the signmaker, see fig. 3.6, and
can be used to draw around when setting out lettering or logos, and to
cut around when stencil or foil cutting. One disc can contain 15–24
circles varying in diameter from 5–50 mm. A template containing
ellipses can be useful for setting out Roman letters.

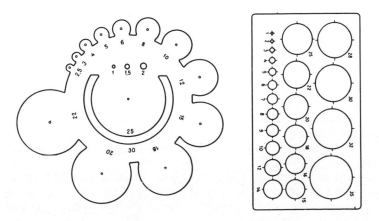

Fig. 3.6   Internal and external circle templates

Paper

Cartridge or drawing paper
This is useful for preparing presentation drawings when selling a sign design to a client, and is obtained in usual metric sizes.

Detail paper
A useful paper for large working drawings – thin, slightly transparent, not brittle, and available in rolls of varying width.

Tracing paper
As it is transparent it is very useful for tracing off lettering when spacing. It is available in a great variety of weights, qualities and finishes. Generally it is more brittle than detail paper therefore tears more easily when used in large pieces. Pencil leads wear down more quickly on tracing paper and they need sharpening very regularly. Tracing paper is available in sheets and rolls.

Scale Drawing

Scale drawing is a simple method of drawing a large sign in correct proportion on a small sheet of paper. For example, a signboard 3 m long by 1.25 m high when drawn to a scale of 1:10 will be one-tenth its actual size, namely 300×125 mm. Drawn to a scale of 1:50 it will be one-fiftieth of its actual size, 60×25 mm.

Any ruler marked in millimetres can be used as a scale rule with the help of arithmetic. For example, one centimetre can be used to represent one metre when a scale of 1:100 is required, or it can be used to represent 50 mm when working to a scale of 1:5. A more simple method is to use a scale rule which is marked out in a number of scales and only needs to be read off.

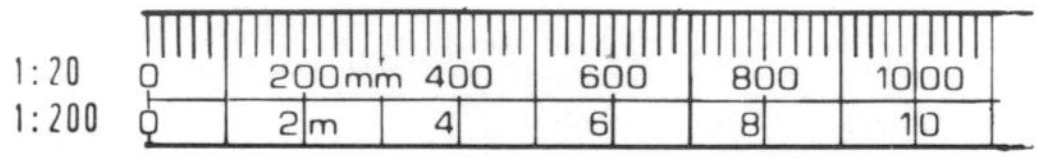

Fig. 3.7   Scales 1:20 and 1:200

Fig. 3.7 shows two scales, 1:20 and 1:200. The top section is marked off for 1:20 and below the line is scale 1:200. The distance between the 0 marker and the 200 mark represents 200 mm to a scale of 1:20 – in fact the distance is 10 mm, 200 divided by 20. Beneath the line the same distance, which is marked 0 to 2, represents 2 m.

A scale rule can be used to measure a line on a scale drawing both for drawing purposes and for taking off measurements when setting out full size.

To draw a signboard 10×5 m to a scale of 1:200 it is first necessary to draw two lines at right angles. Then place the scale rule along the horizontal line with the 0 marker on the angle and mark off the length at 10. Swivel the rule round so that it is vertical with the 0 on the same mark and make a point at 5, the line between 4 and 6. When a line is drawn horizontally from the 5 mark and a vertical line from the 10 mark they will meet to form a rectangle 10 × 5 m to a scale of 1:200.

The rule is used to measure off by placing the 0 marker on the angle of the rectangle and reading the mark at the end of the line.

The common scales are:

1:5   for details of fixings on scale drawings and also when working layouts for small signs;

1:10   for scale drawings of most signs when working out layouts;

1:20 ⎫
1:50 ⎬ common for scale drawing of sign boards;
1:100 ⎭

1:200 ⎱ for large signs and showing position of signs on building
1:500 ⎰ elevation.

Methods of Preparing Full Size Drawings

The sort of drawings that a signmaker is most likely to need to do are precise full size enlargements of a typeface or a company logo. Because there is so little room for error in either of these fields a commercial approach is to use some form of mechanical apparatus to enlarge from supplied artwork or a publication. The type of equipment which can do this is usually expensive and only a large quantity of this type of work will justify the capital outlay. The alternative is to copy the originals which often requires a reasonable degree of draughtsmanship and a knowledge of geometrical drawing to help produce an accurate drawing. When setting out directly onto large signboards or locations projectors are of little value and the signwriters drawing knowledge and skill is the only way to enlarge from supplied artwork.

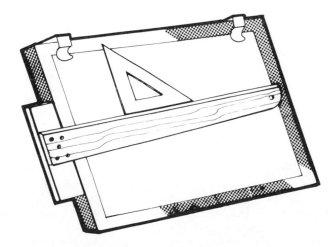

Fig. 3.8   Paper clipped to board with T-square and set square ready for drawing

Draughtsmanship

Draughtsmanship is the skill of drawing accurately. The following will help to produce accurate drawings.

Keep the pencil sharp otherwise the drawn line will have a measured thickness. This will result in the intersections of diagonal lines and bisecting curves not giving a precise point but one which could vary by up to 1 mm.

Wherever possible fix the drawing paper to a drawing board or setting out bench with tape, pins or clips so that horizontal lines can be drawn against a T-square, and vertical lines drawn against set squares set up on the T-square, see fig. 3.8. If the paper moves and lines are drawn with rulers against measured marks onto a guessed parallel, small errors will occur which will spoil a finished job.

Use geometrical methods for measuring or dividing lines rather than a ruler. Errors are easily made when reading off a ruler, particularly when the light is not good or a number of measurements are necessary.

Geometrical Drawing

The followiong methods of drawing can be of considerable value when preparing working drawings or when setting out on site.

Bisecting

Bisecting is a method of dividing a line precisely in half. Not only does it produce a centre line but offers the means of drawing a centre line precisely at right angles to the original line.

Place the point of the compass on one end of the line, open it to any radius which is more than half the length of the line. Draw an arc above and below the line. Move the point of the compass to the other end of the line and with the same radius draw two more arcs to cross the first two. A line drawn between the two crosses formed by the arcs will be exactly central to the original line and at right angles to it. See fig. 3.9.

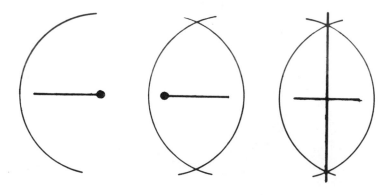

Fig. 3.9   Method of bisecting a line

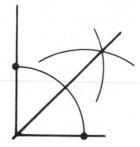

Fig. 3.10 Method of bisecting an angle

An angle can be bisected to produce an exact centre line from the intersection, see fig. 3.10. Place the point of the compass on the angle and draw a curve between the two lines at any radius. Place the compass point on one end of the curve where it touches the line, open it to more than half the length of the curve and draw an arc. Repeat the process at the other end of the curve and with the same radius cross the first arc. A line drawn between the crossed arcs and the angle will be exactly in the centre of the angle. For example, a right angle bisected will produce a 45° angle.

These methods are invaluable for drawing letters and helping to draw geometrical shapes.

Dividing a line into equal parts
This method will be used when the line to be divided will not divide accurately by measurement, e.g. a 545 mm line required to be divided into eight parts.

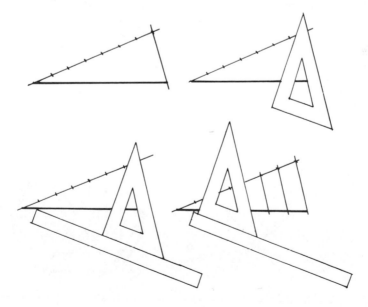

Fig. 3.11 Dividing a line into an equal number of parts

Draw a line at any angle from one end of the line to be divided. Measure along this new line the number of divisions required. Any convenient measurement can be used for the divisions providing every one is exactly the same. Another method is to use dividers opened to any distance and stepped off along the new line to the number of divisions required.

Draw a line from the last division of the new line to the end of the original line, then lines drawn parallel to this one will divide the original line into the required number of parts. The most practical method of drawing parallel lines is to place the long edge of a 30/60° set square exactly against the connecting line. Place a straightedge at the angle of the short side of the set square and hold it firmly in position. The set square can be moved along the straightedge to the divisions on the measured line and lines can be drawn through to the original line. See fig. 3.11.

Finding the centre of a circle

Draw two lines, each to touch the circumference of the circle and at any position but not opposite each other. Bisect each line and where they meet is the circle centre. See fig. 3.12.

Constructing a right angle

When working on a board or bench a right angle can be drawn accurately with a set square, but when working on a large sign or area a set square is too small for accuracy. In these circumstances the 3.4.5 method of drawing a right angle is a practical solution.

Two lines are at right angles if one measures 3, the other 4 and the hypotenuse (a line joining the two points to form a triangle) measures 5. Therefore if two lines are drawn at what appears to be right angles the vertical one needs to be marked off in a measurement which is divisible by 3 (e.g. 900 mm; or 1500 mm), and the horizontal line in a length divisible by 4 (e.g. 1200 mm; 1600 mm; or 2000 mm). The line joining the extremes of these two points should be 1500 mm; 2000 mm; or 2500 mm. If it is less the vertical line needs to be redrawn at a slightly greater angle away from the hypotenuse. If it is more the vertical line needs to be redrawn angled towards the hypotenuse.

Fig. 3.12
Finding the centre of a circle

Fig. 3.13
Constructing a hexagon with a set square

Geometrical shapes
Many logos are contained within geometrical shapes which if drawn only slightly inaccurately will look so much worse when painted. The most common shapes which may cause setting out problems are the polygons and the ellipse.

Polygons
These can all be contained within a circle, and have straight sides of equal length. They are named according to the number of sides they have.

Pentagon = 5 sides; Hexagon = 6 sides; Heptagon = 7 sides; Octagon = 8 sides; Nonagon = 9 sides; Decagon = 10 sides; Undecagon = 11 sides; Duodecagon = 12 sides.

The even sided polygons generally are easier to construct than the odd sided ones. The easiest method is to construct them within a drawn circle.

Within a circle
A circle has 360°, so any polygon whose number of sides can be divided into 360 exactly can be constructed with a protractor or set square. For example, a hexagon requires 6 angles of 60°, see fig. 3.13, an octagon requires 8 angles of 45°, a nonagon nine angles of 40°, and a duodecagon twelve angles of 30°. The hexagon, octagon and duo-decagon can be drawn with standard set squares, but the nonagon will need to be drawn with an adjustable set square or a protractor.

Stepping a hexagon
The easiest method of constructing a hexagon is to step off the radius of the circle around the circumference, which will always fit exactly six times.

Duodecagon with a compass
A duodecagon can be constructed by drawing semi-circles of the circles radius from the four points where the vertical and horizontal diameters touch the circumference. See fig. 3.14.
  To draw all other polygons one of two methods can be used.

Fig. 3.14 Constructing a duodecagon with a compass

Trial and error
Open the dividers to any distance and step it around the circumference. If too many divisions are made the dividers need to be widened and tried again. If too few divisions occur the dividers need to be closed a little and tried again. It may take many adjustments before the exact measurement is found. The method can be time consuming and messy.

By projection
Draw the diameter and divide it into the exact number of parts as the polygon has sides, e.g. a pentagon requires the diameter to be divided into five parts. The line can be divided by the method described in fig. 3.11. Put the compass point on one end of the diameter and open it up to the length of the diameter and draw an arc beneath the circle. Draw a similar arc from the other end of the diameter to cross the first arc. Draw a line from where the arcs cross, through the second division on the diameter, and continue it until it touches the circumference above the diameter. The distance between the left hand end of the diameter and this mark will step around the circumference by the number of sides required. See fig. 3.15.

All these methods describe how to divide the circle circumference into the number of sides required. The final stage in all of them is to draw a straight line between each point.

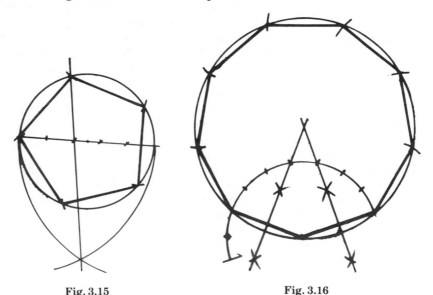

Fig. 3.15	Fig. 3.16
Constructing a pentagon by projection	Constructing a nonagon on a given line

Constructing a polygon on a line
Occasionally it is not possible to draw a circle first when constructing a polygon. But if the length of one side is known it is sufficient information to draw a polygon. The following is one of many methods, see fig. 3.16.

Put the compass point on one end of the line, open it to the length of the line and draw a semi-circle. Divide the semi-circle into the equal number of parts as sides are required. Set squares can be used to help this stage when drawing hexagons, octagons and duodecagons. Trial and error will have to be used for other polygons. Draw a line from the end of the original line to the second division on the semi-circle. Bisect both of these lines and where they meet will be the centre for a circle which will touch the end of both lines and whose circumference will divide equally into the number of sides required.

Ellipse
Small ellipses, up to about 40 mm long, can be drawn with templates. Larger ones need to be set out geometrically. There are many methods of drawing ellipses, but the two most practical ones which can be adapted to large scale setting out are based on the trammel and on using focal points.

Trammel method
Set out the major axis (the longest diameter) and cross it exactly central and at right angles with the minor axis (the shortest diameter). Make a trammel from a strip of paper or card, or a wooden batten and make a mark near one end. Place the mark against the extreme point of the minor axis and mark off half the minor axis (the point where the axes cross). Move the trammel so that the first mark is on the extreme point of the major axis and mark off half the major axis.

Place the trammel along and below the major axis with the first mark on the extreme point of the axis. Swivel the trammel down a short distance and manoeuvre it until the half-minor mark is touching the major axis and the half-major mark is touching the vertical part of the minor axis. Put a pencil or chalk mark by the outside mark. Move the trammel again and when the two inner marks are in contact with

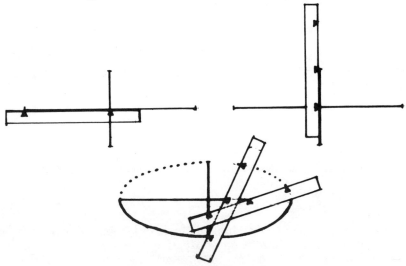

Fig. 3.17   Drawing an ellipse with a trammel

their respective axes put another mark at the outside marker. Continue this process around the whole axes until a series of dots have been made which can be joined up carefully by freehand drawing into an ellipse. See fig. 3.17.

Focal point method
Set out the major and minor axes as before.

Open the compass to half the major axis, place the point on the end of the minor axis and draw two marks on the major axis. These are the focal points.

Fix a pin in each of the focal points and one in the end of the minor axis which was the centre for the two focal points. Tie a piece of thread or fine string to one of the focal point pins, stretch it tight around the top pin, and secure it to the second focal point pin. Replace the top pin with a pencil, and keeping the thread taut, draw a curve which will touch the extreme points of the axes.

If a small groove is cut in the pencil lead about 2 – 3 mm away from the point the thread will catch in it and will not constantly slip out as the curve is drawn.

When this method is used for very large setting out a beam compass or a piece of string tied to a pencil can be used to mark the focal points if the compass is not big enough to span the required radius.

Rubber suckers can be used if pins cannot be driven into the surface but the resulting curve may not be very accurate because the rubber may stretch as the tension of the string is applied to them. See fig. 3.18.

Fig. 3.18   Drawing an ellipse by guiding a pencil along a string stretched between pins fixed in the focal points

Enlarging
Any logo or similar device which needs to be enlarged for reproduction and is not contained within or based upon a geometrical shape can be accurately enlarged by 'squaring' or proportional scales, see fig. 3.19.

Draw a shape around the original device to touch its extreme points.

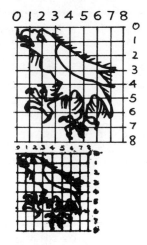

Fig. 3.19   Enlarging by 'squaring'

If these lines are drawn horizontally and vertically to form a square or rectangle the task will be made easier. Divide the length of the shape into an equal number of divisions and divide the width into an equal number of divisions. When vertical and horizontal lines are drawn through these points the shape will be covered with a grid. The shape of the grids may be squares or rectangles.

Draw the shape which is to contain the full size drawing of the device. If a perfect reproduction is required the shape must be in correct proportion to the small one. For example, if the original copy has been contained within a rectangle 80 × 45 mm, the full size shape must be twice, or three times, or ten times these measurements, namely 160 × 90, or 240 × 135, or 800 × 450. Or any other proportions of the original.

Divide the full size shape into the same number of divisions as the original and draw in the grid. For easy reference the grid can be numbered on both the small and large drawing.

It is now necessary to mark off on the FS drawing the points at which the device touches each of the grid markings. If a series of dots is placed on the drawing first these can be joined up later with a clean, free drawn line. The size of the grid used depends upon the intricacies of the device and the free drawing skill of the person doing the enlargement. There is less need for interpretation when the 'squares' are put very close together but a tight grid makes it difficult to see the device.

On rare occasions a device may need to be enlarged to a different proportion to the original. For example, a shape which fits into a square can be enlarged to fit a rectangle. The result does look very different. When this is required the proportional scale method is the only one which can be used. Mechanical enlargers can enlarge only in proportion. The method is to draw the full size shape to the required size and divide it into the same number of divisions as the original.

When enlarging from a book illustration or a piece of artwork that

Fig. 3.20   Fret patterns constructed within a net

cannot be marked the grid can be drawn on a piece of tracing paper laid over the original. This method may be used also when enlarging any small original because grid lines may obliterate the shape and make copying very difficult.

Patterns in a net
Many repeating patterns are contained within a net and can be reproduced comparatively easily by calculating the number of squares carefully, and drawing the pattern between them. Fig. 3.20 shows some common patterns which are constructed within a net.

Enlarging Apparatus

Apart from photographic enlargers there are many pieces of equipment on the market which will increase the size of a printed typeface or logo. They all use lenses in some form or other, are expensive, and have various limitations.

Enlarger
The standard type requires the original to be placed on an illuminated shelf beneath a transluscent table upon which the enlarged image is transmitted. The operator can control both the lens beneath the transluscent table and the illuminated shelf until the right size image is obtained in sharp focus. When tracing paper is placed on the table the image can be seen through it and can be drawn.

This type of equipment has a limted enlargement range, perhaps no more than six times. If a bigger image is required it has to be done in stages. The enlarged drawing placed on the shelf and enlarged again, and the process continued until the required size is obtained. A further restriction occurs when the transluscent table is not big enough to take the full size drawing.

Epidiascope or episcopes
Epidiascopes can project an image onto a screen or paper and produce a greater enlargement than that obtained with standard enlargers. Some of the original epidiascopes used as visual aid equipment were very large and heavy and could project horizontally only. This required all drawing to be done on a vertical surface which can be difficult.

The modern types are smaller and can be used to transmit images vertically as well as horizontally, see fig. 3.21. In a workshop with limited space a convenient method of mounting them is on a vertical track above a flat drawing bench. The scope can be moved up or down until

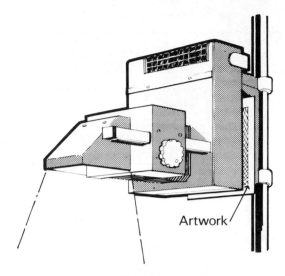

Fig. 3.21   An episcope

the right size is obtained then fixed in that position by tightening the securing bolt. Drawing on the bench is more comfortable than working upright. These enlargers may produce an image up to twenty times the original. Most of them require a special lens to enlarge less than twice as big as the original. Some models can be adapted to reduce the size of the original.

Projectors
A cheaper method of projecting is to use a simple slide projector. This has the advantage of being much cheaper to purchase than the other two pieces of equipment, but it is less convenient to use. Transparent slides of the original have to be made before they can be used with a projector. Simple logos can be traced onto a piece of acetate sheet and projected, but more complicated ones may need to be photographed on to a slide before they can be used.

A projector is most conveniently used by a signmaker whose work is limited to a few typefaces. These types can be purchased as dry transfer lettering in small sizes and cut up into slide sizes and mounted. When the jobs which require these types need to be done the appropriate slide is selected, projected onto a sheet of paper and the image's outline drawn.

Projectors may be restricted when used for small enlargements because some machines cannot be adjusted for close focus and there is difficulty in getting close enough to draw when projecting over short distances.

Heraldry

The signwriter will often be required to paint coats of arms. Such jobs take one of two forms. Either a repaint of an exiting heraldic device, or

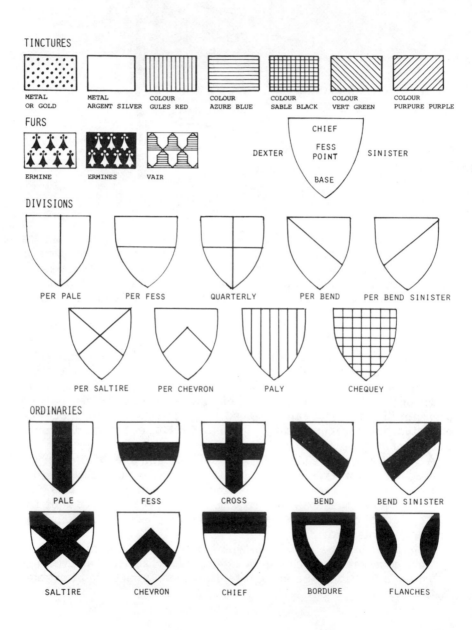

TINCTURES

METAL OR GOLD | METAL ARGENT SILVER | COLOUR GULES RED | COLOUR AZURE BLUE | COLOUR SABLE BLACK | COLOUR VERT GREEN | COLOUR PURPURE PURPLE

FURS

ERMINE | ERMINES | VAIR

CHIEF
DEXTER FESS POINT SINISTER
BASE

DIVISIONS

PER PALE | PER FESS | QUARTERLY | PER BEND | PER BEND SINISTER

PER SALTIRE | PER CHEVRON | PALY | CHEQUEY

ORDINARIES

PALE | FESS | CROSS | BEND | BEND SINISTER

SALTIRE | CHEVRON | CHIEF | BORDURE | FLANCHES

Fig. 3.22 Common heraldic terms

a new painting from written or drawn information. For both jobs the signwriter needs a fundamental knowledge of heraldy to avoid making mistakes.

Heraldry is a precise art which follows rules laid down by a controlling body hundreds of years ago and which still apply. All heraldic arms must be registered with the Royal College of Arms and once recorded can be used by that family or that authority for perpetuity. If a coat of arms is reproduced differently to that recorded in the College it is no longer the arms of that person. It is possible that the changes will depict the arms as that of another person. For these persons it is necessary for a signwriter to know the basic forms by which a shield may be displayed and to have a working knowledge of the heraldic language.

There are many books published on heraldry to which the signwriter should refer when working on any heraldic design. The following glossary of heraldic terms should provide just enough information to make the task of checking instructions easier.

Heraldic terms
See fig. 3.22.

Colours or tinctures
These are in three groups:

Colours which are: gules (red); azure (blue); sable (black); vert (green); purpure (purple).
Metals which are: or (gold); argent (silver)
Furs which are ermine and vair.

Colours are shown in their brightest form so that they are always distinctive, and contrasted against the metals, which may be painted also in yellow or white respectively.

It is a common rule of heraldry that no colour shall be placed on a colour, and no metal on a metal.

The ermine furs are depicted in four different ways, two of them with white backgrounds and two with black. The whites should be shown against colours and the blacks against metals.

The term Proper is used when a device is required to be painted in its natural colour.

Hatchings
The name given to the method of showing the tinctures in line so that they can be reproduced in black and white.

Divisions
A shield can be divided into two or four parts and each arrangement has a title which is preceded in a description by the words 'party per' or 'per'.

Ordinaries
Bands are often placed on shields in set positions, each one has a name and all are called ordinaries.

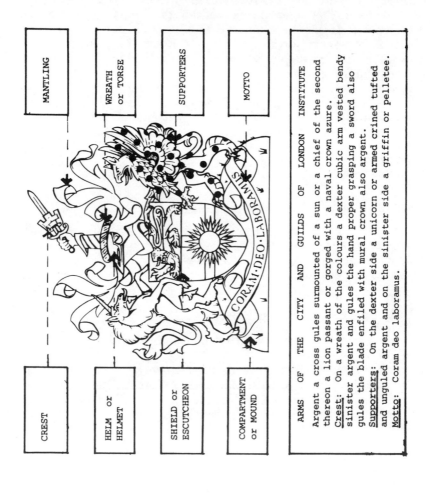

MANTLING

WREATH or TORSE

SUPPORTERS

MOTTO

CREST

HELM or HELMET

SHIELD or ESCUTCHEON

COMPARTMENT or MOUND

ARMS OF THE CITY AND GUILDS OF LONDON INSTITUTE

Argent a cross gules surmounted of a sun or a chief of the second thereon a lion passant or gorged with a naval crown azure.
Crest: On a wreath of the colours a dexter cubic arm vested bendy sinister argent and gules the hand proper grasping a sword also gules the blade enfiled with mural crown also argent.
Supporters: On the dexter side a unicorn or armed crined tufted and unguled argent and on the sinister side a griffin or pelletee.
Motto: Coram deo laboramus.

Fig. 3.23 A full or complete heraldic achievement (reproduced by kind permission of the City and Guilds of London Institute)

Charges
Any design or device which is placed on a shield is referred to as a charge, including the ordinaries.

Field
The background of a shield, which can be an overall tincture, or a division, or have small devices placed all over it, like a chequer-board or a scattering of fleur-de-lys.

Dexter
The left hand side of a shield as seen by the spectator, but the right hand of the wearer.

Sinister
The right hand side as viewed, but the left hand as worn.

Chief
The top part of the shield.

Fess point
The centre of the shield.

Blazon
The written description of a shield. All coats of arms are registered by their blazon. Over many years and after many reproductions heraldic artists are inclined to slightly change the shapes and arrangements. The one sure way of checking whether an illustration is accurate is to compare it against the blazon. See fig. 3.23.

The rules of blazon are: the field must be described first; the chief takes precedence over any other part of the shield; dexter takes precedence over sinister; the tincture of the charge is stated immediately after the name.

Emblazon
The painting of a coat of arms.

Full or complete achievement
A term sometimes used to describe a coat of arms which is emblazoned with a helm, crest, mantling and supporters, see fig. 3.23.

Escutcheon
The shield, the essential feature of a full achievement. Many arms consist of a shield only.

Helm
The helmet which is placed on top of the escutcheon. The type of helmet denotes the rank of the holder. Royalty will use gold or silver helmets. Most other ranks will use a helmet in profile and painted as steel. Helms are not part of the blazon but are emblazoned if the holder has a crest. See fig. 3.23.

Crest
A device fitted to the top of the helm and described in the blazon (fig. 3.23). Some arms consist of escutcheon and crest only.

Mantling
A cloth originally draped over the top of the helm. Generally shown in a decorative form as if cut into ribbons and twisted. It is designed and emblazoned to fit the shape available around the crest. Often shown as colour on the outside with a metal or fur lining. Mantling is not described in the blazon and is normally included when a helm and crest are emblazoned. See fig. 3.23.

Torse or wreath
The mantling twisted into a band and placed on top of the helm but below the crest. Always shown in the same colours as the mantling and always of six knots, the first being of the lining metal or fur. Forms part of the blazon. See fig. 3.23.

Supporters
Animals or humans standing either side of the shield. On rare occasions other forms are used. Not all coats of arms have supporters. They are fully described in the blazon. See fig. 3.23.

Mound or compartment
A firm base upon which the supporters and the shield stand. Usually a grassy hill is used. Rarely part of the blazon. See fig 3.23.

Motto
Commonly shown in a ribbon. The wording of the motto is described in the blazon but the method of displaying it is left to the designer or heraldic painter. See fig. 3.23.

Four
Coatings

All signs require some form of coating whether it is to colour or protect the sign substrate, or to produce the lettering or symbols on them. Although used for different purposes the coatings for painting or signwriting may have similar composition yet are sold under different labels. No matter how expensive a sign may be in labour costs to produce and regardless of the skills applied to achieve a beautiful finish, the signs life span is dependent almost entirely on the selection and application of the right type of coatings.

For these reasons a signmaker needs to have a knowledge of coating technology so that the right type of material is used to protect or paint a sign, particularly in severe conditions, and that materials used together are compatible.

Composition of Coatings

All coatings contain a medium and a thinner. The medium is the film former, it converts from the liquid coating to the hard film. It provides the adhesive and flowing properties to the coating, and influences the kind of sheen to which it dries. The medium also produces the film that will resist moisture, abrasive washing or chemical attack. This essential component is available in many forms, each one having particular virtues and identity, so that a coating can be selected which will achieve the qualities required.

The thinner makes the medium into a usable form so that it can be applied easily and evenly whether by brush, spray, roller or squeegee. Because mediums are available in so many forms the range of thinners is almost as big, and the selection of the right thinner for the coating is often as critical as the selection of the coating.

With the exception of bitumen mediums are transparent. Although many coatings are required in this form (e.g. varnishes), the majority need to have opacity or covering power to obliterate the substrate. Also they must have colour. To provide both opacity and colour fine powdered solids called pigments are added to the thinned mediums to make paints. In some instances the pigments also help the medium to protect the substrate. Depending on the nature of the medium other components may need to be added to either make the coating dry or make it more flexible.

Driers are added to coatings containing drying oils to make sure that they dry within a few hours. Catalysts or hardeners or curing agents need to be added to some types of resins to make them harden. Plasticisers in the form of oils or resins are put into some quick drying coatings to make the dry film less brittle.

Some paints are manufactured in a jelly-like state so that a thick coating can be applied with little tendency to sag. These coatings are called thixotropic.

Mediums

Coating film formers may be: drying oils, such as linseed oil; resins, originally extracted from trees now mostly synthetic; mixtures of drying oils and resins which combine the slow drying and elasticity of oils with the toughness of resins; nitrocellulose, which is natural cellulose dissolved in an acid; chlorinated rubber, a treatment of synthetic rubber which has many specialised uses; and, bitumen, a black natural or synthetic material with great water and chemical resistance. Table 4.1 shows the characteristics of the most common mediums.

Coatings which have the same medium, but are made by different manufacturers usually can be mixed together. A small sample should be tested first. If they are incompatible they will thicken into a sticky mixture or the pigment will 'float'. Coatings which contain drying oils usually can be mixed together without problems.

Table 4.1   Characteristics of common mediums.

Type	Properties	Uses
Oil only		
Linseed Oil	Slow drying Destroyed by strong alkalies Mixes well with lead based pigments	Red lead primers White lead primers Calcium plumbate primer Oil stainers
Resins only		
Shellac	Natural resin Readily dissolved in methylated spirit Produces hard, brown film	Knotting French polish Button polish
Polyvinyl Acetate (PVA) and Acrylic	Synthetic resins Clear and non-yellowing Good adhesion Suspended in water	Emulsion paints and varnishes Masonry paints Timber primer Adhesives Screen inks

Table 4.1 contd.

Type	Properties	Uses
Polyurethane and Epoxy	Synthetic resins Very hard films Resist water, chemicals and abrasion Require hardener to dry Very expensive	Floor paints or clear coatings Chemical resistant coatings Bar top paints for clear coatings
Oil and resin		
Oil Modified Alkyd Resin	High gloss Flexible film Destroyed by strong alkalies Resists weather Very widely used	Undercoats Gloss finishes Eggshell paints Varnishes Some metal primers Signwriters enamels and colours Some screening inks
Oil Modified Polyurethane Resin	Generally harder and tougher films than alkyd	Gloss finishes Eggshell and gloss varnishes
Tung Oil Modified Phenolic or Coumarone Resin	Water resistant Alkali resistant	Alkali resistant paints Boat varnishes
Nitrocellulose	Rapid drying Hard film Chemical resistant Spray applied	Vehicle refinishing paints and lacquers
Chlorinated Rubber	Water and chemical resistant Very flexible Quick drying	Chemical resistant paints Water resistant paints Road marking paints
Bitumens	Black Resist water, acid and alkalies Cheap Softened by heat Bleed through oil paints	Damp-proof compounds Bituminous paints Brunswick black Black Japan

Thinners

The right thinner for the coating is the one that reduces the viscosity, but does not dissolve the dry film. Because of the vast range of mediums it is always advisable to follow the manufacturers instructions concerning the correct thinner to use. In extreme cases the wrong thinner could cause the coating to thicken into an unusable mass, or it could dissolve the undercoat and lift off all the coatings down to the substrate.

Thinners begin to evaporate once the material has been applied. Their speed of evaporation influences the way the coatings are applied. Water and white spirit are reasonably slow and paints thinned with these can be comfortably applied by brush. Methylated spirit evaporates quickly and coatings that use this thinner must be applied in a few minutes. Cellulose paints dry so rapidly because of their highly volatile thinners that they can be sprayed only.

Many thinners give off flammable or dangerous vapours. There are statutory regulations controlling the storage and use of some thinners – see the end of the chapter. No spirit-thinned coatings should be used in large quantities without adequate ventilation being provided to prevent either asphyxiation or explosion.

Thinners must evaporate completely. If any residue is left in the film it can slow the drying or stop it completely. Also it can reduce the efficiency of the dry film. Both paraffin and petrol may leave harmful residues and should not be used as thinners. Table 4.2 shows the characteristics of the common coating thinners.

Tale 4.2   Characteristics and uses of common thinners.

Type	Characteristics	Uses
Water	Cheap Non-flammable Readily available Non-toxic	Thinning all emulsion paints Washing brushes used in emulsion paints Few screen inks
White Spirit	Extracted from crude oil Flammable	Thinning all coatings containing drying oil including signwriters colours and many screen inks Cleaning brushes and screens used for oil based colours Thinning and dissolving Brunswick black Dissolving tallow (glass decoration)

Table 4.2 cont.

Type	Characteristics	Uses
Methylated Spirit	Alcohol Highly flammable Evaporates quickly	Thinning button polish and French polish May dissolve dry emulsion paint
Cellulose Thinners	Special blends of powerful solvents prepared for use with specific coatings Highly flammable Evaporate rapidly Expensive Dissolve oil based dry films	Thinning all cellulose coatings Cleaning spray equipment used for cellulose paints
Polyurethane Thinner	Similar properties to cellulose thinners	Thinning 2 pack polyurethane coatings Cleaning spray equipment and brushes used with polyurethane
PVC and Acrylic Screen Ink Thinners	Similar properties to cellulose thinners	Thinning screen ink for plastic surfaces Cleaning printing screens used with pvc and acrylic inks
Solvent Naphtha	Highly flammable Dissolves oil based dry films	Thinning chlorinated rubber paints Thinning some primers Cleaning brushes used in chlorinated rubber paints

Notes

Turps substitute is either white spirit or a mixture of white spirit and other solvents. Suitable as a cleaner of brushes and screens and generally reliable as a thinner of oil based paints.

Paraffin is suitable for cleaning brushes used in oil paints and may dissolve some screen inks.

Flash point is the temperature at which a thinner gives off a flammable vapour. With the exception of water all the listed thinners are flammable. Some, like cellulose thinners, have a very low flash point and may produce a flammable vapour at well below a normal room temperature.

Pigments

Pigments are obtained from one of three sources:

Earth or natural – which are clays or minerals mined and ground to a very fine powder. They are available in a limited colour range but are cheap and reliable when used in exposed situations.

Inorganic – mixtures of chemicals or the result of the action of chemicals or heat on various metals. A large range of traditional colours are produced all varying in price and reliability. All white pigments are inorganic. The availability of coloured inorganic pigments is diminishing, those retained are kept principally for their colour.

Organic – dyestuffs produced principally from derivatives of crude oil. This is the most common source of coloured pigments. An almost limitless range of colours are produced from this source, most of them expensive and varying in reliability.

Pigments have been produced from all these sources over very many years resulting in an extensive range of colours being available. Manufacturers of artists paints still produce a wide range of colours, but decorative and industrial paint manufacturers have limited the number of pigments they use to those which are generally reliable and will produce coloured paints which keep their colour and offer a minimum health hazard. Even so paints and signwriters colours do react differently and a knowledge of pigment properties can aid a signmaker when selecting and mixing colours for both painting signs and signwriting.

Essential pigments qualities are:

Colour
Each pigment has its own characteristic colour which influences its choice when used in its full strength and when mixed with white or coloured pigments to produce other colours. For example, chrome yellows are available in a range from primrose (a pale greeny yellow), through lemon (strong standard yellow), to middle (rich mustard type yellow). When mixed with white they produce a range of colours from cream to pale sunshine yellow. When mixed with blue they produce good greens.

Staining power or tinting strength
This is the amount of pigment required to change white or other base colour to the desired colour. Some stainers such as raw sienna have poor staining power and a considerable amount of the pigment is required to convert white to a deep cream. But prussian blue is a very strong stainer and very little is required to change white into a pale greeny blue.

Opacity
Opacity refers to the covering power of pigments. This is of vital importance to the signmaker because most signwriters colours and screen inks are expected to be able to obliterate a surface in one coat. Paint manufacturers usually indicate on their colour cards those colours which have poor opacity and the selection of these should be carefully considered when preparing a specification. Some colours, such as lime green and orange, have poor opacity and may take three or four coats before the surface is obliterated. Most signwriters colours are selected because of their good opacity, but some colours have better obliteration than others. Brights reds, particularly crimson, generally are more transparent than browns.

Light fastness
The ability of a pigment to withstand the effect of light is known as light fastness. A fugitive pigment will quickly lose its brilliance when exposed to strong natural light. A light fast pigment resists the effect of light and will retain its full colour after long exposure. Some pigments have better light fastness when used at full strength than when they are reduced with white. Most stainer and signwriter colour manufacturers select pigments which offer the greatest resistance to the destructive effect of light. Information on the performance of their colours can be obtained from the manufacturers and should be carefully followed when a sign containing a number of colours is to be used in an exposed place.

Toxicity
Some pigments contain substances which are poisonous so must be used with care. Lead for many years was the basis of many pigments, but its use was seriously curtailed from about the middle of this century. There are still a few metal priming paints which contain lead and some of the traditional inorganic stainers are still made from lead. It is important that toxic pigments should not be used on signs which are in easy reach of children or animals. Paints containing lead must be clearly labelled to that effect.

Table 4.3 lists some of the pigments which are available as signwriters colours, together with their principal properties. The key to the ratings is: VG very good; G good; F fair; P poor.

Table 4.4 lists the pigments used in the manufacture of paints and states their properties and uses.

Table 4.3 Common pigments available as signwriters colours.

Name	Colour	Origin	Staining Power	Opacity	Poisonous
Titanium oxide	White	Inorganic	—	VG	No
Ochre (Oxford, Yellow, Golden)	Brown yellow	Earth	G	G	No
Raw sienna	Brown yellow	Earth	P	P	No
Lead chrome (Lemon, Middle, Orange)	Bright yellow to rich orange	Inorganic	G	G	Yes
Zinc chrome (Primrose)	Green yellow	Inorganic	F	F	No
Raw umber Burnt umber	Deep brown	Earth	G	G	No
Burnt sienna	Red brown	Earth	F	G	No
Vandyke brown	Deep brown	Earth	F	P	No
Venetian red Indian red	Purple and Brown-reds	Earth	G	G	No
Scarlet (poppy)	Rich red	Organic	VG	G	No
Crimson (Alizarin)	Blue red	Organic	G	P	No
Ultramarine blue (French blue or Permanent blue	Rich blue	Inorganic	F	F	No
Prussian blue (Chinese blue or Antwerp blue)	Deep green blue	Inorganic	VG	P	No
Phthalocyanine blue (Winsor blue)	Rich deep blues	Organic	VG	VG	No
Phthalocyanine greens (Winsor Green)	Rich deep greens	Organic	VG	VG	No

Table 4.3 contd.

Name	Colour	Origin	Staining Power	Opacity	Poisonous
Chrome greens	Light medium or deep greens	Inorganic	G	G	Yes
Cerise Mauve	Rich red-blue and blue-red	Organic	F	G	No
Vegetable black (Drop black) (Ivory black) (Lampblack)		Inorganic	G	G	No

Table 4.4   Base pigments used in paints.

Titanium oxide	White pigment used in all types of paints. The base of signwriters white colour.
Zinc phosphate	White, non-toxic pigment used in metal primers and universal primers.
Calcium plumbate	Cream coloured pigment containing lead. Used in priming paints for galvanised iron and hardwoods.
Red lead	Rich orangy-red pigment used in primers for iron. Toxic. Mixed with Brunswick black as acid resist.

Driers

Paints and varnishes are composed so that they will dry within a practical time span. Some, like cellulose paints, dry very rapidly and can be recoated within minutes. Others, like alkyd gloss finishes, dry slowly and cannot be recoated for at least eight hours after application. The speed of drying depends on the method by which the medium converts to a solid film, and by the action of additives in the coating. Coatings based on drying oils contain driers which absorb oxygen very rapidly from the air and pass it on to the medium so that it dries within eight hours. Without driers oil paints could take many days to dry. Cellulose paints and emulsion paints do not contain driers and depend upon their conversion to a solid film by the evaporation of their thinners.

Two pack coatings, such as polyurethane, dry because a chemical action occurs between the two materials when they are mixed together that changes the resin into a solid film. Until the components are mixed the coating will not dry. The two materials are mixed together just before they are used, and once mixed can be used for about five hours after which time they will have dried to such a state that they can no longer be brushed or sprayed.

On occasions the signwriter uses oil stainers which contain no driers therefore they will have to be mixed with a material that ensures that they will dry within a few hours. If they are mixed with a standard undercoat or gloss finish or varnish there is usually no need for further additives because all three materials contain driers which will ensure that the coating will dry. When used on their own they need the addition of a drier which can be obtained as liquid oil drier or terebine. Only a small amount is needed to make the stainers dry. The most common material used by the signwriter as a drier is Gold Size which is a varnish that contains a high proportion of liquid oil driers or terebine.

Drying

Coatings dry by a variety of methods, the process generally going through a number of stages.

The first stage is evaporation of the thinners which starts immediately the coating is applied and may take between a few minutes and a couple of hours depending on the coating and the type of weather or room temperature. As the spirit evaporates the coating begins to thicken and become sticky. This is known as flashing off or setting up. When set up the coating film still feels sticky but has lost its flowing properties. It is essential that the coating is fully applied before it has set up or stopped flowing to obtain a smooth, even film. Cellulose paints set up within seconds of application and for this reason can only be sprayed because the brush cannot be used fast enough to apply it before it has set up. Oil based paints can take up to half an hour to set up, after this time the film is so sticky that if it is brushed further it becomes very uneven and will remain in that rough state when it dries.

When the atmosphere is warm during application the thinners evaporate more quickly and the setting up time is shorter. In a cold or wet atmosphere the evaporation is very slow and in extreme conditions the coating may not dry at all.

Some coatings dry entirely by evaporation of the thinners. They are quick drying paints and can be difficult to apply. They are cellulose coatings, french and button polishes, chlorinated rubber paints, some screen inks, and Brunswick black and Black Japan.

Other coatings dry by one of the following processes after the thinners have evaporated.

Oxidation

Coatings which contain drying oils combine with the oxygen in the air and change their structure from liquid to solid. The oxidation process can be slowed down and sometimes stopped if insufficient air is circulated, or if the air is damp, cold or dirty. Coatings which dry by oxidation are metal primers, undercoats, gloss and eggshell paints, and varnishes. The normal touch dry time is 8-12 hours.

Coalescence

Vinyl resins which are suspended in water join together when the water evaporates to form a continuous film. The resin particles coalesce. If the atmosphere or surface is cold or damp the evaporation will be slowed considerably and the coating may take many hours to dry. Coalescing coatings are usually touch dry in two hours. Coatings which dry by this method are emulsion paints and varnishes, pva adhesives, and masonry paints.

Polymerisation

Two pack coatings harden by polymerisation. The resin will remain in a liquid state for an indefinite period but once mixed with the curing agent a chemical action starts which gradually converts the resin into a solid. Once the process has been started it cannot be stopped. Heat will speed the hardening and moisture may slow it down. Coatings are usually touch dry in 6-8 hours and the dry film is extremely hard and tough. Two pack coatings are: polyurethane and epoxy paints and clear finishes, some adhesives, and etch primer.

Dry Films

Reversible films

Coatings which dry by evaporation contain resins dissolved in a thinner. When the thinner evaporates the resins join up in a continuous film. It is a physical change only, therefore the resins have not changed their nature so can be redissolved by the same thinners. Dry films of these coatings are known as reversible because they can be softened by their original thinners. Cellulose paints, french polish, chlorinated rubber paints and Brunswick black are reversible and their dry films will be softened and eventually removed by the action of their thinners. This property makes them very difficult to recoat by brush, because the new coat is dissolving the old. Also they cannot be used in areas where they may be splashed or washed with solvents.

Non-reversible films

Coatings which dry by oxidation or polymerisation are the result of a chemical change and the dry film cannot be softened by their original thinners. Once dry they can be overcoated without problems and are used much more widely than reversible film coatings.

Types of Coatings

Primers or sealers

These are the first coatings applied to any new or uncoated substrate. They make the bond between the surface and the following coats and if coatings flake off a surface or are chemically destroyed by the surface it is often due to the wrong primer being selected. Primers are specialised materials, each having properties that make them ideal for coating certain substrates. When used on very absorbent surfaces they are often called sealers.

Undercoat or surfacers
These are coatings which contain a high proportion of pigment and are applied between the primer and the finishing gloss paint. They obliterate the substrate and provide an ideal surface for the finish. Generally they have poor flexibility so as few coats as possible should be applied to avoid the paint system cracking. Undercoats are often used as signwriting colour.

Finishing coats
These are matt finish (no sheen), eggshell or satin (slight sheen), or glossy. They may be opaque (paints), or transparent (varnishes or lacquers). All these coatings can be used for signwriting.

Signwriters colours
Heavily pigmented paints available in either thick paste form (tube or tin) which are thinned with white spirit to make them appliable; or, enamel form for direct application without thinning. The paste colours are most suitable for use on eggshell finish or emulsion or masonry paint. For writing on gloss paints or varnish, particularly newly applied coatings, the paste colours should be mixed with gold size, varnish or a little enamel to prevent the film cracking or crazing severely. The paste colours are widely used on glass, either in a slightly thinned form or mixed with varnish or enamel.

For signs on very exposed sites it is advisable to write direct with enamel or first coat with the paste colour and second coat with enamel.

Some manufacturers of signwriters enamel supply them to match their range of cellulose refinishing paints to make vehicle signwriting easier. Enamels should always be used when signwriting directly on vehicles.

All signwriters colours contain driers and will dry within a few hours of application. Most set up quickly and can be second coated with care within a couple of hours.

Stainers
These are pigments ground in a medium and available in tubes or tins for mixing with base paints to produce ranges of other colours. Generally they are available in two forms:

Oil stainers which are like signwriters colours but contain no driers and can be mixed with oil based coatings only. If mixed with gold size or varnish they can be used alone like signwriters colours but may not dry as quickly or have as much opacity.

Universal stainers which can be mixed with any paints, but cannot be used alone even when mixed with gold size. When universal stainers take up more than 20% of the volume of the final paint there is a possibility that the paint will not dry.

Screen inks

The word ink is a generally accepted term for any paint made for printing through a screen. They are heavily pigmented, viscous coatings available in a large range of colours and qualities. There are fast drying inks which dry by evaporation and are sometimes reversible; slower drying inks which contain oils and dry by oxidation producing matt or glossy non-reversible films; those which require heating to make them dry; those which are intumescent and foam up when heated and produce a thick, embroidery type finish; fluorescent inks for good visibility in poor light; transparent inks for mixing with metallic powders or for sealing other inks.

Screen inks are prepared for the substrate to which they will be applied. Some are made specially for application to paper and card; others for plastics; some for painted panels; many for fabrics. Although white spirit is a commonly used thinner, some inks require the special thinners recommended by the manufacturers.

Special coatings

There are paints which are prepared for application to chemically active surfaces which would destroy conventional paints, or for use in extreme exposed conditions. These include alkali resisting paints for use on concrete or cement rendered surfaces; road marking paints for use in car parks or factory floors; nitro-cellulose paints on vehicles; two pack polyurethane paints used on floors and aircraft.

Table 4.5 lists most of the common coatings available together with their medium, thinners, type of film produced, their main uses and restrictions. The key for abbreviations is: WS – white spirit; MS – methylated spirit; Special – those recommended by manufacturers; NR – non-reversible; R – reversible.

Table 4.5 Properties and uses of common surface coatings.

Types	Medium	Thinner	Film	Use and Restrictions
Primers				
Red lead	Linseed oil	WS	NR	Priming iron and steel Poisonous
Zinc phosphate	Linseed oil	WS	NR	Priming iron and steel Priming timber Non poisonous
Zinc chromate	Oil/alkyd	WS	NR	Priming all metals Non poisonous

Table 4.5 contd.

Types	Medium	Thinner	Film	Use and Restrictions
Calcium plumbate	Linseed oil	WS	NR	Galvanised iron Hardwoods Poisonous
Etch primer	Polyvinyl butyryl	Special	NR	Pretreatment of aluminium
Acrylic	Acrylic	Water	NR	Interior timber
Alkali resisting	Tung oil/ resin	WS	NR	Plaster Concrete Cement rendering Non poisonous
Leadless timber primer	Oil/resin	WS	NR	All timber Non poisonous
Undercoats				
Oil	Oil/resin	WS	NR	Between primer and gloss finish
Acrylic	Acrylic	Water	NR	Between acrylic primer and gloss finish for interior signs Plaster and concrete
Surfacer	Nitrocellulose	Special	R	Between primer and finish for vehicle refinishing
Opaque Finishes				
Emulsion matt	PVA Acrylic	Water	NR	Interior signs Signwriting over emulsion or masonry paints
Emulsion silk				
Masonry paint	Acrylic	Water	NR	External walls Seldom used for signwriting because of aggregate content
Cement paint	Cement	Water	NR	
Eggshell or satin	Oil/resin	WS	NR	Interior signs Signwriting over eggshell or emulsion
Gloss paint	Oil/resin	WS	NR	All types of signs Very durable Signwriting over gloss, eggshell or nitrocellulose

Table 4.5 contd.

Types	Medium	Thinner	Film	Use and Restrictions
Nitrocellulose	Nitrocellulose	Special	R	Vehicle refinishing Cannot be applied over oil paints Cannot be used for signwriting
Clear Finishes				
Oil varnish	Oil/resin	WS	NR	Sealing natural signs Protecting sign-written signs Pencil varnishing on glass
Marine varnish	Oil/resin	WS	NR	Sealing exposed signs Signs on boats
Gold size	Oil/resin	WS	NR	Adhesive for gold leaf Drier and binder for signwriting colours Binder for metallic powders
Knotting	Shellac	MS	R	Sealing knots before priming
French polish	Shellac	MS	R	Natural wood finish for inside or protected signs
Button polish	Shellac	MS	R	Quick drying sealer for interior timber signs
Polyurethane varnish: matt, eggshell or gloss	Oil/resin	WS	NR	Natural wood finish for signs not exposed to moisture Protecting sign-written signs
Emulsion glaze	Acrylic	Water	NR	Sealing interior timber
Special Coatings				
Road marking paints	Chlorinated rubber	Special	R	Signs on roads, car parks and factory floors

Table 4.5 contd.

Types	Medium	Thinner	Film	Use and Restrictions
Two pack polyurethane	Polyurethane	Special	NR	Coating or sign-writting floors Aircraft finishing
Brunswick black	Bitumen	WS	R	Acid resist for glass decoration

Storing Coatings

All paints and varnishes deteriorate during long storage so it is a false economy to keep large stocks of little used coatings.

Oil paints skin over on storage and gradually thicken. Skins have to be cut off carefully before the paint is re-used, but invariably small pieces are left behind which must be strained out otherwise the finish will be spoilt. In time paints thicken to such an extent that they cannot be made to a usable state with thinners.

Cellulose, chlorinated rubber and bitumen paints do not skin over but do gradually thicken. Usually they can be reduced with thinners.

Emulsion paints can be destroyed by very cold conditions. On very long storage they can corrode their metal containers. They should not be stored outside or in non-insulated sheds.

Varnishes can be sensitive to cold and long exposure to cold conditions can thicken them considerably making their application difficult, reducing their abiity to flow out after application, and sometimes delaying their drying time. They should be kept at a constant, reasonable temperature of about 15°C.

Tube colours can set hard. This happens particularly with ultra-marine blue and vandyke brown but other pigments can be affected. The pigments may sometimes settle out of the oil in which they are ground and only oil will squeeze from the tube. By replacing the cap and thoroughly shaking the tube the components can be reunited usually. The oil should not be drained off otherwise the balance of the mixture is disturbed and there may be problems with adhesion or drying when they are used.

Stirring
All paints which have been stored must be thoroughly stirred or shaken to redistribute the pigment through the medium. Unless this is done the paint may have poor opacity or dry to the wrong sheen or colour.

Varnishes must not be stirred or shaken. This may introduce air bubbles into the coating which after application may leave tiny craters in the film.

Thixotropic paints do not need stirring unless they need to be strained or mixed with other paints. By stirring they become liquid and can be poured. When left for a few minutes they revert to their natural jelly like state.

Fire precautions

Any coating which uses a thinner that has a flash point below 32°C is considered to be highly flammable and must be stored with care to avoid fire hazards. Most coatings come within this range. Those with the lowest flash point are nitro-cellulose, two pack polyurethane, and coatings containing methylated spirit. There are special regulations controlling the storage of large quantities of these materials, and advice from the local authority should be obtained when more than 50 litres are being kept.

Regardless of the quantity in store it is safer to store cellulose materials and all thinners in a fireproof container. The safest measure is to put them in a lockable, metal bin situated outside. Only small quantities should be kept in the workshop.

Five
Colour

Colour influences the attraction and legibility of a sign as much as the type and arrangement of the letters. As much attention must be given to selecting colours as to all other aspects of designing signs.

There are many areas in which the signmaker has no control over the colours of the sign because they have been precisely specified in official publications. Warning signs for use in factories and other work places not only state the size of the sign, the type of letters or symbols, but also the exact colours in which they must be painted. This applies to road signs also.

In circumstances where the signmaker has to decide what colours are to be used a little knowledge of colour theory and phenomena will be of value.

Light and Colour

All light contains certain wave lengths of colour. When the light strikes a coloured surface some wave lengths may be absorbed and others may be reflected. Those which are reflected are picked up by the eye and translated into effects which are called colours.

The purest form of light is that emitted from the sun and is known as white light. When this light is bent by passing it through a glass prism or a droplet of water the coloured waves are separated. If this image is projected onto a white screen the separate colours will be seen. Nature does this when sunlight is broken up by raindrops, the reflected image being a rainbow. These separate colours are called the spectrum, and contain six colours: red, orange, yellow, green, blue and violet, see fig. 5.1.

Artificial light has a spectrum also. Each type of artificial light produces a different spectrum and not all of them contain the six colours produced by natural light.

Because the coloured surface can only reflect or absorb the colours in the light which is directed at it the effect produced by the surface can be different under different light. Therefore a colour seen in daylight can look entirely different under artificial light.

A white surface reflects all light directed at it, and black surfaces absorb all light and reflect none, see fig. 5.2.

A red surface reflects the red rays and absorbs the rest. A blue surface reflects the blue rays and absorbs the rest.

A surface which appears white under natural light will appear a different colour when a light of another colour is shone on it. For example, a yellow light will reflect only yellow waves and the surface

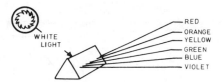

Fig. 5.1   White light bent by a glass prism to produce the spectrum

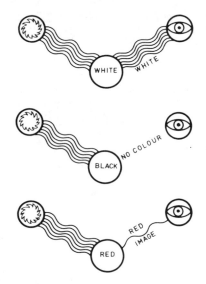

Fig. 5.2   A coloured surface is the result of the rays of light it reflects to
the eye

will appear yellow. If the yellow light is shone onto a red surface no colour will be reflected because the light contains no red rays to reflect. The affect will be black or a dark dull colour. This is why people's lips look black under the yellow sodium street lights.

Additive and Subtractive Colour

Completely different effects are produced by mixing coloured lights and coloured pigments. An arrangement of certain coloured lenses in a lamp can produce a beam of white light. In no way can any mixture of coloured pigments produce a white paint. The mixing of coloured lights is called additive colour, and the mixing of pigments is called subtractive colour. A knowledge of additive colour is essential to the neon and illuminated sign maker but has little value to the signwriter or screen printer. Subtractive colour or pigment mixing is of value to the signwriter and screenprinter when selecting colours for signs, when considering the effect of signs under various lights, and when matching colours.

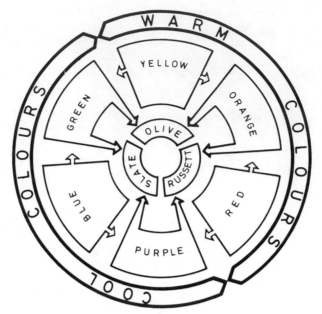

Fig. 5.3   A pigment mixture colour circle showing primaries, secondaries
and tertiaries

Colour Circle

In order to relate the spectrum colours so that they can be used in
many ways they are conveniently arranged on a circle. Fig. 5.3 shows a
simple pigment mixture circle. This circle illustrates the following
important colour terms and relationships.

Primary colours are those which cannot be produced by the
admixture of other colours. In theory they are the base of all other
colours. The three generally accepted primaries are: yellow, red and
blue.

Secondary colours are situated between the primaries and are mixed
from the two colours either side of them. Green is a mixture of yellow
and blue, orange from red and yellow, and purple from blue and red.
Neutral grey is the colour obtained when the three primaries are
mixed together.

Tertiary colours are the mixtures of the secondaries. When colours
are mixed together they lose some of their brightness. Secondaries are
less bright than the primaries that produced them and tertiaries are
less bright than the secondaries.

Natural order of colour refers to their arrangement on the circle so
that yellow is at the top and purple at the bottom. Yellow is lighter in
tone than purple and is acceptable in that form. If the arrangement is
reversed and purple is made lighter than yellow it is an unnatural
order and many people react against it.

Tone refers to the amount of light colours reflect. Yellow reflects
more light than purple and is a light tone. Tonal contrasts are

essential considerations when selecting colours for signs.

Shade is a colour containing black. Shade is a dark tone.

Complementary colours are those opposite each other on the circle. Yellow is complementary to purple, and red is complementary to green. Primaries are complementary to secondaries. Complementaries mixed together can form neutral grey because all three primaries are involved. This can be useful knowledge when colour mixing because the addition of a complementary can grey down or reduce the influence of a predominant colour. For example, if a colour seems slightly too red the addition of a little green will grey the red and the red predominance will be reduced.

Warm colours are those which give the appearance of warmth. They are the yellow, orange and red range of the circle. Most warm colours are referred to also as advancing colours and give the impression of being nearer or more visible. Yellow and yellow orange are commonly used as warning colours, because, even in poor light, they are esily seen.

Cool colours have the opposite effect of warm colours. They are the blue, green and purple range of the circle. Cool colours are also retiring colours and generally have less visibility than warm colours. Blue and green signs are less visible and there are many occasions when this quality is required of a sign.

Other colour terms

Hue describes the characteristics which distinguishes one colour from another. e.g. Yellow is a different hue to red, and pink has a red hue.

Value is the relationship each colour has to a range of grey tones from white to black, see fig. 5.4. If white is 10 and black is 0, the value of yellow, which is a light tone, would be about 8 and purple would be about 2.

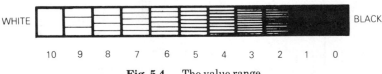

| WHITE | | | | | | | | | | | BLACK |
| 10 | 9 | 8 | 7 | 6 | 5 | 4 | 3 | 2 | 1 | 0 | |

Fig. 5.4   The value range

Chroma means the greyness of a colour. If bright yellow is numbered 14, as it is greyed down by mixing with neutral grey the number reduces until it contains all neutral grey and becomes 0.

These three terms were originally used to describe the characteristics of colour in a system known as the Munsell Scale. They are commonly used as descriptive terms now. It is much easier to define the tone of a sign colour by quoting an approximate value than to talk about 'light colours' which could be interpreted differently by many people. Signs which are required to be brighter or greyer can be described in chroma terms and be more readily understood. For example, a client could ask for a sign to be painted in a 'lightish grey green' and a look at a selection of paint manufacturers colour cards could identify a large number of colours which meet the description. A description such as a 'mid-chroma green of value 3' is much more positive and would make selection easier and more accurate.

Colour Blindness

Not all people see colours in the same way. There is a small percentage of people whose eye mechanism is sufficiently irregular that different effects are produced when looking at certain colours. Complete colour blindness is extremely rare but colour deficiencies are much more common. The most common form is a red/green deficiency and people suffering from this disability have considerable difficulty in distinguishing the lighter greyer tones of red and green.

When selecting colours for signs which must be read by a large number of people every care should be taken to avoid colours which are close in tone particularly those with green or red hues.

Effect of Artificial Light

Colours will change their appearance under different lights. It is essential that colours for signs are selected under the type of light in which they will be viewed. Changes can be very dramatic and a sign's legibility can be destroyed completely when its illumination is changed.

There are five main sources of artificial light, each having different colour characteristics, see fig. 5.5.

Daylight (natural light)
Daylight is the purest form of light. Colours in this light will be seen in their most brilliant form.

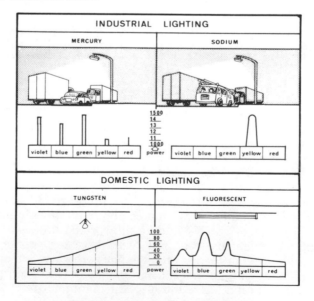

Fig. 5.5   Spectrums of artifical lights

Tungsten light
This is the most common type of domestic lighting, emitted from a bulb containing a tungsten metal wire which becomes white hot when heated. It produces a full spectrum but the red/yellow waves are much stronger than the blue/violet waves. Under tungsten light yellows and reds appear bright, but blues and violets look dull.

Fluorescent light
Fluorescent lights are the most common type of lighting in offices and factories. They work when powders coated to the inside of tubes glow when ultra violet light is directed at them. Although there are very many different coloured tubes available, generally they produce a spectrum stronger in the blues than the reds. These lights make blues and purples look bright, but dull down reds and yellows.

Mercury vapour
This is a rare type of illumination except for certain street lighting. It is a very violet light having a very weak red content. Blues appear bright, although more violet, and reds lose their colour entirely.

Sodium discharge
Sodium discharge is a common type of street lighting. It is a very yellow light with both reds and violets missing from its spectrum. In this light only yellows can be seen clearly. For this reason many emergency vehicles are painted yellow so that they show up well under sodium lighting.

Table 5.1 shows some of the effects of artificial light on the principal hues.

Table 5.1 Effects of artificial light on colour.

Colour of surface in day light	Street lights		Domestic/commercial lighting	
	Sodium	Mercury	Tungsten	Fluorescent (natural)
Red	Brown	Brown or black	Bright red	Dull cool red
Blue	Brown or blue	Deep violet	Dull green/ blue	Bright blue
Green	Brown-yellow	Dark green	Yellow green	Cool blue green
Yellow	Yellow	Green-yellow	Intense-yellow	Green yellow
White	Light yellow	Blue white	Cream off-white	White

Fig. 5.6   Legibility depends on the tonal differences between lettering and background

Colour and Legibility

Lettering will show up when its colour is in a tone contrasting to the background colour. No matter how different colours may appear when separate if they are of similar tone they will not show up when put together. For example, bright red lettering will not be visible if applied to a bright green sign because they are of similar tone, both are about value 3. If the red lettering colour is shaded slightly to a value 2 and the background tinted to a value 8 the sign will be most legible.

Black and white offer the greatest contrast but there are practical and aesthetic reasons why they are not used for signs very often. White reflects all colour therefore in bright light it can cause glare, making the sign difficult to look at. In places where colour scheming has been very carefully carried out, such as a reception hall, or restaurant or exhibition, white signs may intrude or affect the balance of the scheme. For many jobs the contrast between background and lettering will be less than that produced by black and white, but in most cases the contrast must be strong enough to be read easily and immediately, see fig. 5.6. For warning signs contrasts should be as strong as possible. For general information signs the contrast can be less and colours can be selected partly for their aesthetic value. For signs which are read at close quarters and are not essential for everyone to see the contrast can be low. When values are very close, such as 4 and 6, lighting on the sign must be very good for it to be legible.

Glare

White glossy signs can cause glare and should be avoided when they need to be read in bright, direct light. Polished metals, particularly stainless steel, reflect more light than white and cause considerable glare in good light. Matt white and satin finish metals provide the same contrast but reduce glare considerably.

After Image

Each colour of the spectrum is picked up by different parts of the eye. When certain parts become overworked by absorbing reflections from a particular colour they rest by bringing into use the parts which absorb the complementary colour. For example, if a red shape is looked at for a few seconds when the eyes are directed away the same shape will be seen on another surface in green. The red absorbing parts of the eye have become fatigued and green, being the complementary colour to red, has taken over to allow the tired parts to recover quickly.

This phenomena is called after image and can cause legibility problems on a sign. If complementary colours in strong chroma are used together the eye tends to concentrate on each alternately and the lettering appears to move backwards and forwards very slightly and rapidly. The effect is not pleasant and will seriously affect the reading of the sign.

After image often occurs with outlined letters. A red letter with a green outline, or a yellow letter with a blue outline, may cause the characters to fluctuate.

Contrasts

Shapes appear to change their appearance when seen in different contrasts. A white letter O on a black background will appear larger than the same letter in black on a white background. Its thickness will appear to slim when shown as black on white. These strong contrasts are rarely shown on one sign but the phenomena may need to be considered when making signs of different colours appear similar in weight and shape. See fig. 5.7.

Fig. 5.7   A black letter on a white ground needs to be thickened to make it appear the same thickness as a similar white letter on a black ground

British Standard Colours

The British Standard Institution publishes a colour card of 100 colours under the title BS 4800 'Paint Colours for Building Purposes'. Each colour has a code and paint manufacturers produce colours to match many of the BS colours in both gloss and emulsion finishes. Confusion sometimes occurs when the manufacturers give names to the colours. This is particularly so when many different names may be given to the same colour.

Architects and graphic designers often specify BS colours for signs in the knowledge that the colours are readily available from most paint manufacturers. It is a practice that avoids the use of vague colour descriptions or colour names which may be different with every manufacturer. The code for each colour consists of three parts. The first part signifies the hue of the colour, and consists of two even numbers from 02 to 24. Greys are identified as 00. The second part is a letter and signifies the greyness of the colour. There are five grades from A which are greys, through B, C and D which are increasingly less grey to E in which colours are shown in their pure form. The third part refers to the weight of the colour and is shown as an odd number. It is an adjustment of the value of the colours and although hues have been affected differently it does permit a comparison of the weight of colours. For example, all colours which have a 39 weight appear to be of similar tone.

Examples of BS colours
08 B 15 is a warm off-white, commonly known as magnolia. The 08 indicates that it has a yellow-red hue; the B puts it in a very greyed category; and the 15 suggests a colour of a light tone which can be compared with 15 other colours for intensity.

Six

Access

Much site signwriting and signfixing needs to be carried out from some form of scaffold. A scaffold may be a simple one step platform or a three lift tubular scaffold. Whatever type is used it must give easy, comfortable access to the job and be safe.

Usually a scaffold is considered necessary only when the height of the sign is over 2 m from the ground. Yet the most difficult heights to signwrite can be 500 mm high and just under 2 m high. For the low signs a technique has to be developed to get the body low enough yet still keep the arms free to produce the strokes. Sitting on a box, or squatting cross legged, or kneeling are all methods that must be tried in order to find a comfortable position. Kneeling pads and knee pads should be used when kneeling is the most convenient position. Without some form of protection knee joints can become very painful and may be permanently damaged when such pressure is applied to them.

In chapter 8 a design for a signwriters box is suggested which can double as a seat for low work and as a platform for work just above shoulder height. It is essential that if a box is to be used for these purposes it must be designed so that it is safe and will not rock or break under the weight of a body standing and moving about on it.

For working at heights above 2 m some standard form of scaffold must be used. On some contracts the scaffold may be already erected for use by other subcontractors, but generally the signworker will have to supply, or arrange the supply of, a scaffold to gain easy access.

When selecting a scaffold the essential rule is to decide on something which is safe to use and suitable for the particular job. The criterion must not be to select a scaffold which is easy to carry to the site. The ideal scaffold may be the one that combines all three qualities, but the first two must be the controlling factors.

Scaffold and the public
Statutory regulations exist which state quite clearly what constitutes a safe scaffold. Not only does the law require that the person using the scaffold is safe, but also that the public in the vicinity of the scaffold are not subject to any dangers. In this respect it is essential that pavements, corridors or staircases are not blocked by scaffolding unless an alternative route is clearly indicated. Also if people are expected to walk beneath a scaffold every precaution must be taken to either warn them of possible dangers from falling objects or erect nets or sheeting to collect debris or tools which may be dropped.

Accepting a contract to signwrite a shop fascia does not give the signwriter any privileged rights to either use the pavement to erect a scaffold or to inconvenience the public.

Types of Scaffold

Stepladder
Stepladders are made either from timber or aluminium. Timber steps are heavier to carry, but may be cheaper to purchase. They are available in sizes between five and nine treads high. See fig. 6.1.

Steps give comfortable access for signwriting or signfixing up to a maximum height of 3 m. A pair of steps are hazardous when the user's knees are above the top step. Not only do they become top heavy when the knees exceed the top level but there is less chance of regaining balance if the user overreaches.

Fig. 6.1   Timber stepladder

Safety checks
Steps must not be used if:
   any treads are broken or missing;
   ropes on timber steps are missing, frayed, or of different lengths;
   stays on aluminium steps are not locked;
   hinges are loose, insecure or rusted;
   not fully opened.

Platform steps
This is a variation on the traditional type of stepladder which provides a wide platform in place of the top tread. The platform can be used to put tools or materials on, or it can be stood on and offers a more comfortable and safer working platform from which to signwrite. The runners usually extend above the platform to provide a hand hold when stepping on and off the platform. It is most commonly available in five tread heights, although higher ones are available. Being light these steps can be very useful to the signwriter who needs to carry equipment in a car or small van and also to move it to many positions on one job.

Trays are available which can be clipped onto the traditional stepladders to provide a platform for tools and materials. They cannot be stood on.

Fig. 6.2   A trestle scaffold

Trestle scaffold
A trestle scaffold is a convenient and easy way to use scaffold which may consist of either two pairs of stepladders supporting a scaffold board, or two pairs of trestles supporting lightweight staging.

Steps and a board provide a working platform for one person. The platform must not exceed 1.5 m long and is secure up to about 1.7 m high. The safety checks apply equally for steps whether used on their own or supporting a working platform.

The scaffold board should be 38 mm thick; have no cracks or splits; and be free from dirt, see fig. 6.3. Boards should overhang the supporting treads by about 100 mm, but must not exceed 150 mm.

Trestles are made from timber and, unlike steps, are specifically designed to support a working platform. Being wider than steps they can be used with a lightweight staging platform which is 500 mm wide.

A lightweight staging platform can be up to 7 m long and when

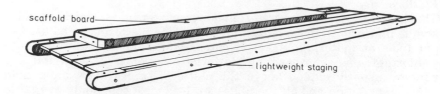

scaffold board

lightweight staging

Fig. 6.2   Scaffold boards are narrower than lightweight staging and
cannot be used for long spans

supported by trestles is secure up to 4.5 m high (fig. 6.3). It can safely
support three persons.

Safety checks
Trestles must not be used if:
   any cross members are broken, loose or missing;
   hinges are loose or rusted;
   not fully opened.
Lightweight staging must not be used if:
   stiles are cracked or split;
   platform is dirty or slippery;
   the overhang is less than 100 mm or more than 250 mm;
   it is over 4.5 m from the ground when supported on trestles.

Trestle scaffolds are ideal for working on shop fascias, see fig. 8.28.

Ladder
A ladder may be made from timber or aluminium, and is available in
single lengths or as a double extension. Triple extension ladders are
available, but rarely used because of their great weight and the
difficulty of extending them. Extension ladders can be fitted with ropes
and pulleys which make them easier to extend. If the ladders are often
used as separate pieces the hand operated type are usually more
convenient because having no ropes they are easier to separate and
refit.
   Ladders give access to a single position which is higher than that for
which trestles can be safely used.

Safety checks
Ladders must not be used if:
   any rungs are missing or broken;
   stood on uneven, loose or soft ground;
   resting on a rung or unstable surface;
   the top is not tied to a firm part of the building or the base is not tied
   (see fig. 6.4), or a person is not standing on the bottom rung to
   prevent it from slipping;
   it is necessary to stretch to one side or to stand higher than 1 m from
   the top to reach the required position;
   if both hands are full and the ladder cannot be held;

Fig. 6.3   A ladder secured and at the right angle

the angle is too steep or too narrow. The safe angle is when the ladder rises four times to one at the base, see fig. 6.4.

Ladders are used for fixing signs about 5 m high. They are rarely used singly by the signwriter.

Convertible ladders
These are small ladders which can be converted into free standing stepladders. They are of two types:
(1)   *Swing round*, which consists of two, three or four sections and when they are put in line they clip together to form a ladder, but when hinged they can form a pair of steps, stabilised by a stay which hooks onto opposite rungs. The three and four section units can convert to a stand off ladder and a low working platform.
(2)   *Slide*, which are of two sections that slide within each other to extend as a ladder similar to a traditional extension ladder. The two parts can be separated and held together by some form of patent clip, or swivel to form a pair of stepladders.

Both types are very convenient for transporting and carrying. The four section swing type packs into a very small unit.
    They can be most valuable to the travelling signwriter but they are limited to the height that they can reach. The average height of the ladder is 3 m and when converted to steps will reach about 1.3 m to the top tread. Some makes have rungs instead of treads and these can be most uncomfortable to stand on for long periods.

Safety checks
The locking devices which hold the sections in place when used as both

a ladder and steps must be fully engaged otherwise they may collapse when climbed on.

Ladder Scaffold

Two ladders, each holding a ladder bracket which in turn supports a lightweight staging platform, form a ladder scaffold. See fig. 6.5.

Ladder brackets are constructed from steel and hook over two ladder rungs. The platform supporting arm is hinged so that it can be laid flat for easy storage and transport, and can be adjusted to suit the angle of the ladder and ensure a level platform.

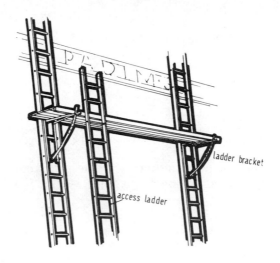

Fig. 6.5   A ladder scaffold

Safety checks

Ladder scaffolds must not be used if:
    either ladder is not tied, wedged or 'footed' to prevent slipping;
    either bracket is severely corroded or the locking pin is loose;
    a third ladder is not available for access to the platform;
    heavy materials or equipment need to be used.

Ladder scaffolds are used for signwriting and signfixing, usually when access is required just above the safe height for trestles, e.g. 5–7 metres.

Mobile Towers

Mobile towers provide a wide, comfortable working platform supported by a metal frame and mounted on castors for easy moving.

The metal frame can be either:
(1)   Steel or aluminium tubes coupled together in the same way that a tubular scaffold is constructed. This type is rarely used by the signworker.
(2)   Patent steel or aluminium frames which either clip or slot

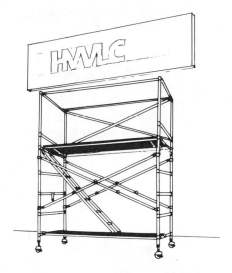

Fig. 6.6   An aluminium frame mobile tower

together or are combined in one unit and unfold into a predetermined size tower. This type is very adaptable and can be easily transported and erected on site, see fig. 6.6.

The safe height to which a tower's working platform can be erected depends upon the narrowest width of the tower. For example if the base of the tower is 1 m wide by 2 m long the safe height is 3 m, or three times the 1 m width. If this height is exceeded the tower becomes top heavy. Manufacturers supply outriders which can be clipped on to give a wider base and permit a safe higher platform to be used.

Safety checks
Mobile tower scaffolds must not be used if:
    the height exceeds three times the narrowest base measurement;
    the uprights are not plumb;
    all joints are not securely locked into place;
    access ladders are leaning against the tower and not built in or securely lashed;
    a guard rail is not securely fitted around the working platform;
    the working platform does not cover the entire standing area;
    the castors are not locked;
    the ground is sloping.

Mobile towers are valuable for exhibition work where fascias and other repeating signs are at a standard level. They are very safe scaffolds for signfixing because signs can be supported by them and there is room to store tools and equipment safely.
    Towers can be used to support working platforms also. When considerable work has to be done above the safe height of a trestle scaffold the safest alternative is to use two towers with a lightweight

staging spanned between them. A 1.5 m base tower will provide a safe 4.5 m working platform.

Moving scaffolds
Trestle scaffold and ladder scaffolds must be dismantled before being moved. It is essential that all materials and tools are removed from the working platform before dismantling starts.

Mobile towers must be pushed along with pressure at the base only. Nobody must be on the scaffold when it is being moved. All castors must be securely locked before the scaffold is re-used.

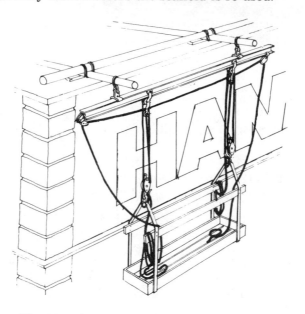

Fig. 6.7   A rope operated travelling cradle

Scaffolds Used but not Erected by Signworkers

Cradles
These are working platforms suspended from poles which project from the roof of a building. The cradle can be lowered and raised by pulling or slackening suspension ropes, or by the operation of a hand or powered winch. Some cradles can be moved across the face of the building also, and these are called travelling cradles, see fig. 6.7.

Cradles are used when signs are painted directly on to large walls or when signs are situated near the top of a large building. They are cheaper to erect than tubular scaffolds, and can be used when a scaffold cannot be erected on the ground because of essential traffic or if the building adjoins a river or a railway embankment.

The cradle or boat can be made from timber with steel reinforcement, aluminium, or glass reinforced plastic. They must have a guard rail around the entire working platform and the working platform must have drain holes so that rain water does not form puddles.

When hand operated the fall ropes are usually made from manilla, when winched the ropes are of wire. Some modern, high buildings have cradles or cradle suspension gear built into the structure.

For other buildings outriggers of steel tubes or joists are fitted on the roof so that a very small length overhangs. The other end is counter-weighted so that no matter what weight is put in the cradle the outriggers will not be lifted.

Safety Checks
Cradles should not be used if:
   suspension ropes are frayed, rotted or have been spliced;
   track stop ends are made from ropes or wire bonds;
   pole lashings are made with rope and not wire bonds.

Cradles must be entered and left at a safe point of access. This may be at ground or roof level or at a large window. Gaining access by climbing up or down the ropes is prohibited.

When using power drills from a cradle it may be necessary to tie the cradle to the building to prevent it swinging outwards when pressure is placed on the drill.

Tubular Scaffold

This is an involved framework built from individual lengths of steel or aluminium tubes coupled together with specially designed metal connectors.

Any height up to 60 m can be safely erected with tubular units. When the scaffold cannot be stood on the ground, or access is required at the top of a large building only, it can be built out from windows or other openings. This type is generally called truss-out scaffold.

Tubular scaffolds are the safest and most comfortable forms of access. They are the most expensive to erect therefore their use by signworkers is limited to the occasions when many other trades or subcontractors are involved in work on the outside of the building. For example, when a building is being constructed or extensively reno-vated and the signs need to be fixed at the same time.

·*Safety checks*
A tubular scaffold should not be used if:
   the upright poles (standards) are standing directly onto soft or uneven ground or pieces of brick. Each standard should have a base plate;
   boards of the working platform are not evenly supported, overhang end supports by more than 150 mm, or have gaps or trippable overlaps;
   working platforms are not protected with guard rails and toeboards;
   height between the working platforms (lifts) exceed 2 m or are less than 1.900 m;
   access ladders are not securely tied to the scaffold and do not extend at least 1 m above the landing stage.

Seven

Signs

Signs can be made from a great variety of materials. there are signs made by blacksmiths, built into walls by bricklayers, put together from tree trimmings by forest workers, and stitched by embroiderers. Signs have been fashioned from concrete, welded onto steel, and burnt out of wood. The Greater London Council is internationally renowned for the blue ceramic plaques that they have placed on many London buildings (see fig. 1.46). Signs are also made from flowers, as seen in some parks and on festival floats.

Although the signmaker has an almost limitless choice most signs are made from timber, metal, plastic and glass. The signmaker may be instructed to use a particular material, or the choice of material may be left entirely to the signmaker.

When instructions come from an architect or a graphic designer it is usual for the sign material to be carefully specified. In these circumstances the signmaker must obtain the precise material and treat it as instructed. If failure results from using a slightly different material or technique the cost of reparation must be borne by the signmaker.

On occasions the signmaker will be given no instructions about the material for the sign and even greater care must be taken to select a material that will be effective in the place that the sign is to be fixed. Not only must it last but it must look well and harmonise with the building or the decor.

To select and use materials for signs an extensive knowledge of the more common substrates is essential.

Timber Signs

Timber is the most adaptable and common material used for making signs. It is easy to work and fix, and is available in such a great variety of forms, colours and weathering qualities that it is possible to find some kind of timber which will suit every situation. Timber signs can be either framed and boarded, or solid.

Framed and boarded signs

Generally the use of boarding is the cheapest method of constructing signs. They can be made by fixing a sheet of thin boarding to a strong timber frame or studding. Or thick boarding can be used with an edge frame to seal the edges and improve its appearance.

Boarding

Hardboard, or similar fibreboard, and plywood up to about 6 mm thickness need to be framed. Thin boards used without frame support will warp or their edges will be damaged. They may be used for temporary signs but will always look cheap if used in any permanent position. Thicker boardings will be more permanent particularly if framed. Hardboard is suitable for interior signs, and plywood for external signs.

In addition to the framing supporting the outside edges 6 mm boarding will need extra cross supports to prevent the boarding warping or twisting. The boarding should be supported every 450 mm. See fig. 7.1.

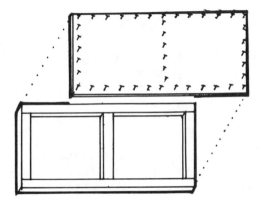

Fig. 7.1 Simple sign made from timber studding to which boarding is pinned

The boarding can be fixed to the frame by pins or screws, which should not be more than 150 mm apart. A PVA wood adhesive can be used instead of pinning which avoids damaging the face of the board.

Frame or studding

For signs up to 6 m^2 a frame made from softwood battens of 50 x 25 mm is most suitable. Larger signs will require a heavier section timber.

The battens need to be fitted or fixed together into a rigid frame before the boarding is attached. The battens are arranged so that the wider face is in contact with the boarding.

There are many ways that the battens can be joined together. The method chosen depends on the cost of the job, or how long it is required to last, or how important the appearance of the edge or back may be to the signs siting.

Methods of joining battens to make frames

Mortise and tenon joint, see fig. 7.2. The ends of one piece of framing is pared down to fit into a corresponding shaped hole cut into the cross piece. It is the strongest and most efficient method of jointing but is also the most expensive to produce. Essential on very large signs.

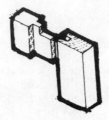

Fig. 7.2 Mortise and tenon joint

Halving joint, see fig. 7.3. Half the thickness of each end of the timbers are cut away so that they fit over each other. A simple and effective joint. The joint needs pinning, screwing, sticking or dowelling to make secure.

Fig. 7.3 Halving joint

Bridle joint, see fig. 7.4. Like a mortise and tenon joint except that the mortise is cut as a groove in the end of the timber to receive the tongue cut in the cross piece. When glued, pinned or dowelled it produces a strong joint.

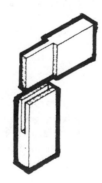

Fig. 7.4 Bridle joint

Fig. 7.5 Mitred joint using dowels

Dowel, see fig. 7.5. Short lengths of hardwood dowel fitted into identical holes cut in the two faces to be joined. When glued the joint is strong. Commonly used with mitred corners.

Corrugated fasteners, see fig. 7.6. Crude fixings which are driven into the two pieces of wood, mitred and butted into position. A cheap and quick method of joining. Not very strong but it is strengthened when boarding is fixed.

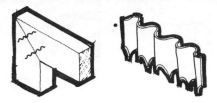

Fig. 7.6 Mitred joint secured by corrugated fasteners

Framing angle pieces, see fig. 7.7. They can be metal L- or V-shaped plates or plastic block joints which are screwed into or onto the angle between the two pieces of wood butted or mitred in position. Stronger than corrugated frames and are less likely to damage the timber.

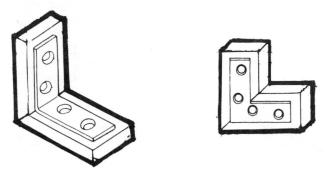

Fig. 7.7 Mitred joints secured by metal angle pieces, in the angle and on the face

Nailing, see fig. 7.8. The cheapest, easiest and least effective method. The nails are driven at an angle to go through both pieces of timber butted or mitred in position.

Fig. 7.8 Mitred joint secured by nails

Screwing. A more effective method than nailing but more crude than jointing.

Edging
To protect the soft and absorbent edge of the boarding the edges of framed signs can be covered with thin strips of timber, pinned or

adhered to the edge of the frame, see fig. 7.9.

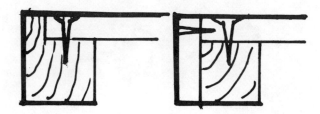

Fig. 7.9 Sign edging by rebated frame and by use of edging strip

A more expensive method is to rebate the face of the frame, cut the boarding smaller than the size of the frame so that it fits into the rebate and forms a flush finish with the top edge of the frame.

Solid signs
Solid timber signs can be made from thick boarding edged with hardwood, or from planks of soft or hard wood.

Edged boarding
Boarding over 10 mm thick does not need to be framed to make it stable. Because most boardings are very absorbent through their edges and look unsightly when cut they are usually covered with an edging strip.

The strip can be a hardwood strip the same thickness as the board, pinned and glued, and mitred at the corners; or, a wider hardwood strip that projects in front of the face to make a frame appearance, or projects beyond the back to make fixing to the wall easier; or, a veneer or plastic edging strip glued to the edge which is suitable for interior signs only. Softwood can be used for edging if the sign is to be painted.

Table 7.1 lists the various type of boardings available either as covers on frames or use as solid boards.

Table 7.1 Various types of boardings available.

Type	Thicknesses in mm	Notes
Hardboard Compressed timber pulp Smooth face, rough back		
Standard	2, 3, 5, 6	Not suitable for external signs Cheap Readily available in standard sheets and cut sizes

Type	Thicknesses in mm	Notes
Tempered (oil impregnated)	2, 3, 5, 6, 13	Suitable for external signs Dearer than standard May be available in standard size sheets only
Decorated coated with enamel	2, 3, 5, 6, 13	Suitable for external signs if back and edges sealed Twice cost of Standard Available in standard size sheets only Needs no further coating Adhere to frame to avoid pin holes in face
Composite board Hardboard either side of honeycomb cellular core	25, 50	Needs no framing Edges require covering with wood or hardboard Very light Easily fixed Not suitable for external signs Available in standard size sheets only Available coated
Wood Chipboard Wood chips bonded by heat with resin.		
Standard	3, 4, 6, 8, 12, 15, 88, 22, 25	Slightly textured surface which requires filling for smooth finish Swells when wet Can be used externally if coated on all faces Available in standard sheets and cut sizes
Moisture Resistant	12, 18	Suitable for external signs Textured surface
Melamine Face Coated on both sides and edges with hard, glossy white paint or wood effect	15, 18	Very smooth surface, ideal for signwriting Matching edging strips available for adhering or ironing on Available in standard size sheets only

Type	Thicknesses in mm	Notes
Veneered Thin wood veneers adhered to back, front and edges	16, 18	Ideal for interior signs requiring natural wood finish Can be varnished or polished Available in standard size sheets only Range of veneers available
Laminated Plastic laminate bonded to face, back and edges	18	Very durable boarding Excellent surface for signwriting Very expensive Available in standard size sheets only Available in range of colours and textures
Plywood Layers of thin timber sheets bonded together. Grain of each ply in opposite direction to ply either side. Finish ply may be of different timbers.		
Standard	4, 6, 9, 12, 15, 18, 24	Available in three grades according to adhesive used to bond plies WBP (weather and boil proof) — resistant to weather, fungi, steam. Suitable for external signs MR (moisture resis- tant) — for damp places. Suitable for protected external signs Interior — for dry conditions only. Delaminates if wet Generally thin sheets available in cut sizes
Marine Specially prepared for exposed places	6, 9, 12	Very expensive Available in standard size sheets only

Type	Thicknesses in mm	Notes
Metal Faced Face, back and edges bonded with unpolished aluminium	4, 6, 9, 12	Very expensive Very durable panels for signs Ideal for finishing in nitrocellulose coatings Available in standard size sheets only
Decorative Veneered with decor- ative timbers	4, 6, 9, 12	Suitable for interior signs requiring natural wood finish Wide range of veneers available Available in standard size sheets only Iron-on or stick on matching edge strips available
Blockboard Sandwich of narrow strips of soft wood between two thin ply boards		
Standard	12, 16, 18, 22, 25, up to 45	Similar properties and uses as plywood Edges need careful covering
Decorative	18	Similar use as decorative plywood

All boardings can be obtained as flame retardant standard. This ensures that they comply with most fire regulations and can be used in public buildings and exhibitions. Flame retardant boards are more expensive than the standard quality boards.

Timber planks

The use of solid timber for signs is usually restricted to small signs, mainly because of cost but also because of the limited sizes in which softwoods and hardwoods are available.

Softwoods are less likely to be used because they are likely to warp on exposure. Also their colour and grain markings are less desirable. Softwoods which can be used are Western Red Cedar, Parana Pine, and Pitch Pine.

Hardwoods are most commonly used for making solid timber signs. They are more reliable when exposed to the weather and generally they are available in a very wide range of colours and attractive grain markings. They are considerably more expensive than softwoods and not so readily available.

Table 7.2 lists the common soft- and hardwoods available with their characteristics and sizes in which they are generally available. If a sign is required in a size larger than the timber is available two or more planks must be glued together.

Table 7.2 Common soft- and hardwoods.

	Characteristics	Sizes
Softwoods		
Redwood	Most common, sometimes called Deal. Very knotty. Pinky/brown colour.	May not be readily available in sizes over 230 mm wide.
Spruce	Sometimes called white-wood. Knotty. Almost white in colour.	
Western Hemlock	Light brown. Very few knots.	
Douglas Fir	Pink brown. Can be knot free.	Can be obtained in sizes up to 280 mm. Larger widths are not generally available.
Parana Pine	Brown/red. Knot free. Expensive.	
Western Red Cedar	Pink brown. Knot free. Expensive. Very good durability on out-side sign.	
Hardwoods		
Beech	Very hard. Close grained. Light cream colour. Needs protection.	
Elm	Strong grain marking. Light brown. Needs protection when used outside.	
Teak	Medium brown with good grain markings. Very durable on outside signs. Difficult to seal. Expensive.	Board sizes vary from wood to wood and from supplier to supplier. Some timbers can be obtained up to 450 mm wide but smaller sizes are more common.
Iroko	Simlar properties to teak, less expensive.	
Mahogany	Rich red colour. Can be used to produce glossy finish. Available in large planks. Expensive.	
Oak	Yellow brown. Heavy. Coarse grained. Good dura-bility on outside signs. Expensive.	

	Characteristics	Sizes
Ramin	Very light colour. Needs protection when used outside. Inexpensive. Easy to work.	
Utile	Red brown colour. Easy to work. Durable on outside signs.	

Hardwoods do not need to be framed or edged but it is often done to improve the appearance of the sign. It is advidable to frame or edge softwood because the end grain is very absorbent and once moisture has penetrated the timber may twist or rot. If frames are used the top length should be bevelled so that rain will run off quickly otherwise it may lay on the edge and eventually be absorbed by the timber. Hardwood signs can have their edges bevelled or grooved to give a further feature, see fig. 7.10.

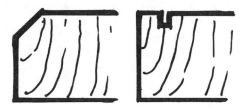

Fig. 7.10 Methods of finishing hardwood signs by bevelling and grooving

Softwoods can be varnished but painting is a more reliable finish. Hardwoods are generally durable without protective coatings. But they do get dirty and become stained and for this reason they are usually sealed and varnished.

Metal Signs

The small signmaker is less likely to have facilities for cutting and working metals therefore metal signs are less common than timber signs.

When they are specified the work of making them is usually subcontracted. Metal signs are very durable and more expensive than timber signs. They are most suitable for permanent signs that must withstand severe weather conditions, or when the signs are continuously and roughly moved about. Some metals can be produced with very decorative finishes and these are specified for their aesthetic quality as well as their durability.

Prefabricated signs
These are made in a similar way to timber signs. The framework is of angle iron and clad with mild steel sheets. Iron and steel readily corrode and must be thoroughly cleaned and coated to prevent rusting.

The signs can be coated with oil based paints by the signwriter or coated with stoving enamel or vitreous enamel by specialist firms.

Decorative metals

Stainless steel. A very hard metal available in a bright or matt (satin) finish. It can be framed or used in sheet form which is fixed direct to wall.

Aluminium. Lighter, easier to work metal. Available in many finishes — polished, satin, anodised, which is aluminium electrolytically treated to produce a more durable finish and available in matt or gloss finish, sheradised, which produces a grey finish, usually matt, created by coating with zinc.

Brass. A traditional sign material which is rarely specified now. Very expensive.

Stainless steel and anodised aluminium are resistant to corrosion but the others do dull on exposure and eventually will form a surface deposit. In order to maintain their brightness most decorative metals are lacquered.

Lettering is usually etched and enamelled on the decorative metals. Screened or foil cut lettering in stove or vitreous enamels are permanent also. Signwriting on signs made from these metals is rare but can be reasonably permanent if the surface is thoroughly degreased with a solvent like cellulose thinners and the signwriting carried out in enamels.

Plastics

Flat signs may be constructed in acrylic sheet, glass reinforced plastic, or plastic laminate.

Acrylic sheet
A common material used in the manufacture of signs. It is a plastic available in sheets and blocks in thicknesses from 2.5–130 mm. There are thinner sheets available but these are in clear quality only and used mainly for moulding into various shaped signs.

Acrylic sheet can be obtained: clear; translucent, which is coloured but allows most light to pass through; opal, which difuses light but cannot be seen through; slightly textured, either as patterns or all over texture which produces a non-glare surface; and, in grades suitable for special use in industry, hospitals and aircraft. It has good weather, chemical and shatter resistance. It is dissolved by some strong solvents and is softened by heat (thermoplastic). Acrylic can be machined, drilled, turned, routed, engraved, and heat moulded. It is widely used in 'illuminated' signs, whether framed into a light box or heat moulded into box shape and lit from within. On occasions it is used as a cladding for a sign and screen printed or signwritten without illumination. Because of its high cost its use as a non-illuminated sign material is very limited. When heated it expands considerably and if fitted tightly into a sign it will distort. The usual method of fixing is to suspend it in an aluminium frame with room for it to expand without causing surface distortion.

There are special screen inks for printing acrylic. Signwriters enamels are generally used for painted letters after the surface has been thoroughly cleaned with detergent and dried.

Glass reinforced plastic (GRP)

GRP is a polyester resin bonded with layers of glass fibres which give the sign considerable strength. It is applied in a liquid form to a preformed mould and hardens to a tough plastic film. When set it is removed and generally painted. It can be produced in flat sheets but it is most commonly formed into shaped signs with or without lettering included in the mould. Any shape can be produced providing the mould has no undercut form which prevents the cast being lifted off when the GRP has hardened. The method of fixing the sign should be incorporated into the making process because screwing into the hard plastic is difficult and weakens the GRP.

The mould can be made from wood, plaster or metal. Before the liquid plastic is applied the mould is coated with a release oil so that the plastic can be lifted easily when it is set. Some of this oil may adhere to the face of the hard plastic and if it is not removed thoroughly can affect both the drying and adhesion of the paint which may be applied to it. GRP signs may be signwritten or screen printed.

Laminate

Thin layers of melamine are bonded to form thin sheets with a hard, smooth surface. It is available in a wide range of colours, patterns and fine textures. The sheets are usually 1–2 mm thick so need to be bonded to a firm boarding substrate. It is an ideal material for signs and can be signwritten or screen printed or masked using oil based paints. The surface needs to be degreased with detergent before painting. Laminated plastic can be painted. It can be engraved and shot blasted also.

Purpose made signs in laminated plastic are made by incorporating the printed text on a thin paper sheet beneath the top layers of clear plastic. This is a specialised process which is carried out during manufacture of the sheet.

Glass

Glass has been used as a sign material since the eighteenth century. In spite of its brittle nature it has retained its popularity principally because it is still widely used as a building material and because the many effects produced by acid etching and burnished gilding cannot be matched on the more durable but much more expensive acrylic sheeting.

Glass signs can be framed in wood or aluminium; glazed into window frames or door panels; or, as toughened glass, fixed direct to a wall.

The most common types of glass used by the signmaker are shown in Table 7.3.

Table 7.3 Glass for signs.

Type	Thicknesses in mm	Uses
Clear Float Glass Manufactured to one standard only which is suitable for all uses. This glass is most commonly decorated.	4 5 6 10 Other sizes up to 25 mm are available.	Small glazing areas and mirrors. Shopfronts, show- cases, commercial glazing. Large shop fronts, counter tops.
Obscured Glass White Flashed Opal One side coated with a thin film of opal	2, 3, 4, 5.5	Windows, doors and small shopfronts which require a degree of privacy.
Obscured Sheet One side of which is sandblasted	2, 3, 4	
Safety Glass Toughened Heated and rapidly cooled so that it withstands weight and impact	5–19	Doors and windows where there is con- siderable pedestrian traffic. Shop fronts, display cases, balustrading.
Coloured Toughened Ceramic colour fused into one surface making it almost opaque.	6, 10	Wall cladding and shop fascias

Toughened glasses cannot be worked or cut, and must be ordered in exact sizes required.

Laminated A sandwich of glass and plastic interlayer	4, 5, 6	High rise buildings where broken falling glass could be hazard- ous. Similar use to toughened.

Tinted and patterned glasses are rarely used by the signmaker.

Finishing Signs

Most signs need either painting or sealing. Hardboard, softwood, boarding, iron and steel, and sometimes GRP need to be painted. This seals the surface and protects it from the weather, abrasion and washing. It also provides a decorative finish and one which can be easily signwritten. Some hardwoods, aluminium, stainless steel, brass, plastics and glass do not need to be painted. Hardwoods are generally sealed so that they do not absorb dirt but still retain their natural colour and markings. The metals may be lacquered which protects them from discolouration or tarnishing.

Painted Signs

Making signs is expensive. No matter what quality materials have been used to make the sign and regardless of the quality of the signwork, the sign will last only as long as the preparation, paint and painting of the sign will allow. These processes are as essential as the selection of the substrates and the lettering skills involved in producing the sign and must not be ignored or skimped.

Repainting
When a sign has to be redone the first decision is whether to completely remove all the existing coatings and start from the bare material, or abrade and repaint. Stripping off previous coatings is not always necessary but it is always a more expensive procedure.

When to strip
(1) When the old paint is so severely cracked, blistered or flaking that the substrate is exposed.
(2) When the old coatings are different to those which are to be applied. Some coatings such as nitro-cellulose or two pack polyurethane can only be applied over similar coatings or to bare surfaces. If applied to oil paints they will lift them. When cellulose or polyurethane paints are to be used and there is the slightest doubt what the existing coating may be it must be stripped.
(3) When French polished. Although French polish can be carefully repolished providing the existing coating is not cracked, chipped or discoloured, the process is risky because the new polish will dissolve the old and a patchy effect could result. The safe policy is to remove old French polish whether it is to be repolished or coated with another material.
(4) When the old sign includes any red paint. Red background, red lettering or any colour containing red, will bleed through lighter coloured paints applied over them and the whole paint may become pink or the red letters will clearly show as pink. Aluminium sealers can be used to seal the red against bleeding but they are not always reliable and coats applied over them do not have good adhesion and may eventually flake. Complete removal is often the quickest and safest method of dealing with bleeding colours.

Methods of stripping old paint systems

Burning off
The cheapest and quickest method of removing oil based paints from

timber signs. There are three methods.
(1) Paraffin blowlamp which is cheap to operate but is heavy to hold and can take up to 15 minutes to fill and light.
(2) Gas torches which operate off liquefied petroleum gas (LPG). The burners either screw direct to a small refillable bottle or can be attached to a cylinder by a flexible hose. Another type operates from a disposable cartridge but is more expensive.
(3) Hot air burners are electrically operated and work on the same principle as a hair dryer but generate considerably more heat. They are very expensive to purchase but can be hired if a number of boards need to be stripped.

All these methods soften the paint so that it can be scraped off easily with a stripping knife or a shave hook. The knives must be used just behind the flame so that the paint is in its softest state and less damage is caused to the surface by having to push the knife hard. Pushing or pulling the knives in the direction of the grain avoids surface damage also.

The stripped surface will always need to be dry abraded to obtain a smooth finish. This is best done with an orbital sander using aluminium oxide or garnett abrasive paper. Burning off invariably scorches the surface slightly and is not recommended if the timber is to receive a clear finish.

Spirit paint remover
A messy and more expensive method than burning off but can be used to remove most paints from most surfaces. It works rapidly and efficiently to remove coatings from metals and glass, but may take longer to soften coatings on timber or boarding. Some plastics may be softened by spirit removers and a test should be made on the back of the sign before a full scale application. It is an essential method of removing coatings from timber which is to receive a clear finish.

The remover is applied liberally with an old brush and left to penetrate from any period between five and fifteen minutes. Some materials may require many applications. When the coating wrinkles and lifts from the surface it can be easily scraped off with a stripping knife or shave hook.

When the surface is stripped all traces of the remover must be removed before dry abrading and painting. Many removers are water washable but a few need to be washed off with white spirit.

Caustic soda
A dangerous material which readily destroys oil based paints. The soda is obtained as crystals and is made into a stripper by dissolving in warm water. Signs can be immersed in the caustic if a large tank is available or the soda can be thickened with a little cold water paste and applied as a thick coating to the sign. Its action is much slower than spirit paint remover but its cost is considerably less. When the old paint is soft it will wash off with running water.

Caustic soda is very corrosive and hands, eyes and clothing must be properly protected when using it. Large gauntlet type industrial gloves are essential and goggles, plastic apron and wellington boots are necessary to protect the other parts of the body. The brush used to put on the soda must not be made from bristle otherwise it will be dissolved.

Wood and hardboard may warp if treated with caustic. The soda will be difficult to remove from them and may damage subsequent paint. Caustic will dissolve aluminium but is ideal for stripping iron and steel.

Dry abrading
A rotary sander with a coarse disc of about grade 80 garnet or aluminium oxide abrasive paper will remove many thicknesses of coatings. It is difficult to control and may damage the surface and it is difficult to get into corners. Also it produces considerable dust and the operator must wear goggles and a face mask as protection. Most suitable for flat timber signs with few coats of paint or varnish.

Treatment after stripping
Surfaces which have been completely stripped of previous coatings should be prepared and recoated in the same way as that described for new surfaces.

Washing and abrading
Previously painted signs in good condition which need to be repainted and signwritten must be clean and the surface abraded to a smooth finish.

Old lettering will 'grin' through new coatings, regardless of the number of coats used, unless it is well abraded so that no edge of paint can be felt around any letter. This is most efficiently done with silicon carbide abrasive paper, commonly known as 'wet or dry' paper. A grade 180 used first will remove the lettering, and a final rub with grade 240 or 320 will smooth the surface and remove any scratches caused by the coarser paper. The paper must be used with water and if a little detergent or sugar soap is put in the water the surface will be cleaned by the abrading process also.

The abrasive paper should be mounted on a block which makes it more comfortable to hold and more of the paper is in contact with the surface compared with holding it in the hand. Electric orbital sanders can be dangerous to use with water but pneumatic sanders are ideal and widely used by vehicle refinishers.

Some vehicles may have been wax polished. This must be thoroughly removed before repainting otherwise the paint will flake off after a short time. Some wax polishes contain silicone which affects adhesion even more. A scrubbing with strong detergent is necessary to remove all traces of vehicle wax followed by thorough wet abrasion.

When the abraded surfaces are dry any bare places can be touched up with primer and any dents or holes can be filled and the surface is ready for undercoating or finishing.

Hardboard signs can be wet abraded providing they have five or six coats of paint on them. A thinner paint system may be cut through with the abrasive paper and the hardboard will become rough and swell by absorbing the water. To avoid this dry abrading is recommended and an orbital sander can be used to speed the process.

Painting Signs

Table 7.4 shows the essential preparation and the recommended primers for most of the common sign materials, whether new or recently stripped.

Table 7.4 Preparation and priming signboards.

Sign	Preparation	Primer for emulsion finish	Primer for oil paint finish
Hardboard and timber frame	Punch nails below surface. Touch nail heads with oil primer. Fill holes with plaster filler.	Acrylic primer	Acrylic primer
Softwood	Ensure nails and screws are below surface. Dry abrade. Coat all knots with shellac knotting.	Acrylic primer	Leadless oil wood primer
Chipboard Plywood Blockboard	Ensure all nails and screws are below surface. Dry abrade.	Acrylic primer	Leadless oil wood primer.
		Primer for cellulose	Primer for oil paint finish
Iron and steel	Degrease with white spirit. Remove rust with wire brush or steel wool.	Cellulose grey or red primer	Red lead Zinc phosphate Zinc chromate
Galvanised Iron	Degrease with white spirit	Cellulose grey primer	Calcium plumbate
Aluminium	Degrease with white spirit. Etch with steel wool.	Cellulose grey or red primer	Etch primer Zinc chromate
GRP	Remove mould oil with detergent.	Cellulose surfacer	Thinned alkyd gloss paint

After priming, signs need as many coats of paint that are necessary to achieve a firm, opaque finish and a film thickness that will withstand the ravages of the weather, or of cleaning. Most exterior signs will require a minimum three coats of paint to remain in good condition for five to seven years. Interior signs do not need so many coats unless they are washed or rubbed against regularly.

All exterior signs must have the same film thickness of paint on the back and edges as have been applied to the face. Backs can be coated with bitumastic paint or 'smudge', a collection of odd ends of paint kept for this purpose.

Tables 7.5 and 7.6 show painting specifications for some of the common surfaces used for signs.

Table 7.5 Painting specification for primed signboards.

Sign	Emulsion finish	Oil paint finish	Nitrocellulose finish
Hardboard and timber frame Softwood Chipboard Plywood Blockboard	2–3 coats	1 undercoat and 1 gloss finish or 2 coats eggshell	Not applicable
Iron and steel Aluminium	Not applicable	1 undercoat and 2 coats gloss finish or 3 coats gloss finish	3–4 coats finish paint

Table 7.6 Painting specification for walls used as signs.

	Preparation	Coating systems	
Plaster wall	Ensure it is dry Make good with plaster	Seal with thinned emulsion paint Apply 2 full coats of emulsion	Seal with alkali resisting primer Apply two coats of eggshell or one undercoat and one gloss finish
Outside walls Rendered Brickwork Concrete	Ensure they are dry Scrape to remove lichen or efflorescence salts Brush to remove grit	Apply 2 coats of masonry paint	
If already coated: dry brush to remove loose coating apply one coat stabilising solution apply one coat masonry paint			

Clear Finish for Hardwoods

Although hardwoods can be painted they are most commonly sealed with varnish or lacquer so that their natural colour and grain are used to their full quality. Many signs are sealed hardwood.

Dry abrading
The grain needs to be rubbed to a very smooth finish. This is best done with an orbital sander although small panels can be finely finished by hand.

Grade 120 or 150 garnet paper or aluminium oxide paper is coarse enough to flatten rough hard grain. Such paper may leave scratches which can be removed with a finer paper, such as grade 180.

Bleaching
Old timber may be stained or new timber may be too dark for the situation or to match existing timber, and in such circumstances the wood needs to be bleached. Household bleach removes stains and colour but sometimes discolours the wood. Oxalic acid crystals dissolved in water is an effective timber bleach but the acid is a registered poison and may be difficult to obtain and can be dangerous to use.

Proprietary wood bleaches are available which are comparatively safe to use and are effective. Some are two pack materials and the manufacturers instructions must be followed carefully.

After bleaching the timber may need further abrading because the water in the bleach can cause the grain to rise.

Filling
Many hardwoods have coarse grain and even after two or three coats of varnish may still be sufficiently uneven to make signwriting difficult. The tiny pores will prevent the brush making clean strokes and will attract the paint causing broken edges and poor finishing. To avoid this the grain needs to be filled.

Grain fillers are available in transparent form, in white, and sometimes tinted to match certain wood colours. They are applied all over the surface with a filling knife or a piece of rag, and when dry rubbed down smooth with glass, garnet or aluminium oxide fine grade paper.

Deep holes are best filled with wood stopper or plastic wood.

Staining
Staining not only makes timber darker or different in colour it enhances the grain. Stain is absorbed into the soft grain to a greater degree than the hard grain producing a bigger contrast between them. Stain also colours the grain filler.

The easiest stains to use are spirit stains or wood dyes which are available in many wood colours. They can be intermixed to produce a wider range.

Stains can be applied by brush or rag. If they are wiped over with a dry rag shortly after application surplus stain is removed from the hard grain to leave an attractive finish.

Some timbers, particularly light oak, ramin and beech are naturally very light and if required to be lettered in gold leaf will provide a poor contrasting background. A thin coat of stain can improve the contrast without destroying the characteristics of the timber.

Table 7.7 shows brief specifications for clear finishing hardwood.

Banners

Banners are widely used for display inside exhibitions and outside at various outdoor events. They vary considerably in size from 500 mm long to in excess of 20 m. Invariably they are purpose made to the size

Table 7.7 Alternative coating systems for clear finishing hardwoods.

Interior signs			
Two coats oil or polyurethane varnish	3 coats cellulose lacquer	2 coats 2 pack polyurethane clear finish	As many coats of French polish necessary to obtain even, glossy finish
Exterior signs			
Four coats oil varnish	5 coats cellulose lacquer	3 coats 2 pack polyurethane finish	French polish not recommended for outside signs

and shape requirements for the particular site on which they are displayed.

Originally, banners were made from cotton duck, a type of canvas, with the edges turned and stitched to give them stability and prevent them from tearing. Large metal eyelets were machined into the hem for holding the supporting ropes. The canvas was either sized or painted with oil paint and signwritten with signwriters colours. Woven materials are rarely used for this purpose having been replaced by PVC sheeting. PVC sheeting for banners is available in different grades and colours. It is always reinforced with a man-made fabric. One side of the material is smooth and offers an ideal surface for signwriting or screen printing, and the back is usually textured.

The material is cut to size from the rolls and the edges are turned and welded to give the banner extra strength and to provide a substantial thickness of material in which to stamp brass eyelets through which the securing ropes are passed. The distance between the eyelets is governed entirely by the requirements of the banner.

On very large banners or those which may be fixed onto very exposed sites the top and bottom hems are made about 150 mm deep with open ends so that timber beams or metal tubes can be inserted which are clamped to a scaffold or a bridge rail. These are called tunnel hems.

Oil paints applied to PVC have poor adhesion and when the material flexes and stretches in use the paint tends to peel off. One of the most reliable paints for printing and signwriting on PVC banners is a screen ink which is specially manufactured for printing on PVC. These inks need a special thinner which may be highly flammable and must be used and stored with great care. The vapour of these thinners is often very pungent and may be dangerous. Good ventilation must be provided during its use. There are low odour inks available. The ink has excellent adhesion to the PVC because the thinners slightly soften the plastic so that the ink and the vinyl form a chemical bond. The ink needs to be thinned when used for signwriting.

PVC ink has two principal problems in use. It forms a reversible film therefore if second coated the thinner in the second coat may soften the first coat and the whole film may pick up or dry very patchy.

Because the ink thinners soften the PVC slightly any painting errors or accidental splashing or spilling may permanently mark the fabrics. This is particularly so with black and red whereas other colours may be removed if wiped off quickly. Small stains which do not wipe off clearly can be touched up with paint which matches the background colour.

Because second coating is difficult the most common method of producing a dark background banner with white lettering is to paint the background in around the letters of a white banner so that the letters are the colour of the banner.

Setting out, marking out and signwriting banners is done in exactly the same way as signwriting more solid signs. The normal technique is to lay them flat on large benches. Very large banners may need to be suspended against a wall. It is essential to have a firm background to the banners.

When a number of identical banners are required it is a common practice to screen print them. The number at which this method becomes practical varies with the intricacies of the layout but as a general rule printing is used when more than five are required. Otherwise the materials and technique are similar to those used for screen printing more stable materials.

Sign Fixing

The fixing of illuminated signs, and very large signs, particularly those in inaccessible positions, is usually carried out by specialist contractors. The fixing of small signs, particularly at ground level, is often required of the signmaker. Signs are fixed either through the face, or by some concealed fitting.

Through the face
Drilling holes through the sign and driving screws or bolts through them into a wall plug is the simplest and often the most effective method of fixing. Screw heads are not aesthetically acceptable and there are many means by which they can be hidden or disguised.

*Countersunk and filled.*This method can be used with wood signs only. The screw hole needs to be deeply countersunk so that the screw head is below the level of the sign. When the screw is tightened the hole is filled with a timber stopper and touched up with colour to match the sign. This type of fixing makes removing the sign at a later date very difficult but it does offer considerable protection from vandalism.

Cappings. A screw is available with a bolt thread in the head into which a domed cap can be screwed after the screw has been fixed to provide a more acceptable appearance. These fittings are commonly used for fixing mirrors and glass. Many forms of plastic caps are available which fit over the head of the screw and cover the grooved head. For hardwood signs screws and cups are often used. These are round head brass screws which fit into a brass cup shaped ring. All cappings are easy to remove when the sign needs to be taken down, but if they are near to any pedestrian area they are very easily vandalised.

Concealed fitting

When face fixings are not acceptable some method must be adopted which is not visible from the face and does not mar the face. There are a few special fittings made for signs but many signmakers develop their own methods.

Keyhole plates, see fig. 7.11. Small round plates which have a shape like a keyhole cut into the centre. They are screwed on or recessed into the back of the sign with the hole at the bottom and the slot above. The hole is slipped over the head of a screw in the wall and drops down over the shank and no direct pulling from the front will pull the sign off. A fixing in each corner is usually necessary. The simplest way to ensure that the screws in the wall match the exact position of the plates in the sign is to make a template. This is done by cutting a piece of paper exactly the size of the sign, placing it over the back of the sign and marking on it the position of each key hole. When the template is placed on the wall in the exact position that the sign is required the holes can be marked on the wall and the screw holes drilled in those places. Suitable for small signs only.

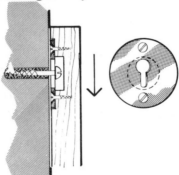

Fig. 7.11 A keyhole plate, and the method by which it is fitted to a screw fitted into the wall

Flush mounts, see fig. 7.12. Two identical steel fittings in which the centre section protrudes slightly. One fitting is screwed to the back of the sign, the other screwed to the wall or batten fixed to the wall. The plates interlock when properly located and can be removed only when knocked upwards. Used as an alternative to key hole plates for similar type signs. Generally two fittings are sufficient although four may be necessary if the sign is almost square shape. A fixing template is essential to locate the plates accurately.

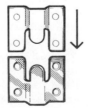

Fig. 7.12 A flush mount

Snap fittings, see fig. 7.13. These are made particularly for fixing prefabricated or cut letters but they can be adapted for small signs. Usually they are made of nylon. A cylindrical fitting is screwed to the wall and a spherical fitting is screwed to the back of the board. When pressed together the board fitting fits tightly into the wall fitting. At least one fitting in each corner is necessary and locating positions need to be carefully marked out with a template as described for key hole plates.

Fig. 7.13 A type of snap fitting. The smaller section is screwed to the sign and fits into the larger section screwed to the wall.

Bolt fixings. Special brass or nylon fixings in two parts which are threaded so that they fit together. One part is fixed to the back of the board, the other to the wall, and a thin spanner is manoeuvred behind the panel to rotate one piece into the thread of the other.

Split batten. Fig. 7.14 shows an angled cut batten at the top of the back of the sign hanging on to a similar angled batten on the wall. Another method is to use two square battens which push onto each other and a screw underneath holds the two pieces together. A more involved version is to use angled batten at top and bottom and slide the sign onto them. Screws through the bottom two pieces hold it in position.

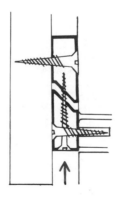

Fig. 7.14 A split batten fitting

Metal and GRP signs can be shaped into a box form and fitted over wood battens or metal angles on the wall and grub screws or recessed nuts inserted top and bottom to hold it in position.

Glass signs can be drilled and screwed through the face with dome capped screws. They can be fitted into a three-sided frame which has been screwed to the wall and the fourth piece inserted and grub screwed into the fixed frame.

Acrylic signs have small strips of the sheeting bonded to the back and are hung into specially manufactured extruded aluminium framing, see fig. 7.15.

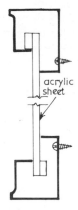

Fig. 7.15 An extruded aluminium section for suspending acrylic sheet

Wall Fixings

Whether the sign fitting is concealed or not there must always be a firm fixing made to the wall.

Solid walls

Invariably the most effective fixing is a drilled hole, plugged with a plastic or fibre tube, and a screw driven into it, see fig. 7.16.

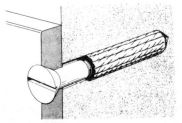

Fig. 7.16 Countersunk screw driven into a fibre wall plug

The holes can be drilled using a masonry bit or hammered using a special percussion drill or a bit struck by a hammer. The depth of the hole depends on the weight of the sign and generally varies between 25 mm and 50 mm. The wall plugs should fill the hole and can be made from compressed fibre and resin, or plastic.

Steel screws will rust and cause stain marks on the wall or on the sign. This can be avoided by either using brass screws which are not as strong as steel screws and very expensive; or, zinc or chromium plated steel screws which have the same strength as standard steel screws and are only slightly more expensive.

Hollow walls

There are a number of fittings available for fixing signs to walls which have only a thin cladding. They work on two principles, either a spring or gravity toggle, or a device which expands behind the board as the screw is tightened, see fig. 7.17.

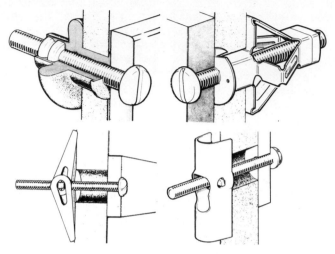

Fig. 7.17 Types of fixings for hollow walls

Holes are drilled in the wall cladding and the toggle on the bolt or the expanding device on a screw is inserted. The toggles either spring open or drop when they get behind the board and as the bolt is tightened they press on the back of the board. The expanders fold up as the screw pulls them forward and they press behind the board.

Another version is like an umbrella and the limbs open up behind the board and tighten as the screw is inserted.

Fixing to Poles

There are many proprietary fixings which are designed specially to grip around a pole. The general principle is to tighten like a belt. When tight the end is bent under using a special tool so that they cannot be undone.

A common method is to bolt through the board and through a hole in the tube and tighten a nut where it emerges.

Fixing Banners

The original method of sewing ropes into the top and bottom hems is rarely used now. It was a method that allowed the banner to be pulled tight from each end and made fast to a firm structure.

The method's weakness became apparent when the ropes got wet. Usually they tightened on wetting but slackened on drying causing the banner to wrinkle and crease.

Most banners are produced with eyelets set in the hem and fixings are made through these. If the banner is to be fixed to a timber fence or frame large headed nails are driven through the eyelets into the wood.

It is not necessary to put a nail through every eyelet as this may cause the banner to crease if it does stretch because of temperature change. A fixing every 1.5–2 metres is usually sufficient.

Fixing to metal structures usually requires nylon ropes to be passed through the eyelets and made fast to the fence or bridge or whatever is behind. The same number of fixings that are used on timber frames is sufficient.

At outdoor events where the banners may need to be fixed to earth banks or hedges the most common practice is to pass ropes through the eyelets which are pulled tight around and fixed to wood or metal stakes.

Large banners which cannot be firmly fitted to the structure have a length of metal tube or timber joists run through the tunnel hems. These are fixed at each end. They may need additional supports in the centre.

Specialist banner firms may supply a free standing structure made from aluminium or timber which can be folded away into a small unit. They are fitted by couplings through holes cut in the back of the tunnel hems.

Eight
Signwriting

Signwriting is the oldest skill associated with signmaking and probably the most difficult skill to master.

Although many different skills have been used to produce signs over the years, the work of the signwriter has always been in demand. It cannot compete with screen printing for speed when producing a number of identical signs. Yet it remains the quickest way to produce a one-off sign, regardless of the surface to which it is to be applied or the intricacies of the design.

Signwriting is a precise art. It is not filling-in predrawn letters, but the painting of letters with a brush to the same precision that a draughtsman will draw a letter with instruments. It is important that the trainee signwriter is fully aware of the standards of finish that a signwriter can achieve. From a distance of 2 m it should not be possible to tell whether a letter has been painted, cut, printed or transferred. Even at shorter distances it may be difficult to detect the painted letter.

It is this high level of proficiency that the trainee must adopt as a standard and accept no other. To reach this level may take many years of concentrated practice, with every sense trained to produce not only a functional sign but one which is aesthetically pleasing.

Signwriters Kit

A signwriter needs few tools, but like most crafts those few need careful selection to produce work of a high standard.

BRUSHES
Some signwriters equipment can be improvised or made, but brushes must be bought. As they are expensive and varied in price, quality and shape they need to be selected with great care. The same degree of care is needed to look after them. The types of brushes available are considerable.

Writing brushes
Writing brushes are sometimes called pencils, pencil brushes, sables, writers, signwriting brushes or quills. The majority of the work done by the signwriter is carried out with these brushes. See fig. 8.1.

It is the hair used in the filling of these brushes that makes them so expensive. The most expensive is sable. Sable hair is cut from the tail of various animals of the weasel family. Although common throughout the world, it is the weasels who live wild in the Arctic or semi-Arctic

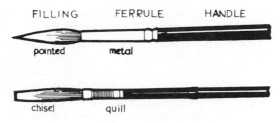

FILLING   FERRULE   HANDLE

pointed   metal

chisel   quill

Fig. 8.1 Ferrule and quill writing brushes

regions of Asia which produce the best hairs. Russia was a main producer but most hair is obtained from China now. Sable is the traditional and most common name used for signwriting brushes, although Kolinsky is used by some manufacturers to describe their brushes. Kolinsky is one of the many weasels from which hair is obtained and it must not be assumed that this is always the best quality 'sable'.

Sable is a light reddish-brown hair. Although very fine it has considerable strength. It holds a lot of paint without too much sag and will spring back to shape immediately the paint is used up or pressure on the filling is relieved. Like all natural hair it has a natural taper so that the tip is very fine which makes it ideal for detailed painting.

The hairs are selected and shaped by hand into a pointed or a chisel (flat edged) filling. They are tied and inserted into either a metal ferrule and glued with resin; or into the wide end of a heat softened birds feather quill which shrinks when it cools to grip the hairs.

Quills are not as widely available as ferrule brushes and generally are slightly cheaper. Sometimes they are available ready fixed to a handle, but the common form is to buy the quills and handles separately for the signwriter to fit together. Ferrule brushes are sold in numbered sizes; quills in bird sizes. See table 8.1 for comparative sizes.

Table 8.1 Brush sizes.

Ferrule	Quill	Approximate diameter in mm
00		1.1
0	Lark	1.3
1	Crow	1.6
2	Small duck (or Large crow)	1.9
3	Duck	2.2
4	Large duck	2.6
5	Small goose	3.1
6	Goose	3.6
7	Large goose	4.2
8	Extra small swan	4.9
9	Small swan	5.6
10	Swan	6.3
11	Large swan	7.1
12	Condor	7.8

These sizes are taken from BS 2808:1969 'Specification for Artists Water-Colour Brushes'.

Pointed brushes come naturally to a point and are suitable for fine lettering and lines. When pressure is applied to the filling it should spread for painting wide strokes. Chisel brushes naturally form a flat edge and are widely used for all types of lettering. Most signwriters carry both types of brushes but the decision to use either a pointed brush or a chisel brush depends largely on the signwriters preference rather than the type of work being carried out.

Ox ear hair or ox hair is widely used in writing brushes as a cheap substitute for sable hair. It is a little darker in colour, feels very fine and has a similar taper to sable which produces a good point or chisel end, but it does not have the same strength or springiness as sable. Some large brushes and many coach liners are made exclusively of ox hair. Smaller brushes usually have a mixture of sable and ox, sometimes called sabox fillings. Some brush manufacturers call their ox hair writers Riggers or Taurus brushes.

Nylon filling brushes are cheaper than sable or sabox brushes. They are very tough hairs but do not have the same paint holding qualities as the natural hairs.

SELECTING SABLE BRUSHES

Most signwriters will have at least one complete set of brushes from 0 to 12. In addition they will have two or three of probably four sizes in the full series.

A signwriter who is often required to do small lettering will have more 0s, 1s and 2s than 6s, 8s and 10s. Some signwriters prefer points to chisels although most will carry both. Some prefer ferrules to quills although most will carry both.

When starting to collect a set of brushes an economic policy is to purchase the even numbers first. A number 2 pointed and 4 and 6 chisel would be sufficient to do most lettering between 50 mm and 150 mm high. The odd numbers can be purchased next, such as 1 and 3 pointed and 8 chisel. Number 5 can be left out because there is little it can do which a 4 or 6 cannot do. Numbers 10 and 12 will be required eventually but their purchase should be left until the signwriter is confident that they can be controlled.

Sable brushes are available in two lengths of hair. The shorter ones are sometimes called ticket writers brushes and are not very useful for the signwriter because they do not hold very much paint. A signwriters speed is related to the amount of time taken to fill the brush, so it is better to select long hair brushes from the start in order to develop a commercial technique.

All quality sable brushes are hand made. The brush maker selects the hairs and manipulates them into a shape to produce a fine point or a true flat chisel edge. They are not cut to make a point or chisel edge otherwise the natural fine tip is destroyed. Some brushes may not achieve the same high standard and for this reason it is important that brushes should be selected rather than purchased by mail order.

A good brush retailer will offer a number of brushes for selection and provide a small pot of water to help compare the finish of the brushes. If the brush is dipped in the water it can be shaped to either a point or a chisel edge. The tip can then be inspected against a good light. The pointed brush should come to one good point with no short hairs projecting to spoil the taper from ferrule to tip. The chisel edge should be perfectly straight and the last 1–2 mm should appear almost transparent, which shows that the fine tip has not been cut off. Another way to check for trimming is to run the thumb and forefinger along the hair from ferrule to tip and not be able to feel when the fingers have reached the end. Signwriters refer to the thick end of a brush as a curb, and if their fingers trip on the curb the brush is rejected. When pressure is put on the filling it should splay out evenly with no short or twisted hairs.

The ferrule should also be inspected carefully. Ferrules are made from either nickel plated metal or aluminium and should be free from seams. Mostly they are crimped onto the handle but some are pinned. It is essential that when the thumb and forefinger are run around and up the ferrule that no seam, pin or rucked crimping can be felt. The slightest irregularity on a ferrule can cause considerable soreness to the skin of the fingers when used for a few hours.

Some ferrules have sharp edges which cut the hairs. This may be detected by working the hairs back and forward a few times and inspect for loose hairs. Quills rarely have roughnesses, but they can be curved or broken. Any brush with these defects should be rejected. Most quills are made from the ends of birds' feathers although some of the large ones, such as swan and upwards may be plastic. Some of these large plastic quills are bound on the outside with wire and where the ends are twisted a projecting roughness may occur. This sort should be avoided.

Fitting a quill
It is possible to shape a handle from a thin dowel using a sharp knife and glasspaper but it is a lengthy process and difficult to retain true symmetry. As most retailers of quills supply handles the need for handmade handles is rare. Handles of worn out brushes can be kept for this purpose also.

The end of the handle should be rubbed down with glasspaper until it will fit into the end of the quill and stop no more than 2 mm away from the end of the hairs. The handle should be a reasonably tight fit but not be forced in otherwise the quill may be cracked. It is necessary to soften the quill end before inserting it on the handle and this can be done by placing it in warm water. After about five minutes when the quill has become very soft and flexible it can be pushed carefully onto the handle. As it dries the quill will shrink and tightly grip the handle. Taping or binding should not be necessary.

ONE STROKE BRUSHES
These are always metal ferruled. They are made similarly to sable writers but the top of the ferrule is squeezed flat to produce a spade-like filling. One stroke brushes were made originally for ticket writing and produce a stroke similar to that of a broad pen. Signwriters may carry a few sizes of them for filling in large letters or painting wide

areas when doing heraldic painting or graphic art. One stroke brushes are available in sable but they use a lot more hair than writers therefore are very expensive. If being used for filling in, sabox brushes are quite suitable. They are sold in width sizes from about 4 mm up to 25 mm.

Fig. 8.2 One stroke brush

LINING BRUSHES
Lining brushes are available in many forms. They are designed to paint fine, straight lines, either freehand or guided by a straight edge.

Coach liner
Coach liners are most commonly available as quills and look like very long haired writers. Pure sable liners are very rare because they are so expensive. The common filling is sabox or ox hair. They are available in a limited range of quill sizes. A lark will produce a line about 2–3 mm wide, a crow about 4 mm, and a duck about 5–6 mm. Many experienced liners prefer to use the quills without any handle. A long handle can make control of the brush difficult when it is held between the thumb and forefinger with the thumb on top. To protect the quill it is safer to fit a short handle of about 60 mm. If full length handles are supplied with the quills they should be fitted and cut off at about 60 mm below the quill. See fig. 8.3.

Fig. 8.3 Quill type coach liner

Sword striper or liner
Sword stripers or liners are shaped like a knife blade and are made in an entirely different way to any of the above brushes and from a different hair. See fig. 8.4. They are made from squirrel hair. Generally it is blue squirrels hair which is used, taken from those native to the colder regions of Asia and America. They are much softer than sable and darker brown in colour. The hairs are bound to a short handle with either copper wire or a narrow metal ferrule. Stripers are available in two or three sizes. Sometimes they are numbered, but generally they are marked in widths from about 8 mm to 13 mm. When wet the hairs should produce a triangular shape meeting in a clean point, and when drawn across a surface should paint a straight line with no short hairs projecting out forming a rough edge.

Fig. 8.4 Sword striper

Lining fitch
Lining fitches are made from white or lily hog bristles and are fitted into a square metal ferrule. Their unique shape is designed so that they can be held at a slight angle and run along the edge of a straight edge. The bristle is much tougher and stiffer than sable so they can be used on rough surfaces such as cement rendering, brickwork, or masonry paint. They are sold in widths from 6 mm to 38 mm. Some manufacturers produce short and long fillings also. Short fillings are easier to control but hold less paint so have to be filled more often. It is possible to fix masking tape around the end of the filling where it meets the ferrule to reduce the effective length of a long filling if it should be difficult to control. See fig. 8.5.

Fig. 8.5 Lining fitch

Like all natural hairs, bristle has a fine tip which should not be cut during manufacture. If individual bristles are examined they should be seen to come to a fine point or maybe break up into two or three fine fibres or flags. When wetted the filling should taper to a fine edge and when pressed onto a surface no short hairs should protrude. The ferrules are usually pinned to the handle and sometimes this may be crudely done so that a large part of the pin protrudes. It is not uncommon for the ferrule to be loose on the handle. Brushes with any of these faults should be rejected.

FITCHES
Fitches have a limited use by signwriters but they may carry two or three in a kit. They are made from hog bristle or nylon fitted into a metal ferrule and available in three shapes. Round, like a sable writer; flat, squashed like a one stroke; and filbert, which is a slightly flattened fitch with short hairs shaped into a 'U' or dome-shaped form. See fig. 8.6. Fitches are available in a great variety of numbered sizes, from 1 (about 2 mm) to 14 (about 16 mm). Flat and filberts are a little wider. A signwriter may use fitches for filling-in but their most useful purpose is when painting a piece of relief decoration, like a cast coat of arms, see fig. 8.7. The bristles can be pushed into deep crevices without the sort of damage which may occur if a sable brush is used.

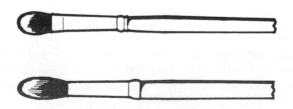

Fig. 8.6 A filbert and round fitch

Fig. 8.7 Fitch being used to push paint into the depth of a relief decoration

CARE OF BRUSHES

Brushes are very expensive and demand great care to justify the cost and ensure their full life and top quality.

Moths and mildew will attack new, unused natural brush fillings, especially sable. It is essential to store brushes in a dry place protected from moths with some sort of insecticide cyrstals or powder.

Brushes should be washed out immediately after use. Any paint which is allowed to dry in the root of a delicate brush such as sable, is both difficult to remove and will destroy the shape of the brush. The brush should be rinsed out in the thinner of the paint being used. If signwriters tube or enamel colour is being used, brushes need to be washed in white spirit. For emulsion paints only water will clean brushes. The brush should be swirled around in the thinner not punched out in the bottom of the container which will only damage the hairs. When all the paint has been removed right down to the ferrule the brush needs to be 'greased'. This is rubbing in a non-setting grease or jelly, squeezing it deep into the filling between the thumb and forefinger and shaping the brush into a point or chisel edge, see fig. 8.8. Petroleum jelly is the most convenient material for this, but tallow, margarine, butter or olive oil can be used. The greasing process has three purposes: it ensures that if any paint has been left in the brush it will not set; it keeps the brush in good shape; and it protects the filling when the brush is being carried around. When working on site it is sometimes difficult to clean brushes thoroughly at the end of a job. But if they are wiped to remove most of the paint and thoroughly 'greased' the paint will be kept soft so that the brushes can be washed at a later date when facilities are better. It is essential that the 'grease' is thoroughly washed out of the brush with white spirit before they are re-used. There are many ways of storing brushes when not in use, see fig. 8.9. The essential concern is to prevent the hair becoming damaged. The simplest way is to lay them flat in a drawer of the box. A more secure way is to lay them flat on a piece of stiff card and bind them with two stout elastic bands. Brush holders are sold which are simple card or metal cylinders with a push on lid. These are often expensive and have little advantage over laying them flat in a drawer.

Sables are available with plastic or metal handles which can be separated into two halves by a thread or push fit. The lower half can be fitted over the filling when not in use to protect it. They are very expensive and not widely used by signwriters.

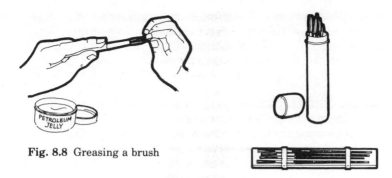

Fig. 8.8 Greasing a brush

Fig. 8.9 Methods of storing and carrying brushes

Other essential signwriting equipment

MAHL STICK

The name is of German origin, meaning painting stick, sometimes referred to as a rest stick. A mahl stick is a vital piece of equipment particularly when working on signs *in situ*. Its purpose is to both steady the hand when painting and to allow the hand to be in the best position for every stroke of the signwriting. It needs to be about 500 mm long, strong enough to support the weight of the hand even after many hours, and flexible so that it will return to a straight stick when the pressure of the hand is released. A convenient thickness for the stick is 12–15 mm diameter. If it is much thinner it can cause the part of the hand resting on it to lose all sensation after a few hours use. If it is too thick it can be difficult to hold after a long period. One end needs to be padded so that it can be laid onto a painted surface without damaging it and also prevents the stick slipping on the surface as pressure is applied. A small pad of cotton wool, covered with rag or chamois leather and bound to the stick with string or masking tape is a practical method of padding. See fig. 8.10.

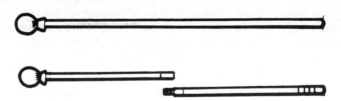

Fig. 8.10 A one piece and a two piece mahl stick

Mahl sticks take many forms. The cheapest sticks are made from cane or dowell. These are very functional but often are too long to fit into the signwriters box and need to be carried separately. Purchased mahl sticks take two common forms. They are in two or three sections which screw together or push into ferrules. Some sophisticated ones are shaped so that the handle part is wider than the rest. Most of them will have a fixed spherical knob made from either wood or cork which will need covering with rag or leather. Being in sections they can be carried in a box easily. They vary in price considerably and some of them are very frail, made with the artist in mind, and will not withstand the more robust and constant use of the signwriter.

BRIDGE OR HAND REST

When working on a sign which is laying flat on a bench, particularly when glass painting, many signwriters prefer to rest their hand on a bridge rather than use a mahl stick. It is a piece of wood supported on two blocks at each end, which can be laid in position with the hand resting on top. A convenient size is about 400 x 70 mm and about 40 mm high. It needs to be made of stout wood so that it does not bend unduly and is able to support many kilogrammes of body weight. The underside of the blocks need to be padded with cork, felt or leather to protect the surface it is rested upon. Some signwriters pad the top with plastic covered foam to make it more comfortable for long periods of use. See fig. 8.11.

Fig. 8.11   Bridge or hand rest

PALETTE BOARD OR THUMB BOARD

The board is held by the thumb of the hand not holding the brush, and is used to support dippers and provides a surface on which the brush may be shaped before signwriting. See figs 8.12 and 8.20. It needs to be big enough, strong enough and light. Palette boards can be purchased, either rectangular in shape or oval, in timber, plywood, plastic or disposable acetate or parchment leaves. A convenient size is about 230 x 160 mm. Many signwriters make their own or have one made. They need to be about 4 mm thick, and can be made from varnished or polished plywood, acrylic sheet, or melamine coated hardboard. Thin gauge aluminium is often used. The thumb hole needs to be chamfered. On the underside where it fits over the thumb and on the top edge where the thumb passes through. Without this the board is very uncomfortable to use. Most manufactured boards are designed for right handed signwriters and this should be checked before purchase. The 'S' shape allows the board to fit conveniently and securely over the Mahl stick. Some signwriters put paper on the board to reduce the amount of cleaning necessary.

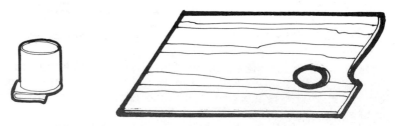

Fig. 8.12   Single dipper (left) and palette (right)

DIPPERS

These are small cylindrical containers for paint and thinner which clip onto the side of the palette board. They are made of non-ferrous metal. The convenient size is about 40 mm diameter and 40 mm high. See fig. 8.12. There are smaller ones which are made for artists and are of little value to signwriters. Some have rims which reduce the risk of spilling, and although this is desirable they do make cleaning more difficult. Double dippers are available also, but these are not always practical because one dipper cannot be emptied without spilling the other.

Cheap dippers are prone to leak, and the bent base which forms the clip may split. These should be checked before purchase.

Some signwriters use small glass or plastic pots instead of dippers. They may be held in the hand omitting the use of the palette board, or they may be stood in a dipper and thrown away after use to avoid washing dippers.

PALLETTE KNIFE

A small flexible bladed knife about 90 mm long which is very useful for mixing or stirring colours in the dipper or on the board. See fig. 8.13.

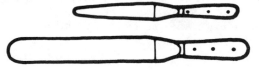

Fig. 8.13   Palette knives

COMPASS

This is not an essential tool because most good signwriters can paint circles or circular shapes accurately with a brush without the need of a drawing aid. They can be useful for other forms of setting out and many signwriters carry one in their kit. A small metal compass can be useful although the larger type with arms about 300 mm long is more valuable. This large type can be obtained in wood or plastic, and the scribing end will hold either a pencil or a stick of chalk. Because the point can do considerable damage to a surface it is often protected by a cork or a rubber sucker. See fig. 8.14.

Fig. 8.14   Large compass for site marking out

CHALK LINE

A line is an essential piece of equipment and is the only certain method of striking a perfectly straight line on a flat surface. It needs to be fine, and very strong and capable of holding particles of chalk. Nylon and other man-made fibres meet the first two requirements but do not hold chalk. A strong unwaxed cotton or crochet cotton, or linen thread is usually the best material. It should be kept on its original reel, or re-rolled onto a typewriter ribbon spool or a larger wooden reel so that it is not easily mislaid.

CHALK
White chalk is the only colour which will not discolour a painted sign, and should be used whenever possible. When coloured chalk is essential the bright colours should be avoided. Red is a particularly poor colour and will permanently stain a painted surface. Brown and blue chalks are the safer colours to use. Non-dust chalk is suitable for marking on a surface but is not suitable for chalking lines. Lump whiting is very useful for chalking lines and drawings, but it is not readily available.

WAX PENCILS
These are available in a small range of colours, but black and white are the only ones needed by a signwriter. These pencils are specially made to mark on glass, plastic and glossy paint and are easily removed, therefore they are commonly used.

MEASURES
A flexible roll-up 3 m tape for long work and a folding wooden metre rule will be sufficient for most work. See fig. 8.15.

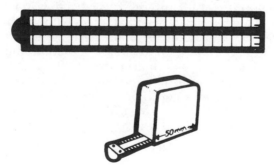

Fig. 8.15   A folding rule and a measuring tape

SIGNWRITERS BOX
The signwriter is a travelling person and does not always know what materials or tools will be required until arrival on site. Therefore it is common practice to carry all the equipment described above to every job. For this a carefully designed and constructed carrier is required. Manufactured boxes are usually too small and very expensive. The best box is a purpose made one, designed to carry the kit which that particular signwriter needs. Any reasonable carpenter can make a signwriters box to a precise sketch. The box should be designed to meet two needs:

(1) to carry all the equipment necessary, without damage or spillage.

(2) to act as a seat for low lettering and as a raised platform for lettering just above head height.

For the second purpose it needs to be made strongly and of suitable dimensions. Fig. 8.16 shows a typical box design. Although most feet will overhang the 250 mm width it still provides a firm reliable base for standing on without being too difficult to carry. The large drawers are ideal for carrying brushes and gilding equipment. The small drawers conveniently hold chalks, lines, knives, rules, gold leaf and a variety of improvised gadgets which are collected over the years. The centre shelf will hold at least ten dippers clipped to it and room for many more behind. The well does hold tins and containers more securely and if paint is spilled it will collect in the well and not run out through the lid. Into this well can be placed tins of paint, tube stainers, and containers for thinners. Thinners containers should have a wide, screw top so that a brush can be easily inserted for cleaning. Paint will collect at the bottom and a wide top makes cleaning out easier. There will be ample room in the bottom of the box for many other things such as varnish, gold size, rags, drawings and mahl stick. The well of the lid can house the palette board by a simple wood twist catch that pushes through the thumb hole. Most signwriters will fit a mortice lock or a padlock for added security.

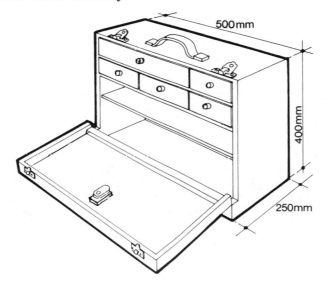

Fig. 8.16 A signwriters box

The Signwriting Process

The ultimate aim of a signwriter is to paint any style of lettering, directly to a prepared ground, with a minimum of marking out, and quickly. This sort of skill requires absolute confidence in the control of the brush, which is achieved only by practice and experience.

The necessary confidence will be achieved faster when the following four points are mastered: (1) correct selection of brush; (2) sufficient quantity of paint of the right consistency in the brush; (3) comfortable position; and (4) the minimum number of brush strokes to paint a letter.

CORRECT BRUSH

The biggest brush possible should be used otherwise boldness of stroke and speed of painting will be affected. There are a few rules to help select the right type of brush for the lettering to be painted. When the brush is fully spread open it should not be wider than the letter stroke. A brush filling will spread two to three times wider than its diameter at the ferrule, see fig. 8.17. Therefore a number 4 writer will produce a stroke about 8 mm wide. Another rule of thumb guide is to assume that a number 1 brush is suitable for 25 mm high letters, and for every increase in height of 25 mm the brush size needs to increase by one. Therefore a number 4 writer is usually most suitable for light or medium weight letters of 100 mm high (4 x 25 mm).

Fig. 8.17   A brush filling will spread two to three times its ferrule diameter

PAINT

Every time that the brush is recharged with paint the rhythm of writing is broken and signwriting stops. So the aim for fast signwriting is to fill the brush as full as possible with paint that is sufficiently fluid to allow a clean stroke to be painted.

The most common way that signwriters prepare their paint is to mix it to what seems the right consistency in a dipper first. Then if it needs further thinning to do it on the board by taking thinners from the second dipper. The right consistency is when the brush can be pulled through a stroke that empties the filling before the stroke runs out. It should also cover or obliterate the surface, and produce a clean edge. If the paint is transparent, or runs readily, it is too thin. If the brush will not move freely or seems to stick to the surface, and will not empty in one stroke it is too thick.

When painting the bulk of the letter, the brush needs to be full. When finishing at corners the brush will need less paint which can be worked out of the brush on the palette board.

POSITION

Fast signwriting will be achieved when the body is relaxed. Reaching high or bending low becomes uncomfortable and tiring after a short time and more time may be used recovering than writing. When working on site it is not always possible to get into the most comfortable position, and can result in jobs taking longer to complete.

Jobs carried out in the workshop should be set up in the most comfortable position.

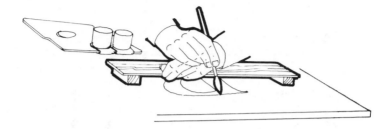

Fig. 8.18 The signwriters position when working flat

Occasionally it is necessary to lay signs flat on a bench to work, see fig. 8.18. This applies often to glass work or when the sign is too large to stand up. But this position is restricting and should not be adopted as a common practice because it will make site signwriting more difficult. The ideal position is to have the sign slightly tilted away from the signwriter, with the height of the lettering being painted just below the shoulder level, and the light above and shining over the shoulder. The simplest way to satisfy these three is to mount the sign on an easel (see fig. 8.21).

Free standing easels can be purchased which allow the height and angle of the sign to be altered easily. These are very expensive and may not be able to hold every size and shape of sign that a signwriter may be required to paint. The cheapest and most adaptable easel consists of two lengths of 100 x 50 mm softwood with 15 mm diameter holes drilled in them every 150 mm, see fig. 8.19. The height needs to be at least 2 m but they can be longer if the workshop walls are high enough to take them and the sort of signs commonly painted need the extra size. Lengths of 15 mm dowel about 120 mm long can be used as pegs. With the two battens leaned against a wall the pegs can be fitted into the most convenient height holes upon which to mount the sign. On very long signs a third batten can be used to support the centre.

If the board cannot be adjusted to the perfect height it is better to stand on a box or small platform than to reach up or stand on tip toe. If the board is too low it is better to sit than bend excessively.

The correct position for signwriting is to have the palette board over the thumb of the non-writing hand with the chamfer underneath and two dippers clipped to the board. The mahl stick firmly gripped in the same hand and the 'S' shape of the board resting over it, see fig. 8.20. The body needs to be 400–500 mm away from the surface being painted, with the feet 500–600 mm apart, see fig. 8.21. Any considerable variations in these distances may result in discomfort or off-balance.

PAINTING
The brush is used to draw letter shapes. It is not used to fill in previously pencil drawn shapes. This needs a close coordination of eye

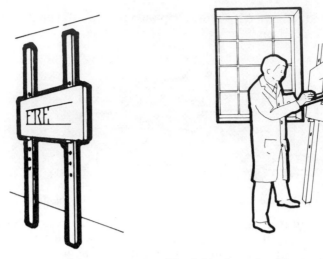

Fig. 8.21 A comfortable signwriters stance

Fig. 8.19
An easel made from two lengths of timber

Fig. 8.20 The signwriters kit ready for use

and hand. The eye must clearly 'see' the shape that must be painted and the message passed to the hand must indicate the minimum number of strokes of the brush necessary to paint that shape. Bold, flowing strokes produce clean, accurate letters quickly. Tentative, dabbing strokes produce uneven, messy letters slowly.

The mahl stick plays a vital part in producing fast accurate signwriting. It needs to be positioned so that the hand is always in exactly the right place to paint each stroke that makes up the whole letter. Sometimes the hand holding the stick may need to be low so that the stick is almost upright. Other times it may need to be almost horizontal, see fig. 8.22. The mahl stick has to be moved many times during the painting of a letter to ensure that the hand is always in the right place. On large letters the mahl stick will need to be moved a lot more. For painting a vertical stroke the hand and the mahl stick can be moved down as a unit, see fig. 8.23. Sometimes the mahl stick can be used as a straight edge and the brush run along it for both vertical and horizontal strokes. It will need to be swivelled when painting curves, using the padded tip as its pivot. Effective control of the brush depends on proper use of the mahl stick.

Fig. 8.22 The mahl stick held horizontally

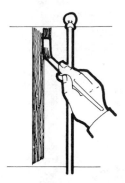

Fig. 8.23 The mahl stick held vertically

The brush is held by the handle at a point just below the ferrule when painting strokes (see fig. 8.24), but the fingers may need to move up the ferrule closer to the hairs when finishing corners, see fig. 8.25. It is held between the thumb underneath and the forefinger on top, with the middle finger resting against the side of the brush to steady it as the brush is moved and twisted while painting. When painting curves the brush is twisted between the thumb and forefinger as the mahl stick is swivelled. Using this technique the elbow of the writing hand invariably remains well below the level of the brush. Whereas the elbow of the mahl stick hand will move much more. Because of the considerable movement of the palette hand it is necessary to fill dippers no more than half full otherwise they will spill their contents.

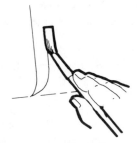

Fig. 8.24 Fingers below the ferrule when painting strokes

Fig. 8.25 Fingers on the ferrule when finishing a letter

For painting strokes the full length and width of the hairs must be used. The tip of the brush should be used only for finishing the letter or painting very fine lines. A sans serif letter P should be painted in six strokes see fig. 8.26. Each stroke overlaps the previous one so that no filling in is necessary. Special care must be taken when painting corners so that they finish with a true square end. The brush should have less paint in it for finishing and if the paint is worked out on the palette board the brush can be shaped into a sharp chisel or point. The tendency of novice signwriters is to avoid the corner and ends tend to be barrel shape, turning into the letter rather than being square. This can be overcome by deliberately swelling out at the corners to obtain a sharp finish. The first few letters will appear to have slight serifs but as confidence increases the swelling will be less exaggerated and the corners will look sharp.

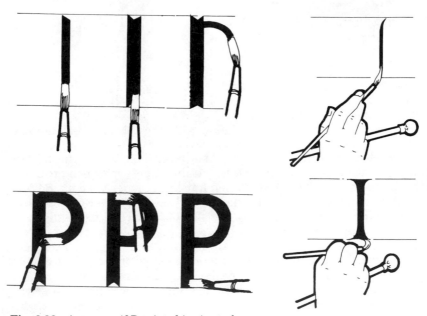

Fig. 8.26   A sans serif P painted in six strokes

Fig. 8.27
A serif is painted as part of the down stroke

The upright stem of the letter is painted with only two bold strokes of the brush. Letters over about 300 mm high will need to be filled in. If the entire letter is painted first in outline the paint will have started to dry before the letter is filled in. A 'fat edge' will then show where the outline paint and the filling in meet and may spoil the appearance. This can be avoided by filling in as the letter outline is painted.

A serif letter should be painted in a similar number of strokes to a sans serif letter. The serif should be painted with the straight stroke and not added on afterwards. The Roman letter shape was designed by the brush so can be naturally painted by brush. The first stroke starts at the top left hand serif with little pressure on the brush. As it sweeps into the straighter part of the stem greater pressure is applied and then released as the brush is guided into the left hand bottom serif, see fig. 8.27.

The brush should always be pulled, with the hand below the level of the hair. In this way the brush can be kept under control. If the brush is pushed or the hand is above the hair there is less control and mistakes or slower painting are more likely to occur.

The eye is inclined to recognise the shape of the letter by the spaces within it rather than by its outline. Therefore the technique of painting the inside shape of a curved letter first is adopted by many signwriters. Once the inside shape is accurately painted the outside shape is painted to match it.

TRAINING

Complete control of the brush is the vital skill of a signwriter. Considerable practice is essential to have this mastery over the brush. The three strokes which are necessary to master first are the straight upright, the circle, and the S-curve.

A method of practising is to snap two chalk lines about 60 mm apart onto a painted panel. Then holding the equipment and standing in the position described earlier a series of upright strokes can be painted to touch both the top and bottom lines. The practice will be complete when every stroke is exactly the same thickness, height and distance apart; and all perfectly upright. The practice should continue with circles and S-shapes and cease only when every shape is accurate and matching the shapes either side.

Control of the brush for smaller letters may take longer to achieve. But the skill involved in painting a 60 mm letter can usually be transferred to 100 mm and 150 mm letters with ease.

Once the trainee is reasonably confident that the brush can be controlled the next step is to paint letters that have been carefully spaced. The first exercises can be signwriting previously drawn and transferred lettering. This aspect of signwriting should not be emphasised and after two or three exercises all practice should be concentrated on painting letters directly to a painted sign with the absolute minimum of marking out with a chalk stick or wax pencil.

Processes in Signwriting

CLEANING

Any dirt or grease on the sign will reduce the adhesion of the signwriting paint making it difficult to apply or shortening the effective life of the writing. A wash with mild detergent, if possible, dried off with a chamois leather is usually sufficient.

SETTING OUT

It may be necessary to set out in one of two ways: (a) direct marking out; or (b) transferring a full size drawing.

Direct

Direct marking means snapping chalk lines for the top and bottom lines of the lettering and sketching out the position of each letter between them. There are three ways by which this could be approached.

(1) On a job where a few words are concerned, in one or two lines and no more than 120 mm high, all the setting out can be done on the sign. With experience a signwriter can accurately determine the height of letter which will fit conveniently into the given space. Before this confident stage is reached a trial or error method can be used.

If the letters are lightly sketched onto the sign using chalk or wax pencil at any guessed size it can be seen immediately whether they need to be bigger to fill the shape more or made smaller if all the letters will not fit in. When the suitable height is found the measurements must be accurately marked each end of the sign, using a sharpened chalk stick or wax pencil, see fig. 8.28. The marks will be the height from the top of the sign, the height of the letters, and the space between the lines. The lines are 'snapped' between these points using the fine thread which has been rubbed with chalk or whiting. A snapped line is always straight, a drawn line can vary. Lines cannot be snapped onto a curved surface. For these signs a long flexible plastic straight edge is needed against which to draw lines.

A line as long as the arms can stretch, which may be up to 1.5 m, can be snapped without assistance. The line needs to be wrapped around the middle finger of one hand and pressed firmly onto one mark. When the line is swivelled away from this point it can be held between the tips of the thumb and forefinger of the same hand. The line when pulled taut by the other hand and placed on the opposite mark can be released by the thumb and forefinger and it will snap into a straight line leaving a thin line of chalk dust between the points, see fig. 8.29. For longer lines one end can be fixed with masking tape, the other held beneath the finger, and snapped with the other hand. Another method is to make a loop in the centre of the line which can be picked up between the lips and plucked while the line is being held taut by a hand at each end, see fig. 8.30. Between these lines the position of each letter should be indicated ensuring that the spacing is right and that margins are equal.

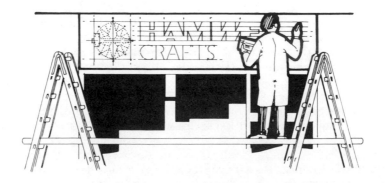

Fig. 8.28 Setting out a fascia board by the direct process

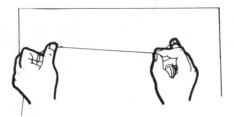

Fig. 8.29 Snapping a chalk line

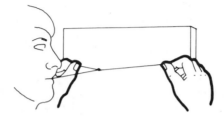

Fig. 8.30 Snapping a chalk line with the aid of the lips

(2) If the lettering or sign is large and difficult to cover in one move, or if the layout is involved it is safer to work out the layout to scale first. This can be done on site. Measure the sign and draw the shape on a piece of paper to a scale, preferably 1:10 which is easy to convert. E.g. if the sign is 3 m long by 750 mm high, the scaled drawing will be 300 mm by 75 mm. On this drawing the size of lettering and layout can be worked out by the similar trial and error method described in (1). When the layout seems right the top and bottom lines can be measured and drawn through and the side margin lines drawn in. The measurements can be taken off from the drawing, multiplied by ten, and marked onto the sign. Snapping of lines and marking position of letters will proceed as before.

(3) A single line of lettering on a sign such as a shop fascia can be set out on a piece of paper without need of a scale drawing. The lettering can be carefully drawn between two drawn lines which may be any distance apart. When the shapes and spacing seem accurate the length of the line of lettering is measured and related to the length of the sign. For example, if the drawn lettering takes up 240 mm and the sign is 4 m long, lettering fifteen times larger than the drawing will fit comfortably into the space (15 × 240 = 3600). The height of the lettering will be fifteen times the size of the drawing. This method can be adapted to other forms of signs. If there are many lines of lettering to be signwritten and each line is of different length it is necessary only to do a drawing of the longest line, that is usually the one with the most letters, in order to determine a suitable height.

TRANSFERRING

Where particular accuracy is needed or where a layout is to be used more than once it is common to prepare or have supplied a full size drawing. In some instances a photograph of the full size layout may be supplied. These can be transferred to the sign by one of two methods.

Chalking

With the face of the drawing on a flat, smooth surface the back can be rubbed in with stick chalk, whiting or a coloured powder. If the drawing is transparent it is necessary only to cover the area of the letters, but on opaque paper it is necessary to cover all the paper. After the chalk is rubbed in the paper needs to be shaken or tapped to remove surplus chalk. Too much chalk will cause a lot of marks on the sign and produces a heavy chalk line which may block the brush when signwriting.

Top and bottom lines need to be snapped on the sign before transferring the lettering. The sizes can be taken from the FS drawing using the method described before. These lines will help to position the drawing in the right place and give guidance when signwriting. If a small piece of the paper is cut away over each top and bottom line at both ends of the drawing it only needs the drawing to be placed on the sign until the snapped lines match the drawing lines to know that the drawing is in the correct position. A piece of masking tape in each corner will hold the drawing in position. When the lettering is drawn over with a sharp, hard pencil or ballpoint pen an impression will be transferred to the sign in chalk. The drawing must be done accurately and rules and compasses or curves should be used. After the drawing has been removed the surface can be dusted quite heavily with a soft brush which will remove the surplus chalk and make the letter shapes more noticeable. Another method is to make up a type of carbon paper by colour chalking a piece of detail paper and placing this, chalk side down, under the drawing to be transferred. The paper can be used a number of times before it needs rechalking or replacing. The drawings are more conveniently handled without chalk getting over everything. They are more easily stored also.

Pouncing

If the same drawing is to be used a number of times it may be quicker to make it into a pounce rather than chalk through each time. The drawing needs to be laid onto a soft surface. A piece of felt or foam is ideal but soft card or three or four thicknesses of paper are suitable alternatives. It is necessary then to prick small holes about 3–4 mm apart around the outline of each letter. Pounce wheels are available for this job which are run around the letters making an even pattern of holes, see fig. 8.31. The most common method is to use a compass point or a needle point with the eye end embedded in a cork so that it can be held safely, see fig. 8.32. The purpose of the soft underlay is to allow the points to penetrate deeply and make a big enough hole. When all the pricking is done the paper needs to be turned over and rubbed with a piece of fine glasspaper to remove the furred paper around each hole.

If this is not done the holes will be closed up again as the pounce is being used. The pounce can be positioned and fixed in the same way as the chalked drawing. When a pounce bag is tapped or rubbed over the drawing the lettering is transferred in a series of fine dots of chalk around each shape, see fig. 8.33. A pounce bag is a piece of muslin or fine material containing whiting or coloured pigment powder and tied at the top with thread.

Fig. 8.31 A pouncing wheel

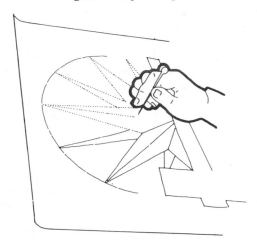

Fig. 8.32 Preparing a pounce with a compass point

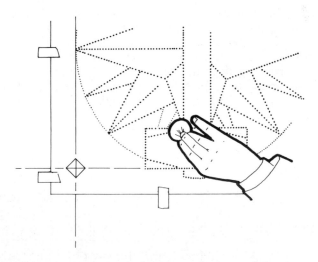

Fig. 8.33 Rubbing whiting through a pounced drawing

SIGNWRITING

At this stage the spelling should be checked. Preferably another person should be asked to check it because the setter out can become accustomed to an incorrectly spelt word which the other person may notice immediately. Using the kit and standing in the position described earlier the letters can be painted. If the lettering is to be a light colour on a dark ground it will probably need two coats for good opacity. The first coat can be signwriters colour, with an enamel second coat, or two coats of enamel can be used. Signwriters colour does seem to harden within a couple of hours and with care a second coat can be applied at this stage without the first coat picking up. It can be a dangerous practice also and may cause the whole film to crack or crocodile, particularly if applied to a recently applied gloss paint or varnish.

The mahl stick knob needs to be clean otherwise a number of dirty spots will spoil the finished job. It must be rested on the sign with care so that the paintwork is not damaged, and so that finished letters are not marred or setting out wiped off.

Regardless of the method used to set out the lettering on the sign it is essential that the top and bottom line for each line of lettering is snapped in. This is the only method of ensuring that the lettering is straight. If chalked or pounced lettering does not always touch the lines it is essential that the letters are painted so that they do. If each letter does not touch the snapped lines the finished lettering will appear undulating and not acceptable. Letters should be painted from left to right. It is a temptation, particularly by left handed writers, to start from the right when a FS drawing has been used for setting out. This method does not allow the same ease of correcting spacing as the work progresses.

Removing errors

Wiping out mistakes must be done with a piece of rag. If only part of a letter is to be removed the rag should be used to push the paint into the letter. If it is wiped across the panel it may mark the surface. The rag must not be used to clean up a letter; it will not leave as clean an edge as a brush (see Fig. 8.34). Wipe out the mistake and paint it again accurately. If the rag does not move the paint cleanly a little white spirit can be applied to it. If too much spirit is used the surface can be marked or the signwriting will be delayed while the spirit is left to evaporate.

Use of tape

A commercial method of speeding the signwriting process is to apply clear self adhesive tape above the top and below the bottom chalk lines before starting to signwrite and to remove it immediately it is finished. This method reduces the need to paint the corners of letters carefully which can be time consuming. There are problems associated with this method. Paint can creep under the tape and cleaning up afterwards can take a long time. Tape can pull off the paint coating of the sign. This danger can be reduced by using narrow tape, such as 6 mm, and by cutting down its sticking power by rubbing the finger along the adhesive edge before fixing. Curved letters which need to project slightly above and below the line have to be touched up after the tape is moved or the tape is pulled away or cut at the points where round letters are positioned.

OUTLINING AND SHADING

Setting out for either of these proceses, which are carried out after the signwriting is similar. A line should be snapped along the top of the extremity of the outline, also along the bottom of the outline or shadow. If this is not done an unevenness can easily result. An outline needs to be a one stroke action so it is necessary to select a brush which will paint the exact thickness of line required.

Running Lines

The signwriter is often required to paint lines on signs. These may be as borders to signs, customising of vehicles, or as part of a layout. Whatever the purpose lines must be straight, even in width, have clean edges and be finished sharply. There are many methods by which lines can be painted.

Fig. 8.34
Wipe signwritten mistakes into the letter   **Fig. 8.35**   Using a coach liner

COACH OR SWORD LINERS

These brushes are specifically made for painting accurate, fine lines and are the traditional brushes. They are best used on well prepared painted surfaces, such as vehicles.

Lines need to be set out and snapped in with a fine chalk line similar to that used for lettering. The brush is filled with paint in the same way that a brush is for signwriting, although getting the consistency of the paint right is more critical when lining. The brush is held between the thumb on top and the forefinger below with the short handle just touching the palm of the hand. The remaining fingers are used to guide the brush and steady the hand against the side of the panel or straightedge placed parallel with the line position. When the brush is full of paint it can be carefully lowered onto the line mark until the whole length of hair is touching the surface. Then, without increasing pressure on the brush, it can be pulled along the line mark leaving a straight, even line, see fig. 8.35. As the paint runs out pressure on the brush should be increased to maintain an even thickness. If the line is too long to be painted in one stroke the brush must be carefully lifted off when the paint has been used up and refilled. Relaying the brush must start well before the end of the previous stroke so that the hairs can be gradually laid down until they match the thickness of the original line. It may be necessary to touch up the beginning and ends of lines with a sable writer in the same way that corners must be finished. Second coating of coach lines can be difficult and every effort should be made to cover in one coat.

Using a coach liner or a sword striper to run horizontal lines in situ presents problems because the loaded filling tends to droop and cannot be manoeuvred onto the line. With practice the tip of the brush can be laid on the line and the rest of the filling swivelled into line and along the line in a smooth dextrous movement.

Fine lining can be carried out with a sable writer, either by a standard signwriting process, or used like a coach liner. Generally this method is slower.

LINING FITCH

Fitches are robust brushes and are useful for painting lines on walls or on any large sign which requires long lengths of lines over about 10 mm wide. Although an even fine line can be painted with a lining fitch they are more commonly used to paint the two edges of a thick line which are filled in after. Fitches are always used with a straightedge. The straightedge needs to be about a metre long and made of thick section wood so that it is not easily pressed out of shape. A piece of 50 × 25 mm wood is not too thick although many signwriters will use 10 mm or 15 mm thick wood. One edge needs to be chamfered. A thin block made from a piece of hardboard pinned at each end of the chamfered side keeps the straightedge off the surface and can be used to bridge over wet paint. It also helps to prevent any paint which gets on the straightedge being transferred to the surface.

The fitch is filled with paint of the same consistency needed for coach lining. The straightedge needs to be placed exactly along the edge of the marked line with the chamfer underneath and held firmly to the surface by one hand on top. The brush is made so that when the tip of the filling is touching the surface the handle of the brush is at a slight angle. Without any pressure being applied to the brush it can be guided along the edge of the straightedge until all the paint is used up, see fig. 8.36. After refilling the fitch needs to be gradually fed into the previously painted line so that the two lines match up exactly. When both sides have been run in the centre part can be filled in with a flat fitch, sable writer, rigger or one stroke. Corners and ends can be touched up with a sable writer.

Horizontal lines are run with the fitch resting on top of the straightedge, not underneath it. Vertical lines are run down the same side of the straightedge. A right handed liner will run the right hand edge first with the straightedge held by the left hand. Then it is moved over to the position of the left hand edge of the line and that edge run in. The left handed liner will work from left to right.

LINING WHEELS

A simple piece of equipment consisting of a small cylinder in which one

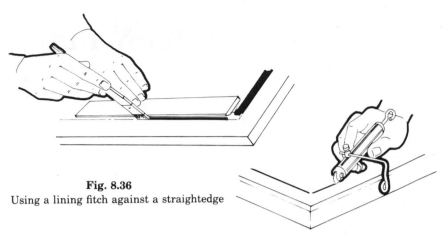

Fig. 8.36
Using a lining fitch against a straightedge

Fig. 8.37   Using a lining wheel guided by a gauge running along the edge of the sign

end is a plunger and the other a serrated wheel. When the cylinder is filled with paint the plunger puts it under pressure and it slowly pours it over the wheel which distributes it on the surface as it is pulled. The wheels will not work when pushed. A set of interchangeable wheels are available from about 2 mm up to 6 mm wide. They can be run along a straightedge or a simple gauge can be attached which guides the wheel along the edge of a panel, see fig. 8.37. Lining wheels are inclined to blob at the beginning of a stroke which can be overcome by putting a piece of tape at the beginning of the line and starting to paint on the tape. Like all lining processes, getting the right consistency of the paint is critical.

TAPE
There are two types of tape that can be used for lining. Ordinary masking tape or clear tape fixed either side of the marked line and painted in between is the common method. There is also a lining masking tape which consists of a band partly cut from a standard masking tape. When the tape is fixed in place the centre piece can be peeled away leaving the line exposed. This is a more accurate method of masking up for fine lines up to about 3 mm.

Tape is commonly used by signwriters who have not been trained to run lines. An experienced liner can paint a line equally as quickly as a person laying tape, painting, and removing the tape afterwards. Also there are fewer problems associated with run lines. Tapes cannot be used on textured surfaces because the paint will run behind where the tape bridges over indentations. Paint is likely to seep under tape which has been applied to smooth surfaces if great care has not been taken to press the edges down firmly. Unless a low-tack tape is used there is a danger that tape will pull off the paint on the sign when it is removed. Tape should be removed when the paint has set up but before it has started to skin. If the tape leaves a mark on a highly gloss painted surface it may be removed when the lining paint is dry by rubbing over with a rag dipped in a mixture of white spirit and water.

Nine
Gilding and Bronzing

Gold leaf has been a popular form of surface decoration for many thousands of years. It was first used by the Egyptians and many examples of their gilding work still exist in museums throughout the world. Because of the high value of gold, many cheaper metals have been produced in leaf form for use as substitutes for gold leaf. In the late sixteenth century the Italians produced a gold effect by applying a yellow tinted varnish over silver or white metal leaf. This technique is still used today, particularly by fairground decorators, although the base metal is more likely to be aluminium now. During the nineteenth century a leaf made from an alloy of zinc and copper was introduced as a gold leaf substitute. This was called Dutch Metal and is still used when a gold leaf effect is required of a temporary nature only. Even though the price of gold has continuously increased the readily available substitute metals have had little effect upon the popularity of gold leaf. The main reason for this is that the other metals look very good when new but quickly lose their brilliance on exposure. Gold may dull when it gets dirty, but does not tarnish and its appearance can be restored by washing.

The signwriter and glass decorator is required to complete many signs using gold leaf but this is not the only work he may be expected to do. During the latter part of the twentieth century the signwriter has gradually taken over the role of the gilder, once the exclusive province of the painter and decorator. Decorative features that are to be finished in gold leaf are often subcontracted to signwriters because they have a more comprehensive knowledge of the skills of the gilder.

Gilding

Gilding is a general term applied to the technique of applying metals in leaf form. Although gold leaf may be the most popular metallic leaf, the term is not limited to the application of gold leaf only.

Bronzing

This is a general term for the application of metallic powders, whether they are dusted onto a sticky mordant or mixed with a varnish and applied like paints. Bronze powders are most commonly used, but the term can be applied to the use of aluminium powders also.

Metallic Leaves

Metallic leaf is produced by beating the base metal until the thinnest possible sheet is obtained. Gold is a very malleable metal and can be beaten to an extremely thin thickness. Other metals cannot be beaten to such a fineness and many of them are thick enough to be handled and cut with scissors. Gold is so fine that it needs great skill, using special tools, to apply it to surfaces.

Up to the middle of the twentieth century gold leaf was produced entirely by hand beating. The gold was rolled into a thin leaf that was still thick enough to be handled, and cut into small squares. These were placed between large pieces of thin gilders skins or parchment and made into a thick pack which was beaten with a heavy hammer, see fig. 9.1. The skilled application of the hammer blows for many hours evenly spread the gold until the small square became the size of the parchments. This thinner sheet was cut into four and the pieces again placed in the packs and beaten until they were the size of the packs. This process would have been repeated until the gold was as thin as it could be without breaking.

Fig. 9.1 Traditional method of hand beating gold leaf

The modern method follows a similar technique but the initial beating is often carried out by machine. The pack is swivelled around beneath the constant action of a hammer head until a thin leaf is obtained. Generally the final beating process is still carried out by hand.

Other metal leaves are produced by machine beating only.

It is estimated that 30 g of gold can be beaten into 1600 leaves which will cover an area in excess of 11 m^2.

Gold Leaf

Gold leaf is available in many grades, colours and forms.

Grades and colours

The purest form of gold is known as 24 carat. This is measured by comparing the density of gold with an equal volume of water. When the gold is mixed with other metals its density is reduced with a resulting fall in its carat weight. Many gold leaves are 24 carat, others vary from $23^3/4$ ct to 16 ct depending upon the quantity of other metals mixed with it. The common grades are:

Triple gold and fine gold which are generally 24 ct. They are the most expensive and have the best durability. Their use is essential on very exposed signs or decorative features, such as church steeple finials, particularly in coastal areas.

Illuminating gold is also 24 ct and is used for gilding lettering or decoration around letters on manuscript books, presentation addresses, freedom scrolls, and similar handmade, one-off works by calligraphers. This is not an area of work in which the signwriter is expected to be proficient.

Regular gold and selected gold are $23^3/4$ to 23 ct and are used most commonly for all interior and exterior signs, particularly when used on glass.

Deep gold is usually a 22 ct leaf and is slightly deeper in colour because of a possible copper content. The colour difference is only obvious when it is compared with pure gold. It is most suitable for all interior and protected exterior signs.

Yellow gold, lemon gold, and green gold all contain varying quantities of other metals and assay between 22 and 16 ct. Like deep gold the colours of these leaves will only appear less like gold when seen with pure gold. They can be used to provide subtle differences on gilded decorative panels or as gold on interior signs.

Double gold and single gold refers to the thickness of the leaf and although generally applied to the 24 ct leaves it may be applied to regular gold also. Double gold is thicker than single but it is not twice the thickness. Double gold is recommended for exterior signs, particularly those in exposed positions.

Forms

Although gold is available in many forms to suit the needs of various industries and crafts the signworker invariably requires it in leaf form only.

Leaves are available in books. Each book contains twenty-five leaves and each leaf is approximately 82 mm square. The book pages, between which the gold leaves are placed, are made from fine rouged paper so that the gold will not stick to them.

Loose gold books contain a separate leaf of gold between each page requiring the gold to be transferred to the area on which it is required by the use of a special brush, see fig. 9.2. It is used for glass gilding and when gilding curved or relief surfaces.

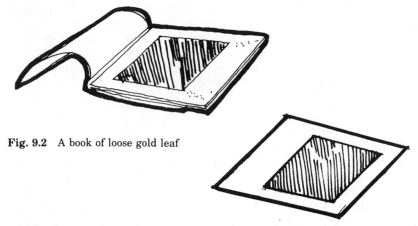

Fig. 9.2 A book of loose gold leaf

Fig. 9.3 A sheet of transfer gold leaf

Transfer gold leaf books have each leaf lightly adhered to a thin tissue paper which is about 90 × 115 mm, see fig. 9.3. The tissue paper can be handled and allows the gold to be applied to the prepared surface without the use of special tools. Transfer leaf is used extensively by the signwriter when working on flat or smooth surfaces. The leaf is attached to the paper by pressure only and so is easily removed when it is applied to a sticky surface.

Properties of gold leaf
Gold leaf is extremely thin. It is finer than human hair and may be as fine as many thousandths of a millimetre. Even in such a thin form it is most durable and will remain in good condition for many years. In many instances gold leaf lettering will survive the material from which the sign is made.

Books of gold leaf will keep for many years providing they are kept dry. When the leaf pages get wet the gold sticks to them. It causes the gold to wrinkle and split also.

Silver Leaf

Silver leaf is rarely used because it tarnishes very rapidly. If used on an external sign, particularly in an area of high air pollution such as in a town or near a factory, the leaf will turn black in a few hours unless immediately varnished. When used on interior signs it needs to be varnished also although tarnishing may take some days to become apparent. It can be used more successfully on glass providing that it is backed up quickly to protect it from the corrosive action of the air.

Unless kept in an airtight box silver leaf can tarnish in store. The edges of the leaf blacken very slightly which may not be noticed until application when each edge shows as a dark line. A recommended practice is to cut off about 5 mm from each edge of the leaves, which have been stored for a few months, before they are used. Silver leaf is available in leaves of 82 mm or 96 mm square, and in books of twenty-five. They can be obtained loose or transfer. The transfer paper is usually a waxed paper so that the metal can be held more securely.

Silver leaf is considerably cheaper than gold leaf and is much thicker. Most gilders apply loose silver leaf in the same way that gold leaf is applied, but often it is thick enough to be handled. Because of its thickness and hardness it is less likely that joints of the leaves can be entirely burnished out.

White Gold

White gold is an alloy of gold and silver and assays at about 12 carat. Its appearance is silver. The gold content considerably slows the speed at which the leaf tarnishes without influencing the colour of the silver.

White gold is much more expensive than silver leaf, but it is much more widely used. Without varnishing on exterior signs it will slowly tarnish. In a clean atmosphere it will keep its colour for a long period inside without varnishing but the recommended treatment for a sign which requires the colour to be retained is to varnish. If it is to be stored for a long period it is safer to keep it in an airtight box.

White gold is available in the same leaf and book sizes as gold. It is always available as loose gold but not all suppliers stock it in transfer form. When transfer leaf is essential the loose gold can be easily transferred. All that is needed is a piece of tissue paper about 90 × 115 mm or an old paper once used for transfer gold from which all the leaf has been used, and a domestic candle. Just one or two rubs over the paper with the candle will deposit enough wax to make the leaf stick to it. With the book opened carefully to expose one of the leaves the waxed paper can be laid on it and lightly rubbed over the back. When lifted the leaf will adhere to the paper and can be applied to the sized surface. The leaf will not be as firmly adhered as purchased transfer gold leaf and will prove to be a little more wasteful. This method of transferring loose leaf can be used for any metallic leaf.

White gold is the most widely used silver leaf, particularly on glass. It is softer than silver leaf and leaf joins can usually be burnished out more satisfactorily although not as completely as gold.

Aluminium Leaf

Aluminium leaf has good colour, does not tarnish and is very cheap. It is also thicker than most other leaves and will invariably show joins. For this reason it is seldom used on glass. For interior signs it produces a most effective permanent silver appearance at very low cost. It can be used on outside signs but will lose its brilliance quite quickly unless varnished or lacquered.

Aluminium leaf can be readily handled and cut with scissors if required. It is available in leaf sizes of about 140 mm square, and as either loose or transfer. It can be obtained in packs of about 250 leaves but the normal form is in books of twenty-five leaves.

Dutch Metal or Schlag Metal

Although originally called Dutch metal it is most commonly referred to as Schlag and is an alloy of zinc and copper. It has a bright gold colour which it retains when used inside buildings, but quickly tarnishes when exposed to polluted air. When varnished or lacquered it keeps its bright metal effect for a long time. It is thick like aluminium so its leaf joins can rarely be burnished out. For this reason it is seldom used on glass.

Schlag metal is available in leaves of between 140 and 150 mm square, and in books of twenty-five leaves or packs of 500. It is readily available in loose and transfer form.

Oil Gilding

Oil gilding is the common term used to describe the process of applying metallic leaf to oil based mordants. It is the method by which the signwriter applies transfer leaf to lettering or decorative features on flat surfaces, and loose leaf to curved or relief surfaces. The other principal method of gilding used by the signmaker is glass or gelatine gilding which is described in chapter 10.

The mordants for metallic leaves are generally known as gold sizes and are either quick drying varnishes or paints, or drying oils. The gold size is applied to a prepared surface, usually by a signwriting process, and when it starts to set and becomes sticky the leaf is pressed or laid on it.

Gold Sizes

Japan gold size
This is a quick drying varnish and is sometimes called signwriters size or quick size. Many manufacturers mark it as 2–4 hour size which suggests that it will acquire the correct tackiness for gilding after two hours but no longer than four hours after application. It rarely lasts four hours and in a warm room may be ready for gilding in less than two hours. Japan gold size is a useful size for signwriters who have a number of small jobs to gild. If it is used on a sign that has a lot of lettering there may be a distinct variation in the colour or brilliance of the gold because gilding will have to be carried out before all the sizing is completed and the slight variations in the tackiness can affect the final gold appearance. Japan size does not allow a very good burnish. It is very difficult to see when applied to a dark ground but this can be overcome by mixing a little yellow oil stainer with the size.

Oil gold size
These are a range of sizes which are made from a blend of drying oils, resins and drying agents, carefully adjusted so that they set in either three hours, twelve hours or twenty-four hours. Many of these sizes are made in France so may be called French oil sizes. Old oil size is another term sometimes applied to the twelve and twenty-four hour sizes.

The three hour size has similar properties to Japan gold size but because it is less viscous it is easier to brush when signwriting. The slow sizes are very thin and need to be applied with care to obtain an even film as any over-application will tend to run or form a fat edge during the many hours that it takes to set.

Oil sizes allow the gold to be burnished to a higher degree than can be obtained with quick size. The slow sizes are particularly useful when large quantities of gilding are being carried out because they can be applied leisurely and remain in a tacky condition for some hours so allowing the gilding process to be carried out with care and precision. They can be used for signs containing a large number of letters which may take many hours to signwrite, or for a large church finial which can be sized in an hour but may take three hours to gild.

Some manufacturers colour the sizes so that they can be seen on a dark ground. Others are colourless and may need to be tinted with yellow oil stainers if used under gold or with white if used with silver.

One of the biggest problems when using slow size is dust settling on it during the many hours between application and gilding. Dust will produce a rough film which will destroy the lustre of the gold. Some form of screen must be applied over the sized area which will prevent dust settling on it without actually touching the surface. Paper screens are safer than fabrics as they are less likely to release tiny fibres. If the sizing is on a ceiling or at a high level there is less problem from dust.

Gloss paint
This can be a most satisfactory size. Preferably a yellow gloss paint so that misses in the gold will not be so obvious. It can be applied in a full coat with less risk of running and if gilded at the right tackiness a high lustre can be obtained. It takes between three and five hours to obtain the right tack but its setting is often less reliable than gold size. A useful size for jobs taking two to three hours to size, like a shop fascia or an exterior coat of arms.

A small quantity of linseed oil added to the gloss paint not only delays the set but prolongs the tack period allowing a more leisurely gilding time.

Tools for Oil Gilding

For the application of gold size the normal signwriting equipment is used, e.g. palette board, dippers, mahl stick and sable writers. Specialist equipment is required for applying loose leaf gold only.

Gilders cushion
The gilders cushion is often called the cush. See fig. 9.4. Gold leaf is placed upon, cut and lifted from the cushion. It is a piece of wood about 200 × 125 mm lightly padded with felt and covered with chamois leather or goat skin. Underneath are two leather loops. One is slack so that the thumb can be inserted to hold the cushion steady. The other is flush with the base of the board into which the knife is sheathed when not being used. One end of the padded face is shielded with a stiff paper screen which is stood up to cover the end and half of each side to prevent the gold being blown about by draughts. The shield can be folded down when not in use and makes the cushion easier to store and carry about. Some shields are made from old legal parchments. The

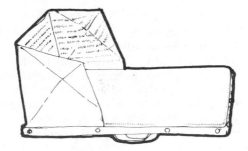

Fig. 9.4 The gilders cushion

cushion needs to be dusted with French chalk regularly so that the
gold leaf will not stick to the leather. Left handed cushions are
available.

Some experienced gilders rarely use a cushion. They work directly
from the book. Although some may hold the book in the hand and take
out full leaves with the tip, the most common method is to place the
book on a piece of wood about 100 × 130 mm. This can be held quite
comfortably in one hand and the thumb can be used to hold down the
turned pages as the leaf is exposed. Having the firm base board, leaf
can be cut also using this method. A gilders knife can be used for this
purpose but many gilders use the finger nail of their thumb or
forefinger or a sharpened end of the tip to cut the gold. The page above
the leaf can be used to aid in the cutting both as a steadier and a
straightedge. If the page is folded along the line where the leaf needs to
be cut the thumb can be placed on a folded page to stop the leaf moving
and the fingernail or tip edge can be run along the folded edge.

This method may not be commonly used in a workshop where
draughts can be controlled but it is a useful technique when working
on site where no control over draughts is possible. Gilders who use
their fingernail for cutting need to keep it a little longer than normal
and also well manicured so that there are no roughnesses to tear the
leaf.

Gilders knife
This is a long, flat bladed knife for cutting the leaf into the required
size on the cushion. See fig. 9.5. The cutting edge of the knife must be
well ground but not sharp. A sharp knife does not effectively cut the
gold but it will severely cut up the leather cover of the cushion. The
blade must be kept clean otherwise it will attract the leaf which will
cling to the knife and become useless. It needs to be washed in
detergent and dusted with French chalk to keep it clean. If a gilders
knife is not available a dinner knife can be used effectively, providing
the cutting edge of the blade is straight. The advantage of a gilders
knife is that the handle balances the blade so if laid down the handle is
heavy enough to keep the blade off the surface.

Fig. 9.5 The gilders knife

Gilders tip

A gilders tip is a very thin row of squirrel or badger hair set between two pieces of card. They are usually a little bit wider than the standard width of gold leaf and available in three lengths of hair: short about 38 mm length cut, medium about 48 mm, and long about 60 mm. The tip is used to pick up the gold from the cushion and to deposit it onto the sized surface. The short haired tips are for small cut pieces and the large tips for full leaves. Very often gilders use one size tip for all jobs because a particular length of hair suits their technique. See fig. 9.6.

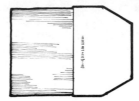

Fig. 9.6   The gilders tip

The hairs of the tip are prepared for picking up the gold by rubbing vigorously against the gilder's hair or cheek. This 'activates' the hairs so that the gold is attracted to them and can be transferred from the cushion to the sized surface. There are two theories why this 'activation' does occur. One is that the rubbing causes the hairs to become charged with static electricity to which the gold is attracted. The other is that the hairs pick up the slightest trace of natural grease which is sufficient to adhere the gold to them. Whatever the cause there are some occasions when no reaction occurs and the tip will not pick up the gold. It is at these times that some gilders rub the merest trace of petroleum jelly on their cheek where the tip is rubbed.

In time the tip hairs become too sticky or greasy and must be washed in warm mild detergent water. Only the hairs must be made wet. If the card handle becomes wet it will soften and either release the hair or buckle out of shape. Clean hair usually picks up more efficiently.

Domed mop

This is not an essential tool, but is a very useful one. They are round brushes in either ferrule or quill, made from squirrel or pony hair. Mops are available in a range of sizes from 6–25 mm in diameter. One about 16 mm often proves to be the most useful. It is used to push the gold into crevices when gilding relief shapes and to remove surplus gold before burnishing, a process known as skewing. A fine fitch or a pad of cotton wool can be used for these processes also but the mop is more adaptable and can be used with a lighter touch.

Fig. 9.7   A domed mop

Surface Preparation

As it is so thin gold leaf will stick most tenaciously to anything offering the very slightest tackiness. Grease deposited on the surface by fingers can be sufficient to hold the gold.

A freshly gloss painted or varnished or French polished surface may offer a surface tackiness which, although it cannot be felt, will cause the gold to stick to it. Coatings which have been applied two or three days previously can still be suspect. If gold does adhere to places to which it is not required it can be very difficult to remove, particularly if it is very close to the sized areas. The added process is time consuming and may result in the surface becoming damaged. Therefore the first process when oil gilding is to ensure that the surface is hard, clean and non-sticky.

Two other qualities a surface should have to make it ideal for gilding are smoothness and to be non-porous.

Surfaces which have been poorly prepared so that they contain many small holes, cracks or coarse grain will not allow a good gilding finish to be applied over them. The coating of the surface must be free from bits and coarse brushwork also. Neither gold size or gold leaf will bridge small holes and these will show up as dark lines in the finished gold. Bits will penetrate through the gold and prevent it being burnished to a good lustre. Porous surfaces will absorb the gold size so that no film will exist for the leaf to adhere to. Or the size may be absorbed unevenly so that some places might hold the gold and others will not, resulting in misses or poor burnish. Surfaces to be gilded must be thoroughly sealed so that the gold size is not absorbed.

When gilding on outside surfaces or signs which will be fixed outside it is most likely that the sign will be coated in gloss paint or varnish because they are the most durable finishes. When fully hard these coatings present little problem to the gilder, but full hardness may take many days to achieve. To avoid any possibility that the surface may be tacky painted signs should be washed with warm detergent and wiped with a chamois leather, and either pounced with French chalk or coated with glaire.

Pouncing with French chalk
A pounce bag (see chapter 8) containing either French chalk or fine whiting tapped over the entire surface to be gilded will absorb any tackiness. Before the sign is set out for gilding all of the chalk must be dusted off using a fine dusting brush or dry paint brush. If any chalk is left on the surface it may absorb the size and produce uneven edges and dirty finishes to the letters. See fig. 9.8.

Fig. 9.8 Preparing a surface by pouncing with French chalk

Pouncing is a most convenient method and would be used on most signs which are normally completed in one day.

Coating with glaire
Glaire is the white of an egg mixed with about 500 ml of warm water. It is applied with a soft brush to the entire sign and allowed to dry, which may take half an hour to one hour. Every care must be taken to ensure that there are no misses in the film. These are most likely to show up after the glaire has dried, when misses will show through as glossy patches. Gold size applied over the dry glaire will penetrate it and adhere to the surface underneath. If any gold should stick to any areas outside the sized letters it will wash off when the glaire is removed after the gilding has been completed.

Glaire must be washed off as soon as possible otherwise it may cause the paint or varnish film to crack or peel. Two or three days may be safe but a longer period may cause problems. If the gilding is likely to take more than three days it is advisable to apply glaire daily to a section large enough to be comfortably sized and gilded.

Glaire can be removed with warm water within six hours of the gold being applied. The really safe period is to leave it overnight.

Kitchen shops sell a simple gadget which easily separates the white from the yolk of an egg. Most gilders separate it by breaking an egg into two halves over a jug and tipping the yolk from one half to the other allowing the white to fall into the jug, see fig. 9.9. Another method is to make a hole in each end of the egg with a compass and blow out the white. The water mixed with the white must not be hot otherwise the albumen starts to cook.

Fig. 9.9 Separating the white from an egg

Glaire is most likely to be used in preference to pouncing when a lot of work is required on the sign which may take some days to complete. If the sign should pick up any dirt and grease during this period it will not cause any problems because when the glaire is washed off surplus gold adhered by grease will be removed also. The use of glaire is recommended also when very fine lettering is being gilded because any chalk on the surface may make signwriting difficult or affect the finish of the letters.

Preparing uncoated surfaces
The largest part of the sign gilders work will be carried out on painted or varnished surfaces but occasionally new or uncoated surfaces may

need to be gilded. The method of preparing bare substrates is largely dictated by the nature of the material.

Timber
Grain unevenness and pore marks must be filled so that a perfectly smooth surface is produced. Timber must be filled with a grain filler over the entire surface, abraded smooth when dry and primed with an oil based timber primer to seal both timber and filler.

Plaster, concrete and stone
The surface must be dry and clean. Because they are absorbent they must be sealed with an oil based alkali resisting primer.

GRP and plastic
Being so smooth these surfaces provide an ideal base for gilding provided they have been thoroughly washed with strong detergent to remove mould oil or other surface greases.

Slate
Usually non-porous enough to need no coating and the size can be applied directly to the clean, dust free surface.

Iron and steel
All rust must be removed and if this is done with steel wool or emery cloth and white spirit the surface will be made clean and free from grease. If the metal can be sized immediately after cleaning and it will not be used in a very exposed condition priming is not essential. Otherwise a coat of zinc chromate primer is recommended, leaving it for twenty-four hours to fully harden before sizing.

Aluminium, zinc and copper
Providing the surface is thoroughly cleaned with steel wool and white spirit gold size can be applied directly to these metals.

Gilding with Transfer Leaf

Transfer leaf is applied to any flat sign.

Sizing
After the surface is prepared the lettering is applied by any of the methods already described. It is important that the surface is touched as little as possible to reduce the possibility of depositing any grease.

The size is prepared by thoroughly stirring the slow sizes, particularly the tinted ones, or mixing sufficient yellow oil stainers with the quick size so that it can be seen easily against the surface.

The knob of the mahl stick or the base of the bridge need to be clean and this is most easily done by dipping them in ground whiting.

The gold size is applied by the normal signwriting technique. It is essential that it is applied evenly and in as full a coat as possible. Particular care must be taken not to make mistakes which need to be rubbed out. The slightest smear of gold size outside the confines of the letter could hold the gold and prove very difficult to remove. The safest procedure if a brushing error occurs is to thoroughly remove the letter with spirit and touch up the area with glaire before resizing.

When to gild

Judging when the size has reached the correct tackiness for the gold to be applied is the secret of good gilding. When the knuckle of the forefinger can be lightly drawn across the surface without marking it and a positive squeak caused by the friction is made the size is right, see fig. 9.10. Some gilders rely upon the pull they feel when the finger nail is placed on the surface. If the size is too wet when the gold is applied many defects may occur. The size film may be broken, the gold may split, and the lustre of the finished gilding will be poor. If the size is too dry the gold will not stick and the letters will have to be resized.

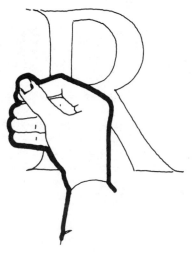

Fig. 9.10 Testing the tack of gold size

When using quick or four hour size it will be necessary to test previously sized letters continuously and gild each one as it becomes ready. If the size is going off in about three hours it is essential to stop sizing three hours before the end of the working day because if the last few letters are gilded after only one or two hours their burnish will be completely different to those which were gilded when the size was harder.

Gilding

When the size is ready for gilding the wide margin of transfer paper is held between the thumb and forefinger and laid in position over the letters but without touching them. With a pad of cotton wool the gold can be pressed firmly against the size and the back of the paper rubbed in a circular motion to press the gold into the size, see fig. 9.11. A light but even pressure is necessary. While holding the gold to the surface with the pad the other end can be pulled away partly so that the letters can be viewed to ensure that every part has been gilded. If there are misses the gold can be swung back in place and rubbed some more.

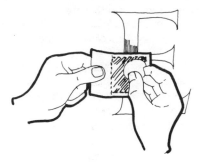

Fig. 9.11 Applying transfer gold leaf

The fingers must hold the paper steady for if it slips while being rubbed the skidding may break the size or show up as a different lustre to the other parts.

Some gilders rub over the paper with the soft part of the thumb instead of a cotton wool pad. This is an effective method but if not carried out with great care may leave finger marks in the size or break the size.

The positioning of the paper over the sized areas must be carefully done to avoid undue waste. For the first batch the edge of the sheet should be placed just overlapping the edge of the size. The next move should be adjacent to the first batch.

If the transfer paper is rubbed on or touches the size it will adhere and when pulled away will leave paper fibres in the size. These places may not gild but if they do they will appear rough through the gold. Many gilders cut off the small edges of exposed paper around the leaves with scissors before gilding to avoid the paper sticking to the size.

Testing for misses
When all the gilding seems complete one of the used sheets of transfer paper should be passed over the letters slowly. Where the gold has been applied it will show through the paper as yellow. Any misses will show through as black and these can be touched up with the gold. If misses are not discovered until the size is dry the pieces will need to be touched up with size or the entire letter may have to be resized and gilded. Quite often touch-ups or regilds will appear a different lustre to the original gilding.

If small missed sized areas will not hold the gold breathing on them sometimes makes them sticky again. It is necessary to place the mouth as close to the surface as possible and 'huff' at the missed areas. The warm moist breath may just soften the size momentarily to grip the gold. The process has drawbacks because the breath can make surrounding areas sticky also and the gold may stick in those places as well. If the surface is glaired the risks are less.

Skewing

Even if gold leaf is pulled quite cleanly from the transfer paper small surplus pieces do occur at the edges of the letter. Touched-up places also leave a little surplus gold. Removing this surplus gold is called skewing. It is carried out with the mop or a large pad of cotton wool, moved around lightly over the gilded area in a circular motion until all the loose gold is broken off.

Most gilders collect this loose gold and when a fairly large quantity is obtained they sell it to goldsmiths at the current market price. The occasional gilder may take many years to collect sufficient skewings to make a marketable quantity. Gilders who take on work which uses many hundreds of books of leaf will have sufficient two or three times a year.

The skewings are collected in a paper bag which is held just below the mop or cotton wool. Traditionally the skew bag was made from newspaper or drawing paper, folded into a triangular bag in a similar way that hats were made for children. This has a wide opening for collecting and a narrow base in which the gold collects. The used transfer papers are placed in the skew bag also. When the gold is melted down for assaying the paper is destroyed. The transfer paper skewings are sometimes called tifflings.

Burnishing

Metallic leaf is polished with a loose mop of cotton wool. If the size has been applied in an even, full coat and the leaf applied when the size was of the right tack the metal will respond to the friction of the wool and take on a full lustre. Once the gold is applied to the size the air is cut off to the size and in theory it will not get any harder. Therefore burnishing should be effective immediately after gilding. In practice size does harden slightly after gilding and burnishing may be more effective the following day.

Gilding with Loose Leaf

Loose leaf is used most effectively on incised or relief surfaces. Common examples are: carved lettering in stone or wood; carved or cast individual letters; plaster, stone, wood or plastic coats of arms or company logos; carved or moulded decorative features on walls or furniture; and metal finials in churches, such as crosses or weather vanes.

Sizing

The gilding process usually takes more time when using loose leaf by the nature of the surface and the method of handling the leaf. Therefore it is most common to use a slow size with loose leaf. It is applied in the same way as transfer leaf and the surface must be prepared with the same care.

Quite often loose leaf gilding is applied to large areas and larger brushes may be necessary such as fitches or even 25 mm paint brushes.

The size is ready for gilding when it is in the condition described for transfer gilding.

Gilding

The leaf may be applied direct from the book as described earlier. This is a process which is most commonly used when large areas are to be gilded particularly when working outside or in draughty areas or where there is a lot of movement. In other circumstances the leaf is taken up from the gilders cushion.

The leaf will crease up or float away with the slightest of draughts. Control of gold leaf can be lost by the movement of the cushion, breathing of the gilder or someone walking by. To keep the leaf under control movements must be kept to the minimum or made very gently, and breathing must be directed away from the cushion.

If the cushion is held as close as possible to the sized area there will be less opportunity for the gold to float or crease while being carried from the cushion to the size.

Experienced gilders will shake many or all of the leaves in a book onto the cushion and draw one at a time from the pile. The inexperienced gilder will find it easier and more economical in gold to place one leaf on the cushion at a time.

If the book is opened so that a leaf is exposed a few shakes will release the leaf into the space protected by the paper screen. By sliding the knife under the leaf it can be brought forward to the front of the cushion. Rarely will it lie flat but this can be improved by laying the tip of the knife edge along one side of the leaf and, with the mouth immediately over the centre of the leaf and about 50 mm away, puff the leaf flat.

If the leaf needs to be cut because the precise piece to be gilded is smaller than a full leaf it is done by drawing the knife through the gold while keeping the edge of the blade flat on the surface of the cushion, see fig. 9.12. The leaf may need to be cut in half, quarters or strips.

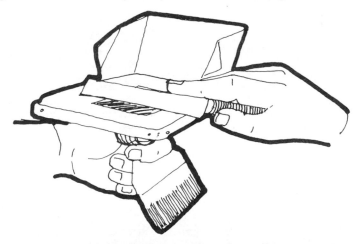

Fig. 9.12 Cutting loose gold on the cushion

The knife should be slipped into the simple sheath beneath the cushion so that it is handy when needed again and where it is less likely to get dirty or greasy. While the knife is being used the tip can be held between the fingers of the hand holding the cushion. When the knife is sheathed the tip can be taken into the gilding hand.

The tip after rubbing in the hair above the ear, or against the cheek, or by the side of the nose, or any other part of the face or body which happens to affect the tip hairs in an effective way, is placed over the leaf or cut piece. The leaf will stick to the hairs and allow it to be transferred to the sized area. As the leaf touches the size it will be attracted to it and readily leaves the tip, see fig. 9.13.

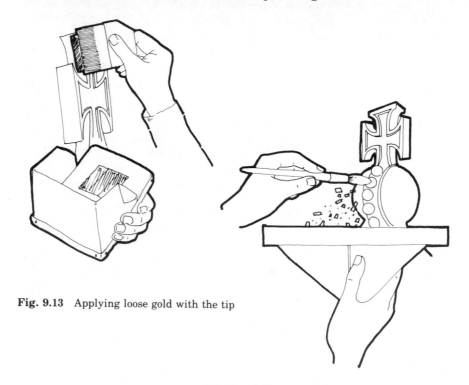

Fig. 9.13   Applying loose gold with the tip

Fig. 9.14   Skewing off surplus gold using a fitch

The process continues, slightly overlapping each piece to avoid misses, until the whole sized area is covered with gold. On surfaces which have deep crevices the temptation to push the leaf into the depths with the tip should be resisted because some size may be picked up on the hairs and make them so sticky that they will not release the leaf to the size.

Skewing
There is always more surplus gold with loose leaf gilding, so the skewing process is essential. The mop is more effective than cotton wool for getting into holes or crevices. Sometimes a clean soft fitch is more able to push the gold into missed places for which the mop is a bit too soft. The skewing process does two things. It removes surplus gold and pushes the gold into better contact with the surface. See fig. 9.14.

Burnishing
The action of the mop during skewing also polishes the gold. A further polishing with cotton wool on the highlights is sometimes necessary.

Highlighting

When the relief in the surface is very deep it is common to gild the highlights only. This is a saving in gold and labour. If the surface is first coated in cream colour or bronze paint and only the parts which catch the light are sized and gilded the effect is of solid gold from a distance.

Distressing

A bright burnished gold effect is not always required particularly in an old building if it is to match existing work. 'Ageing' a piece of new work is sometimes called distressing. The simplest method is to mix raw or burnt umber oil stainer with white spirit and a small quantity of liquid oil driers or terebine and brush it all over the surface. It is essential to punch it deep into the crevices where dirt is most likely to collect.

When the highlights are rubbed clean of colour with a big pad of clean rag the aged appearance can be most effective. Careful control of the wiping will match most surrounding, truly old surfaces.

Water colours can be used also, made from thinned emulsion paint or poster colour and are suitable for interior surfaces.

Varnishing

Gold leaf should not be varnished because it destroys the burnish which gives the special quality of true gilding. Most other leaves need protection to prevent them from tarnishing and this should be applied as soon after gilding as possible.

When working over aluminium leaf or Dutch metal the varnish may be tinted to give some interesting and decorative effects. Varnish tinted with yellow chrome or ochre oil stainers applied over aluminium gives a close resemblance to gold. Amber transluscent enamels give a similar effect. Red, blue and green tinted varnishes are often used over aluminium and Dutch metal for effects on fairground panels.

Bronzing

The original method of producing metallic powders was to mechanically hammer thin pieces of foil until they broke up into small fine flakes. Although this process is occasionally used, the usual method is to hammer atomised metal in a large ball mill. The fine particles of metal are rolled around in a large cylinder filled with small hard balls for many hours until the particles are broken into a very fine powder. The powders are then passed through various types of machines which polish them to a brilliant finish. The degree to which they are polished influences the price of the final powder.

The flakes may be as thin as 0.25 micron. The diameter of the flakes varies from 50 micron, which are the coarse powders, to fine ones as low as 4 micron.

Types of Metallic Powders

Bronze powders
Bronze is an alloy of copper and zinc with a small quantity of aluminium added. Although it is commonly used as an imitation gold it is available in a wide range of colours from Pale (which is most like gold) to Rich or Copper. There is also a Penny Bronze powder which is very dark.

They are available in grades also. Standard which is the most coarse powder and is most often mixed with a medium into a paint. Lining which is much finer and has a wide use for bronzing picture frames. It can be obtained as fine and extra fine also. Burnishing quality is finer still and when used to dust onto a size can be burnished to high lustre.

There are tarnish resistant qualities also. These have been coated during manufacture with a material such as silica. These powders are very expensive.

Aluminium powders
Aluminium powder is much more rarely used than bronze and seldom available in more than one grade. It is cheaper than bronze. It is made in a similar way although sometimes a wet process is used when the particles are dispersed in white spirit.

Methods of Bronzing

Dusting
This process follows the same principles as gilding. The size is applied and when it reaches the right tackiness the powder is dusted on.

When good quality powders are used some fine finishes are achieved. When used inside the effects are long lasting but when exposed to the atmosphere they tarnish quickly unless varnished.

Surface preparation must be carried out with the same care as for gilding. A surface of very slight tackiness will hold the powder and will not release it even after thorough washing and leathering. Pouncing is essential before sizing and even the use of glaire is recommended on some jobs which have lettering or intricate design work.

Gold sizes used for gilding can be used for bronzing but they should not be left quite so long before applying the powder. The area round the sign should be covered with clean paper before the powder is applied to collect all the surplus. This can be re-used.

The powder is dusted onto the sticky size with a mop or a rabbit's foot, see fig. 9.15. Rabbit's feet were commonly used for this purpose and so were readily available. They are not so easily obtainable now, but are ideal applicators of bronze powders and are cheaper than mops. The mop or foot is dipped in the powder and liberally applied to the size. Gentle swirling ensures that all of the size is covered. The surplus can be brushed off onto the paper with the same tools.

Fig. 9.15   Dusting on bronze powder with a rabbit's foot

When completed the whole surface can be washed and leathered and when dry the bronzing can be burnished with cotton wool.

Mixing

Bronze and aluminium powders can be mixed with varnish and applied as a paint. The effect is not as good as dusting, the lustre is considerably less, but it is less messy and quicker.

Retailers who specialise in gilders or signwriters materials usually have bronzing mediums which are special varnishes for mixing with bronze powders. Polyurethane varnishes, oil varnishes or Japan gold sizes can be used but on occasions they react with the bronze powders and become so thick as to be unappliable. If the medium is acidic or contains sulphur it may destroy the lustre of the powder, or even turn it black. For spraying, bronzing cellulose lacquers are available for mixing with metallic powders.

The quantity of powder to medium may vary depending on the quality of the powder and the colour of the surface to which it is applied. The most practical method of gauging the quantity is to add a little powder to the medium and try it on the surface until a suitably opaque and lustrous film is obtained. It is advisable to strain the mixed paint through a nylon mesh before use. This filters out any coarse pieces and ensures a more even distribution.

The paint can be applied in the usual way using signwriting technique for lettering, or fitches for large areas, or brushing or spraying it onto cut foil or film. Bronze paints are often stickier and more viscous than signwriters paints so are slow to use and may not be manoeuvred into such fine finishes. They need to be stirred regularly otherwise the powders settle out.

Paints

Prepared metallic paints are available in a variety of qualities and forms. There are heat resisting paints, high lustre paints which dry to a glossy finish, oil based medium, cellulose medium, or water thinned paints. Generally they are cheaper than either of the other methods of using metallic powders. They can give an equal quality finish to mixing but will probably be less effective than dusting.

Metallic screen inks are available in a range of colours.

Ten

Glass Decoration

Glass has been a popular material for decorating for hundreds of years. The beautiful stained glass windows of medieval churches are some of the earlier examples. It has been scratched with sharp tools, and incised with grinding stones to produce engraved and brilliant cut glass. During the middle of the nineteenth century the technique of etching glass with acid was perfected and brought the art of glass decoration into the area of the signmaker. Later sand blasting of glass became popular and although it proved to be a quicker and more commercial method of decorating glass it only added to the methods by which glass could be worked, it did not replace acid etching. The Victorian period was the period when most glass decorating was carried out. A large part of the decorated glass of the period was used in pubs and restaurants and remained a popular form of decoration throughout the first part of the twentieth century. Victorian and Edwardian revivals during the 1960s and 1970s have kept the art alive.

Glass decoration has remained a specialised craft, but has always been on the fringe of the sign industry. Many signwriting firms had a glass decoration shop and many of the basic techniques of painting, gilding and, to a lesser degree, acid etching glass have been expected of signwriters over the years.

There still remains a demand for decorative glass and glass signs. It is essential that the skills required to do this work are not lost.

Methods of Glass Decoration

Basically glass can be worked in seven ways to produce decorative effects or signs. Some of the more beautiful examples have combined many of these methods to produce the decorative effects.

(1) Engraving
   The highly skilled technique of scratching glass with sharp tools either by hand or with mechanical aids such as electrically operated reverberating needles or the edge of grinding wheels. It is an art which has rarely been practised by signmakers.

(2) Brilliant cutting
   Designs cut deep into glass by the very skilful manipulation of the edges of rotating stone discs. The common effect is to produce deep, three dimensional patterns. Many of the fine examples of Victorian glass included brilliant cut areas. Cut glass is an example of this technique also. Like engraving it is a highly specialised skill and

rarely part of a signworkers job. When required on a sign job the work is usually subcontracted.

(3) Sand blasting

This is the bombarding of the glass with fine, sharp grit which destroys its transparency. Although sand was used originally non-silica materials such as carborundum are used now. The grit is propelled by compressed air and directed onto the glass through a nozzled tube. The glass is first covered with a tough, self adhesive tape, from which the areas to be blasted are cut out. The tape acts as a resist and protects the part not to be cut. The blasting nozzles can be controlled with such skill as to produce a large range of textures and very intricate design work. Portraits can be cut by the very skilled sand blaster.

The original resist used for sand blasting was made by coating blotting paper with many coats of gum arabic. When the gum had hardened is was fixed to wet glass and the shapes cut from it. With care standard masking tape can be used as a resist. Self-adhesive plastic wall and shelf coverings are used also.

(4) Acid etching

The corroding of glass with an acid to produce a great variety of tones, textures and decorations. Very widely used during the Victorian period and still practised. See fig. 10.1.

(5) Glass painting

A form of signwriting which is applied to the back of glass so that its appearance is enhanced by the translucency of the glass. Generally accepted as one of the signwriters' skills.

(6) Glass gilding

The application of metallic leaf to the back of glass which produces mirror-like brilliance. The metallic leaf is applied with an entirely different adhesive than those used for oil gilding but the technique is similar. It is often combined with glass painting and sometimes with acid etching to produce signs and decorative panels.

(7) Mirroring

This is a specialised process of applying a highly reflective coating to the back of glass. Sometimes used to marvellous effect with acid etched, sand blasted, and brilliant cut decoration.

It is the skills of acid etching, glass painting and gilding which are explained in this book.

Glass is worked on the back

Except on rare occasions when signwriting is done on the face of the glass, all glass decoration is carried out on the back of the glass so that all work is in reverse. It is a very costly error to discover that when the finished sign is viewed from the front everything is back to front.

Smoothing edges

Glass is handled and moved a number of times during the processes of

Fig. 10.1   An acid etched glass panel in many tones

decorating so it is important at the beginning of the job to smooth off any sharp edges. This can be done by rubbing with a coarse carborundum stone. A smoother finish can be obtained by rubbing the ground edge with a grade 240 silicon carbide paper used with water.

Acid Etching

Acid etching is sometimes called glass embossing or aciding. There are six principal processes in acid etching. (1) Preparing the acid; (2) Applying the resist; (3) Containing the acid; (4) Texturing; (5) Aciding; and (6) Cleaning off.

Preparing the Acid

Hydrofluoric acid
Hydrofluoric acid corrodes glass. Although the acid and its effect on glass was discovered in the late seventeenth century its decorative use was not exploited until the early part of the nineteenth century.

The principal of acid etching is to protect the part of the glass not to be decorated with a resist and to apply acid to the exposed parts until it has eaten its way into the glass far enough to achieve the type of texture required.

Hydrofluoric acid is used in two forms, either diluted, or as white acid.

Dilute acid
Hydrofluoric acid is available in various strengths. The most common one is 60%. A 50% acid is weaker and a 70% is stronger. It is never used in the strength that it is obtained but is diluted with water. A very strong acid may break down a resist, cause a dirty edge to the decoration or etch irregularly. It may cause the glass to become stained, which would show up if the areas were gilded after. To use an acid in its full strength is expensive also.

For normal texture work the acid needs to be mixed with 3 parts water. For toning, working over white acid treated glass, the dilution may vary from 2 parts water to 5 parts water. Generally a weak acid takes longer than a strong acid to etch glass so some glass decorators use weak acids and leave them on for a long time whereas others use stronger acids for shorter periods of etching.

When etched with dilute acid the glass still retains its translucency, so in this form it is used with other materials to produce textures which show up when gilded. Dilute acid is used over specially applied resists to produce interesting textures, or is mixed with mica chips to produce stipple effects. Its other use is over glass which has been previously textured with white acid. White acid gives a frosting effect and when later etched with acid a series of tones of frosting are obtained.

White acid
White acid is hydrofluoric acid mixed with washing soda. It produces a

frosting effect on the glass, which allows light to pass through but obscures clear vision.

Hazards of using acid

Hydrofluoric acid is a registered poison and can be obtained through controlled outlets only. Small quantities may be purchased from a pharmacist. Large quantities are obtainable from a small number of licensed acid dealers. It is supplied in plastic containers, clearly labelled with both its content and a poison warning which must not be removed. If it is decanted into another container similar labels must be securely fixed to it.

The acid gives off a pungent and dangerous vapour and must be used only where an effective extraction unit is available.

Rubber or plastic gloves must be worn during the entire period when the acid is being used to protect the hands from accidental splashing or when handling bottles which may have traces of acid on the outside. Wearing a plastic apron and rubber boots is essential also to protect clothes from the corrosive effect of the acid and to protect the user from accidental spillage. Eyes are most vulnerable and if they are exposed to the acid it will cause excruciating pain and may permanently damage vision. Clear safety goggles will protect the user against this hazard and must be worn at all times when using acid. Other exposed areas of the face can be rubbed with petroleum jelly to protect the skin from the effects of acid fumes. Avoid leaning over the acid during its etching period. The fumes can cause damage to the respiratory organs.

When acid is in use the room must be sealed and a warning sign displayed so that only the person experienced in using the acid has access to the room.

Acid burns to any part of the body must be treated by a doctor as soon as possible. A degree of relief will be obtained by placing the affected part under cold running water for fifteen to twenty minutes. Only medical treatment will alleviate the pain and ensure that no permanent damage does occur.

Preparing white acid

White acid is a mixture of hydrofluoric acid and washing soda. The proportions of the mix is critical, but because of the varying qualities of the two materials it is not possible to state precise quantities.

A reasonable guide is to add 1 litre of acid to 2.5 kg of soda, or any proportional variation on these quantities. Soda does absorb water and will produce a weak mix if its water content is high. Acid can be of varying proofs and if above 60% the white acid will be too strong if used in the above proportions. The only way to get a proper acid is to mix the materials in the above quantities, test its action, and adjust as necessary.

Testing can be carried out on small pieces of clean glass. The acid should take about one hour to affect the glass. After this time the etched glass is washed with water and inspected.

If the acid is of the right strength the glass should have an even frosted effect. A weak acid will leave the glass still transparent and a scum will be left on the surface which is soft and can be removed easily. If the test shows this result add about 250 ml of acid, mix thoroughly and test again. A too strong acid will leave a scaly scum on the surface and when held in the right light small sparkly patches will show. When this occurs add another 500 g of soda, mix well and retest.

Getting the white acid to the right strength can take a long time but is an essential process. Most glass shops will mix up a large quantity of the acid to last them four or five weeks so that the mixing process is done only ten times a year.

The raw mixture will be so thick that the stirring stick may stand up in it. So when the strength is right it must be thinned with water to the right consistency for use. It will probably need to be doubled in volume with water.

The acid should be mixed in a plastic bucket. A type which can be fitted with a lid is both useful and safe for storing the acid after mixing. After a time scum forms around the inside of the top of the container and as the plastic is flexed it breaks off and falls into the acid. If these pieces are not strained off before use the hard scum will cause patchy embossing. To avoid this some acid shops store white acid in wooden butts which tend to hold the scum so that it does not fall into the acid.

Applying the Resist

A resist is a material which is applied to glass to protect it from the corrosive effect of the acid. The quality of the finished decorative glass is dependent upon the type of resist used and the skill in applying it to the areas of glass not to be etched. The process is sometimes known as stopping out.

Brunswick black
A book published in the middle of the nineteenth century gave as a recipe for a resist paint: 'Mix black with boiled oil and litharge, boil until thick, thin to working consistency with copal varnish'. A few years later another book on glass decoration recommended Brunswick black as a resist which did not need the messy preparation of the first one. Brunswick black, together with Black Japan, have remained the traditional resist paints ever since. Both have a bitumen base, which is resistant to acid, and produce reversible films so are easily removed with white spirit after the aciding. Some firms market it under the name Embossing Black. Mirror backing paint can be used as a resist also, and although efficient is more expensive than Brunswick black. Originally the Brunswick black was applied to the areas not to be etched with a sable pencil by fixing the full size drawing to the face of the glass and painting the resist in the required areas on the back of the glass. It is rarely used in this way now because of the risk of the acid penetrating the black, particularly around the edges. The modern practice is to thicken the Brunswick black with red lead powder which offers a more reliable brush applied resist.

Painting resist in this way is kept to a minimum and may be the method only when toning over white acid etched glass. The most reliable method of resisting is to coat completely the back of the glass with Brunswick black, see fig. 10.2a, apply lead foil to it, cut out the areas to be etched from the foil, and remove the black from the cut out areas with white spirit. The double layers of resist are less likely to let the acid through to the areas not to be etched.

When the prepared glass is to be immersed in an acid bath for etching it is necessary to completely coat every face of the glass with Brunswick black.

The black does not have to be a dense coat providing that there are no misses in the coating. The coating must feel dry before it is covered with foil or acided. Some glass decorators leave it for about an hour to reach this stage where others leave it overnight before working over it.

Lead foil
Lead foil is a more reliable method of resisting and is applied either to a Brunswick black coated glass or direct to the glass. As the process of etching glass can be so expensive in labour hours, errors must be avoided and fewer problems arise if the double layer of resist is used. Brunswick black under foil not only offers a reinforcement to the resisting, it helps the lead foil to adhere well to the glass also. The lead foil can be applied directly the Brunswick black is hard enough not to pull off or soften when the foil adhesive is applied. Again, some glass decorators will carry out all the processes on one day whereas others like to leave the black to dry overnight before applying the foil.

The lead foil which is most suitable as an acid resist is one which is tin coated. This is sometimes called embossing foil. Ordinary lead foil is dirtier to handle because of its unsealed surface and may prove to be porous. Foil is available in two or three thicknesses or gauges. Although the thinnest gauge (0.025 mm) is available in rolls it is usually available in sheets about 900 × 300 mm and can be bought in small quantities. It is this grade which is most commonly non-tinned and may be subject to pinholing which makes it unreliable for aciding. The heavier gauge (0.05 mm) is most commonly sold in rolls and by weight and can be purchased in large quantities only. It is about 300 mm wide. The heavier gauges are less likely to tear and are preferred by most glass decorators.

Lead foil can be adhered with petroleum jelly, but except for very small jobs it is rarely used because of its cost and the difficulty of getting a smooth, even film. The most common adhesive is one made from a mixture of tallow and wax.

In their natural and purchaseable state tallow and wax are very thick or solid so need to be made thinner by heating before they can be mixed. This is most safely carried out by placing the material in a tin or metal container and then standing it in a container of simmering hot water. Direct contact with a hot plate or gas ring could cause the tallow or wax to burn.

Tallow is an animal fat and may be difficult to obtain in small quantities. Dripping is an edible form of tallow and is readily available in small quantities and can be used when tallow is not available.

The most common wax used is beeswax. This is particularly hard and expensive therefore paraffin wax is sometimes used instead. For small quantities ordinary household candles can be melted down.

When the tallow and wax have been heated to a liquid state they can be mixed together easily. During the summer or when working in a warm shop the mixture will remain reasonably pliable and a 50/50 mixture of tallow and wax will generally produce the right consistency. In cold conditions it may be necessary to increase the tallow content to make it soft enough to be used. If the cooled mixture does need making harder or softer it can be made liquid again by heating and a little melted tallow or wax mixed in until the right blend is obtained.

Some glass decorators add a very small quantity of boiled oil or gold size at the hot mix stage to make the cooled block a little harder. Others add a half eggcup full of sweet oil which has the opposite effect. Some craftsmen add a little coloured pigment also so that the finished material is more distinctive.

If the mixture is poured into a small tray or biscuit tin lid which has been lightly coated with sweet oil it will quickly cool into a slab which can be cut into pieces about 100 × 60 mm. When this cake of wax is rubbed over the glass it will leave a thin film of grease of just sufficient thickness to hold the lead foil, see fig. 10.2b. A more even film can be obtained by rubbing this coating with a rag pad which has been previously coated with the wax/tallow cake. The lead foil is pressed onto the greased surface so that it is smooth and in close contact with the glass over the whole surface. The heavier gauge foils can be placed directly on to the waxed area because they are less likely to crease in their rolls. But the thinner gauge sheets are difficult to handle without creasing and these should be rubbed out before they are laid on the adhesive. If the sheets are laid on a smooth, hard surface, like a piece of glass, and rubbed with a pad of rag, working in a circular motion from the centre of the sheet to the outside edges, the creases will be removed.

The foil should cover the whole glass surface or the black painted area. When more than one sheet is necessary they should be overlapped, but by no more than 5 mm, spreading a little adhesive under the overlap first. To ensure good contact with the adhesive the foil can be rubbed with a pad of rag or a thick piece of upholsterers felt, see fig. 10.2c, about 100 × 60 mm by 15 mm thick. Rubber rollers and rubber squeegees are sometimes used for smoothing down, but generally they do not achieve the right contact with the glass and they are more likely to tear the foil. If the foil is torn accidentally during the laying process it is easily patched with another piece of foil cut big enough to overlap the torn area by at least 10 mm all round and stuck down with the wax/tallow.

Any surplus foil hanging over the edge of the glass should be cut off with a sharp knife because if it is handled the edges may be pulled up.

When the foil is smooth the full size drawing of the decoration is laid on the glass in exactly the right position and fixed so that it will not move. The simplest way of ensuring its exact position is to draw a horizontal and vertical centre line on the drawing first, and snap the

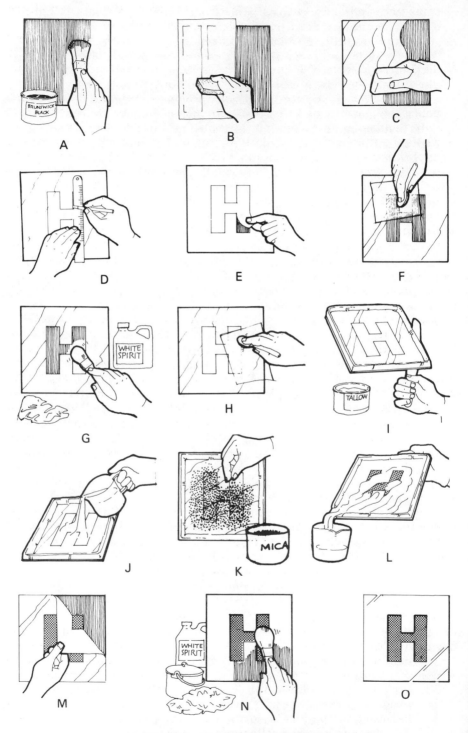

Fig. 10.2   Processes in acid stippling

same lines on the foil with a chalk line. When the drawing centre lines match the glass centre lines the drawing is in the exact position.

Before fixing the drawing check that it is in reverse. Work is being carried out on the back of the glass so the image from the glass decorators position should be backwards so that from the face of the glass it will be seen in its correct position.

If the drawing is on opaque paper it should be traced onto tracing paper before applying to the glass otherwise the lines will not be seen with the design in contact with the glass. An alternative method is to make the drawing translucent after fixing it in position by wiping the paper with a piece of rag dipped in a mixture of white spirit and linseed oil. This process also makes the drawing have a better contact with the foil.

The drawing can be fixed in position by placing heavy weights around the outside or applying small pieces of masking tape around the edge of the drawing. The disadvantage of using tape is that it may pull off the foil when the drawing is removed.

The drawing is transferred to the foil by scribing over the outline with a sharp pencil or ball point pen. There should be no need to chalk the drawing first because the lead will be marked quite clearly by the scribe pressure only. If the drawing is to be used a number of times it may be practical to make it into a pounce as described in chapter 8.

With the drawing removed it is necessary to cut from the foil those parts of the design which are to be acid etched. If the design is intricate it is advisable to mark carefully on the foil those parts which are to be removed. The marked sections are then cut using a very sharp knife.

The knife for this work needs to be small and round so that it can be held between the thumb and forefinger and twisted around curves in the same way that the signwriting brush is used. There are special cutters which can be purchased for this work which have replaceable blades that screw into the end. Some decorators use surgical scalpels but these generally have flat handles and are not so manoeuvrable as round cutters. The most common cutter is one that the decorators make for themselves from rods of silver steel, see fig. 10.3. The method of making these cutters is described later. Whatever cutter is used it should have a pointed blade, kept very sharp on an oil stone during the entire cutting process.

Fig. 10.3 A silver steel cutter

Cutting must be clean and aids such as straight edges (see fig. 10.2d), French curves, circle templates and compasses should be used whenever they are appropriate. Overcutting in corners must be avoided as the acid may penetrate through the cut and will show when the area is gilded. The cutter should be kept upright at all times because a slanting blade will undercut the foil and tend to lift it up.

When each shape has been cut around, the pieces of foil over the areas to be etched can be lifted off (see fig. 10.2e). If there are places where the knife has not cut right through the foil these must be severed with the knife and not pulled away which might cause the foil to tear. When all the foil which is not needed has been removed the design to be etched will appear in the foil resist in the Brunswick black first applied. This allows an opportunity to examine carefully the cutting and to make any adjustments before the black is washed off.

Paraffin or white spirit applied with a rag or brush to the cut foil areas will quickly remove the Brunswick black, see fig. 10.2g. Too much spirit may penetrate beneath the foil and remove the black which may weaken the resist so only enough spirit on the brush to soften the paint is necessary. The final smeary residue of black can be cleaned off to perfectly clear glass with a clean rag.

The edges of the foil may have been disturbed during the cleaning process and to make sure that it is in good contact with the glass all the edges need to be rubbed down. This is done with a hard smooth object like a spoon (see fig. 10.2h), or end of a ball point pen, or a piece cut from a large cardboard roll. To avoid damaging the foil a piece of tracing paper should be placed on the surface first so that the direct contact is with the paper and not with the foil. This rubbing down process should be carried out after cutting and before cleaning off to prevent the paraffin creeping under the foil, see fig. 10.2f.

Repeat patterns
Much of the traditional decorative etched glass has elements in the design which are regularly repeated. This happens particularly in the corners where border lines are twisted or interlaced to form decorative features. To make sure that all the corners look alike on each panel and throughout a series of identical panels the repeating shape is cut from a piece of very heavy lead foil and used as a cutting template. It is placed in the exact position after the design has been transferred to the foil resist and cut around carefully with the knife. Glass decorators keep these templates and are able to use them on many jobs over the years.

Other resists
Self adhesive plastic films which have a wide use for lining shelves can be used as an acid resist. It is more expensive to buy than lead foil but is more readily available particularly in small quantities. The plastic film usually has an easily peelable backing paper and when this has been removed the film can be firmly pressed onto the clean glass. There is less chance of the film creasing or getting air bubbles if it is held away from the surface and just a small amount is lowered to the glass and smoothed with a pad of rag until tight before lowering more.

The design can be transferred by chalking the back of the drawing and drawing over it in the way described for signwriting. Cutting and lifting is carried out in the same way as for foil.

Plastic film is not as reliable as foil and Brunswick black and should be used for small areas of work only.

Screen resists
When a number of identical glass panels are to be etched resist can be

screen printed. The screen is made in the conventional way, but the paint used is Brunswick black thickened with red lead powder or a special acid resist supplied by screen ink manufacturers. Foil cannot be used with this method so the process is recommended only when the design is simple.

Containing the Acid

To etch glass the acid must be in contact with it for any period up to one hour. So that it does not run off the glass in that period a wall needs to be built around the panel so that the acid is contained in a puddle over the exposed glass for as long as it is necessary to produce the required texture.

The easiest and most common method is to build a fat wall, see fig. 10.2i.

Fat wall

The 'fat' can be either tallow, or a mixture of tallow and wax similar to that produced for adhering lead foil. Either needs to be in a smooth easily workable consistency and this can be achieved by working them hard on a piece of glass with a large palette knife. This breaks down their colloidal state and makes them into a consistency like that of butter. The wax and tallow mixture may need to have extra tallow added to make it soft enough to use.

When the 'fat' is the right consistency it is loaded onto the palette knife so that the entire length of the blade has an even thickness of fat. The fat is then transferred to the edge of the glass to form a wall about 15–20 mm high around the entire perimeter. The technique of beating the fat on the glass, picking it up on the blade of the knife, and transferring it to the edge of the glass requires considerable dexterity and practice.

The building of the wall is made easier by holding a strip of glass about 15 mm away from the edge of the glass and packing the fat into the gap. The glass needs to be about 300 × 80 mm, brushed with a very dilute form of acid just before use so that the fat will not adhere to it. The glass will ensure a vertical plane to the inside of the wall and the knife will form a sloping edge on the outside.

When the acid has completed its action it will be poured off the glass by making a breach in the wall and tipping the glass. During this process the acid may run around the edge and mark the face of the glass. To avoid this, when the fat wall is complete, a smear of the fat is rubbed on the face of the glass at the point where the pouring off will be most convenient.

As white acid has a much slower corrosive action the smearing of fat on the face of the glass is not necessary. If the entire face side is coated with a paste of whiting and water it will be sufficiently protected from dribbling acid.

Foil and fat

When etching is required right up to the edge of the glass a fat wall cannot be used because it needs to be applied to part of the glass. In these circumstances a concertina folded strip of foil is used held together with fat, see fig. 10.4.

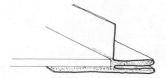

Fig. 10.4   An acid wall made from foil and wax

It is made by cutting a number of strips of foil about 140 mm wide and as long as the glass sides or about 300 mm long if the glass is very big. The edges of the glass should be rubbed with the block of tallow and wax used to adhere the foil so that they are protected if the acid gets between the wall and the glass. The face of the glass is coated with the fat in a strip about 30 mm wide around the entire panel. The coated glass is placed over about 30 mm of the lead foil strip which is laying flat on the bench so that it is well stuck. The remaining area of foil is coated with fat and bent so that it stands up around the edge of the glass when the other side can be coated with fat. The foil is then folded two or three times to produce a thick foil wall adequately coated and stuck with fat.

When strips have to be joined together they must be overlapped by at least 20 mm and sealed with fat. Great care must be taken that no fat gets onto the glass which is to be etched because it will act like resist. An alternative method to using the foil wall is to carry out the decoration on a piece of glass which is about 100 mm bigger all round than needed. When the etching is finished the excess can be cut off. By this method the containing is done within a fat wall. This method cannot be used when toughened glass is being decorated because such glass cannot be cut.

An alternative method of etching is to immerse the prepared glass in a shallow tank of acid. It is not a common practice but it does eliminate the process of building a fat wall.

Texturing

Brights
Glass exposed to dilute hydrofluoric acid can be felt as having been corroded but there will be no visible effect on the glass. On heavily decorated glass panels certain small areas are left as clear glass to give both added texture to the design and to maintain a degree of visibility through the panel. These transparent glass areas are known as brights and may be areas which have been etched with dilute acid or areas which have been left untouched.

White acid
When exposed to white acid glass becomes frosted. It has an all over diffuse texture which still allows light to pass through. As an example

of the amount that white acid diffuses glass, if the etched glass is held against a printed sheet the type is clearly readable, but once it is moved away by as little as 10 mm the letter shapes cannot be seen.

White acid can be used all over a glass panel so that it remains translucent (allows light to pass through) but is no longer transparent (cannot be seen through). Where normal 3 or 4 mm glass is being used it is most likely that obscured glass would be specified but for heavier glasses or toughened glass they may need to be white acid etched to produce the obscuring quality. A similar effect can be produced by sand blasting. The most common use for white acid is as part of the various tones employed to produce decorative glass, particularly the traditional French embossed glass.

Toning

The effect of dilute hydrofluoric acid on white acid etched glass is to produce subtle changes in the tone of the frosted effect. Half tones are produced by one exposure to the acid. Full tones are the effect of two exposures to acid.

Tonings are produced by first white aciding the total area to be decorated. When this is completed a resist such as Brunswick black is applied to the areas which are to remain white acid and leaving the area to be toned exposed. This is then etched to produce the half tones. When completed the areas to be left in half tone are coated with resist and the exposed area is again etched to produce the full tones.

The finished job will show the glass decorated in three tones of obscured glass. When contrasted with clear glass or brights around or within it the effect is very ornamental. See fig. 10.1.

Tonings are sometimes referred to as satin finishes. Toning acids may vary in dilution or time of exposure. An acid of 4:1 or 3:1 may be used for the half tone and left for 25 min for the weaker mix and 15 min for the stronger mix. Full tone or full satin may use a weaker acid such as 5:1 left to etch for 25 min. Glass decorators work in a variety of ways to produce tonings and the proportions and times stated above can be used as a guide only. The novice decorator needs to carry out a variety of test pieces using different mixtures and exposing for various times. These need to be carefully documented and referred to for all jobs until a reliable technique is established.

When matching a new piece of decorative glass to an existing piece a range of experimental dilutions and exposure times may be necessary before the precise tonings effects will be produced.

Stipple

Fine flakes of mica are not dissolved or affected by hydrofluoric acid, and if they are mixed with the acid they prevent it corroding the glass evenly.

When this action is carefully controlled the texture produced on the glass is like a fine hammered effect or a fine rough cast.

A variety of stipple effects can be achieved by using different grades of mica flakes. Fine flakes produce a tight small texture like that of orange peel. Large flakes produce a texture like coarse leather.

Generally, glass decorators produce three types of stipple: fine, medium and large.

The effect is produced in one of three ways.

(1) The mica flakes are sprinkled onto the poured acid, see fig. 10.2k, and moved around with a soft hair brush until an even distribution is obtained. This method is reliable only on small areas.

(2) Mixing the mica flakes with the acid before pouring. The mixture must be stirred so that the flakes are evenly distributed through the acid.

(3) To stick the mica flakes to the glass with gum arabic before applying the acid. Gum arabic is available in resin form and is melted down by heating in a saucepan or dissolving in very hot water. In this liquid state it is brushed onto the resisted glass and the mica flakes shaken over it until an even coating is obtained. The gum must be left to dry before the acid is poured and the decorators who use this method generally leave it overnight before aciding. This process is carried out before the fat wall is built.

Stippling can be gilded and produces a matt gold effect which when contrasted with burnished gold looks most decorative. Stippling can be toned with white acid to produce a greater range of decorative textures.

Stippled glass allows more light to pass through than white acid glass. Print can be read through the glass up to a distance of 25 mm.

In the early days of glass etching the stippled effect was obtained by sprinkling ground fluorspar or fluoride or calcium into the acid. Fluorspar is the natural stone from which hydrofluoric acid is produced. It is a mineral found widely in the UK, the most common type being Blue John spar.

Bromish
This is a traditional texture produced by applying a resist paint to the glass with a very coarse fibre brush. The name is thought to be a corruption of brooming and the brush used to apply the resist is like a small broom. The brush is loaded by rubbing it on a board thickly coated with the paint and then dragged across the glass to be textured. The paint will be applied very unevenly and will give the impression of tree bark or very rough timber grain. Achieving an acceptable texture requires a lot of practice. See fig. 10.5.

Fig. 10.5   Bromish, one of the acid textures

Brunswick black generally is too thin for this use and may flow out after application to spoil the effect. If thickened with red lead powder it tends to stay in the places where the brush puts it.

When the resist is hard, the fat wall is built and acid applied in the usual way. The acid will corrode only the glass not touched by the resist and when cleaned off the graining texture will be very apparent (fig. 10.5).

A variation on the effect can be produced by applying the resist to white acid glass and toning the bromish.

Sponge stipple
Another traditional texture is achieved by applying the resist paint in a dabbing action with a flat coarse sponge. The effect is like a very coarse large stipple.

The sponge is loaded with paint in the same way as the brush for bromish and the technique of obtaining an even effect takes considerable practice.

Like bromish, sponge stipple can be toned over white acid.

Using textures
Textures can be used to produce decorative glass panels without any painting or gilding. French embossing is a traditional example of glass decoration using only white and dilute hydrofluoric acid.

Textured glass is widely used with painting and gilding to produce an infinite range of decorative effects. The etching processes are always completed before painting or gilding is started.

Original glass embossing effect
In a book published in 1874, *Sign Writing and Glass Embossing*, a process of decorating glass is described as being a new technique and strongly suggests that white acid was unknown at that period. The technique is still used today and sometimes is referred to as imitation French embossing but it should be called original embossing.

The glass is prepared in the usual way and the background is coated with resist paint. The pattern is etched with 3:1 dilute hydrofluoric acid and the resist removed. Only by holding the glass at various angles will the embossed pattern be visible.

With the glass laying on a padded flat bench the embossed side can be rubbed with a block of glass which has been dipped in a slurry of carborundum powder and water. Very slowly the carborundum powder will grind the flat, non-etched areas and destroy its transparency and the etched areas will show up as clear glass.

In 1870 fine emery powder or fine sand was used as the abrasive and the grinding was carried out with either a glass block or a flat block of copper. The modern carborundum cuts faster than emery but as then the process takes a long time.

Aciding
Acid is applied to the prepared glass by pouring or immersion.

Pouring Acid

This is the most convenient and most widely practiced method.

The resisted and fat walled glass is laid on a flat bench and made perfectly level. If it is sloping to any degree the acid will run to the lowest point and may not be in contact with all the glass. A small boat spirit level should be used to check the level by placing it on the glass and checking it in two directions. If levelling is necessary the simplest method is to push small wooden wedges under the low corners until the spirit level bubble is exactly in the centre position.

The acid is best decanted from the storage containers into a plastic jug with a wide pouring lip. The acid is poured over the glass slowly and the jug held as close to the glass as possible to avoid splashing, see fig. 10.2j. The acid should be poured until the entire surface is covered. A depth of 2–3 mm is usually enough.

Acid time

The acid is left to act upon the glass for different periods of time. White acid will need at least one hour to have the desired effect. A 3:1 acid for stippling or bromish needs 20–30 min. Tonings vary according to the strength of the acid and the type of toning required.

Removing acid

When the exposure time has elapsed a wide necked jug is placed under the point where the fat had been spread on the glass face, and the fat wall is broken with a palette knife. If the glass has been wedged a slight tap on the wedge furthest from the breached wall will cause the acid to pour into the jug. If no wedges have been used the blade of the palette knife under the opposite edge will tip it sufficiently to move the acid. See fig. 10.2l.

If dilute acid has been used the fat wall may not be needed again and can be scraped off with a palette knife and put into a container. All traces of acid need to be cleaned off with ample cold water either by hosing down if the facilities allow it, or by placing the glass under a running tap. A few minutes washing is necessary to ensure that no acid is left on the glass.

After white aciding the glass needs to be soaked in water for a further hour. The fat wall should not be removed after the acid has drained off so that water can be poured on. It is advisable to wash the glass face first with water before mending the fat wall and pouring clean cold water onto the glass.

The soaking of white acid is necessary to remove the hard scum which forms on the surface. After soaking the glass needs to be scrubbed with a nail brush and hosed or washed with running water. When the fat wall is removed the etched glass should be carefully examined and any patches of scum still remaining should be scrubbed until an even texture is obtained.

Reclaiming acid

Dilute acid can be re-used. If it has been used with mica this needs to be filtered out by pouring it through a funnel with a nylon stocking inside it.

There is a problem with reclaimed acid. As used acid tends to be weaker than the original mix it may be necessary to add a little more acid to the reclaimed mix in order to obtain similar results.

Immersion in Acid

With this method the entire piece of glass is immersed in a shallow tank of acid. The tank needs to be lead lined or made of glass reinforced plastic, and the base must be perfectly flat otherwise a lot of acid will be needed before there is sufficient to cover the glass.

Immersion tanks are very useful when a number of pieces of glass are to be etched at one time so they are more likely to be used in glass decorating shops involved in high production work. Using tanks obviates the need for building fat walls but it does require the entire glass to be coated in resist.

At the end of the etching period the acid is drained off through a tap at one end and without removing the glass water can be poured or hosed on to clean off all the surplus. When white aciding the drain tap can be closed and the tank filled with water to allow the scum to be soaked off as described earlier.

Disposing of acid
Acid must not be washed or poured away down drains which discharge directly into the local authority sewer. The acid for disposal must be sealed into plastic containers, clearly labelled with their content, and taken to special disposal areas which are designated by the local authority.

Cleaning Off

When all traces of the acid, scum and fat wall have been removed the resist can be taken off. The foil should pull away easily leaving the embossing black to be removed with white spirit, see fig. 10.2m. A light scrubbing with a paint brush is sufficient to dissolve and move the black, see fig. 10.2n. Wiping with clean rags removes the final traces and a wash with detergent will leave the glass sparkling.

White acid effects will be clearly seen even before the resist is removed but dilute acid brights or stipples will be seen only when the resist is cleaned off and the glass viewed at different angles in a good light. See fig. 10.2o.

Cleaning off is the final stage for a French embossed panel but for other forms of decorative glass work there may be many processes of both painting and gilding to follow.

Other Methods of Glass Etching

Acid based screen ink
This is not widely used or the material widely available. It is a

colourless compound which contains hydrofluoric acid and is applied in the normal way through a non-water soluble screen stencil. The depth of etching is very slight and would be acceptable for a number of identical low priced panels only.

Chemical etching
A company called Tyrella have developed a material which is not an acid but does affect the surface of glass sufficiently to impede the passage of light and show a texture. Mainly used for decorating glasses and vases.

Laser cutting
Equipment has been developed which uses a fine, laser beam to cut patterns in timber, plastic and glass. It is unlikely that its use will be very widespread in the sign industry.

Glass Painting

Many signs are produced on glass. They may be a single word on a glazed panel of a door or a very involved decorative panel involving many colours with perhaps gilding and acid etching. The only occasions when the signwriting or painting is carried out on the face of the glass is when the back of the glass is not accessible, or when the glass is obscured or painted, or when it is a mirror. Face painting of glass is not very durable because it cannot be protected sufficiently against cleaning. Also the lustre and brilliance which glass gives to decoration carried out on the back is lost.

If a glass sign includes acid etching this process must be completed before the painting or gilding is started. When painting and gilding are to be combined there is no order of procedure which can be adopted for all jobs. There is a danger that painted decoration may be disturbed by the gilding size so gilding may be finished first but if gilded lettering has a painted outline it is practical to finish the outline before gilding.

Cleaning Glass

Because glass has such a hard, smooth surface paint does not readily stick to it. Glass paints have to contain varnishes which make them sticky and ensure the best possible adhesion. If any dirt, moisture or grease gets between the paint and the glass the adhesion of a well-prepared glass paint will be considerably reduced and if it survives during the many painting processes it is unlikely that it will last long once the sign is in position and regularly cleaned.

Considerable care must be taken to clean glass before any painting processes start. If the job takes many days to complete the cleaning process should be repeated each day because the surface attracts condensation and regular handling will deposit some grease on the glass. A mixture of whiting and methylated spirit applied thickly all over the back of the glass with a piece of rag and wiped off with clean rag directly the spirit has evaporated is a simple and effective cleaning method. The spirit dissolves any grease and the whiting absorbs it, as well as any moisture on the surface. It is not advisable to use this mixture to clean painted glass at it may disturb the paint. A careful wipe with a damp chamois leather is recommended for cleaning daily between processes.

Once the glass is cleaned it should be handled as little as possible. The knob of the mahl stick or the base of the bridge must be clean so that they do not distribute dirt on the glass as the work progresses. Dipping in French chalk or whiting before starting is a simple way to ensure that the stick and the bridge do not deposit any dirt.

Glass cleansers should be avoided. Some of them contain additives which may leave a film on the glass which could seriously affect adhesion. If working on a piece of glass which has been *in situ* for some time it should be thoroughly washed with detergent to remove any film left on by cleaners. When working on site in cold weather or near a place where cooking or washing is being carried out it may be necessary to direct a fan heater on the outside of the glass to prevent condensation which would destroy adhesion of the paint.

Setting out

All setting out must be carried out on the face of the glass otherwise the materials used to mark the glass may affect the paint's adhesion. Also it reduces the number of times the painting side needs to be handled which also reduces adhesion.

For simple signs lines can be snapped with chalk or drawn with wax pencils and the lettering marked between them with a wax pencil in the same way that a sign is set out for signwriting.

Setting out on the face of the glass allows the lettering to be marked the right way around, whereas setting out on the back requires the lettering to be drawn in reverse.

For more intricate signs a full size drawing should be prepared and taped on the front of the glass. Drawings made on fine tracing paper can be seen clearly from the back providing a soft pencil has been used. If the image is very faint or the drawing is on opaque paper it can be made more translucent by wiping over the fixed drawing with a mixture of linseed oil and white spirit. This method also makes the drawing have a better contact with the glass so making it easier to follow with a brush through the thickness of the glass.

Paint for Glass

Most glass painting is carried out with opaque paint. On occasions translucent colour is used.

Opaque paint
The most common colour used on glass is black because much lettering and some design work is outlined and black is the most effective colour. Originally glass painting black was made by the signwriter from

lampblack pigment ground to a smooth, stiff paste with varnish or gold size. In 1860, *The Practical Guide to Sign Writing and Gilding*, by William Sutherland, recommended mixing lampblack with milk for painting glass which was not exposed to too much wet. In his experience, milk bound black was less likely to peel off than a varnish paint. Because lampblack has become very difficult to obtain, most glass painters use signwriters black obtained in tubes or tins. The manufacturers of this colour recommend it to be used without further mixing except to thin it with white spirit. Yet signwriters use it in a variety of ways. The most common mixture is with gold size or black enamel. Both of these materials tend to improve its adhesion. To avoid the necessity of second coating and to give it maximum adhesion the black should be thinned just sufficiently to make it easy to apply. Tube colours may be less reliable for glass painting than the tinned colours. The tinned paints can be stirred thoroughly whereas tube colours can be very oily which not only affects their adhesion but makes them less opaque. When other colours are necessary the specially prepared signwriters colours are the most reliable to use. Signwriters enamels have good adhesion to glass but usually have poorer opacity than the tube colours.

Unlike painting signs the first coat applied to glass is the one that is always seen. Any defects in the paint film will show regardless of the number of coats which may be applied after. The most likely spoiler of glass paint is dirt or bits of skin and these can be avoided by straining all paint through a double thickness of nylon before use. If the paint is decanted from the mixing jar to a clean dipper with a piece of nylon mesh stretched over the top it will be clean and ready for use.

Translucent colour
Non-opaque colours are used to give a stained glass effect or produce a shaded or blended effect on design work or lettering, especially with gilding. They are obtained ready prepared or can be mixed from tube oil colours mixed with varnish. The best results are obtained with stainers which have poor opacity such as Prussian blue, raw sienna, crimson, and veridian green.

Straining of translucent colours is essential because any tiny piece of dirt will show as a dark dot in the coloured film. Also they have poorer flowing properties than is imagined and when used on large areas need to be stippled after application either with the tip of a fitch or with a small stencil brush to remove the brush marks.

Painting

Painted glass decoration can be signwritten or cut from lead foil and painted.

Signwriting on glass
The tools used for glass writing are similar to signwriting, but there are a few differences in technique. Work is carried out in reverse and it is important to check regularly that the appearance from the front is

the one that is required.

The marking out is always the thickness of the glass away from the brush so it is essential that the eye, brush and markings are in line otherwise the shapes may appear distorted when viewed from the front.

Glass is very hard and smooth so it is much more difficult to control the brush and the mahl stick. Great care must be taken to prevent the brush skidding and the mahl stick slipping.

Outside corners need not be painted cleanly. They can be brushed to outside the marking out and cut to a sharp finish when the paint is dry with a very sharp knife against a steel rule, see fig. 10.6.

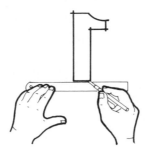

Fig. 10.6   Sharpening corners of glass signwriting when the paint is dry

Outlining

Outlined letters are common on glass. The outline must be bold and precisely painted so that it does not vary in thickness to any degree.

When outlining a letter it is essential to concentrate on the shape of the letter contained within the outline as much as the quality of the line. It is easy to lose a letter shape while attempting to master the control of the brush to paint an even line. Errors will show up particulary when the letters are eventually painted in or gilded.

If a Roman letter is outlined a more acceptable effect is often obtained if the outline is blocked at the extreme point of the serif, see fig. 2.8. An outline which is painted to meet at a point at the end of a serif often appears very long and distracts from the letter shape. When the letter is filled in it is the shape that is read not the outline and the blocked end will not be obvious.

Painting

On large areas it is not always possible to spread paint very evenly and the patchy effect may be seen from the front. This can be overcome by stippling the first coat while the paint is still wet with a stencil brush.

Generally a thicker coat of paint can be applied to a glass panel laid flat on a bench than one *in situ*. This can be an important factor when pricing a glass job to be painted on site.

If second coating is carried out before the first coat is dry there is a strong chance that the paint will pick up. This will show as a patch from the front and cannot be hidden. Only removing all the paint and repainting will remedy the defect.

Foiling on glass

An alternative to signwriting is to adhere lead foil to the glass, cut out the shapes to be painted, paint and remove the foil. Generally this method allows a thicker more even coat of paint to be applied and produces a sharper finish to the letters or decoration. It is a useful method when many colours are being used and particularly when blended affects are being carried out. This is because the foil masks the outside areas so the blending brush can be used with greater freedom to produce the required effect.

The process is similar to that used for resisting glass when acid etching, except that a different adhesive is used.

Adhesive

The foil is adhered with gelatine. Gelatine is available in three forms.

(1) As empty capsules which are made principally for the pharmaceutical industry to fill with drugs. These can be purchased through most gilding material suppliers.

(2) As a powder, probably called gilders size. It is a less pure gelatine than the capsules, but most suitable for adhering foil. It is less readily available than capsules.

(3) As a powder prepared for cooking purposes. A very pure form is icinglass. Available from most provisions stores.

The gelatine needs to be soaked in a little warm water for about ten minutes. About four capsules or a teaspoonful of either of the powders mixed with 500 ml of hot water is a generally acceptable mix. The hot water should be poured onto the soaked gelatine and stirred thoroughly until all traces of the gelatine have been dissolved. If the gelatine will not dissolve it may be necessary to simmer the mixture on a hot plate for a few minutes.

The gelatine is applied to the clean glass with a large soft haired brush and the smoothed foil is applied to it in the same way and with the same appliances as used when acid etching, see fig. 10.7a.

Some glass decorators work on the foil immediately it has been applied but there is a risk when the size is so wet that the foil may move as it is being cut or that the edges of the cut foil may not be tight enough and the paint may creep under. If the foiled glass is left overnight the size will set and there will be less possibility of defects.

Foil can be fixed with a thin even smear of petroleum jelly also. Although cutting can be safely carried out immediately the foil is adhered there is a problem in removing all traces of the jelly from the exposed areas before painting. The slightest amount left on the glass can cause the paint to either not dry or be pulled off the glass when the foil is removed.

Applying and cutting

The processes of transferring the drawing, cutting the foil, lifting from

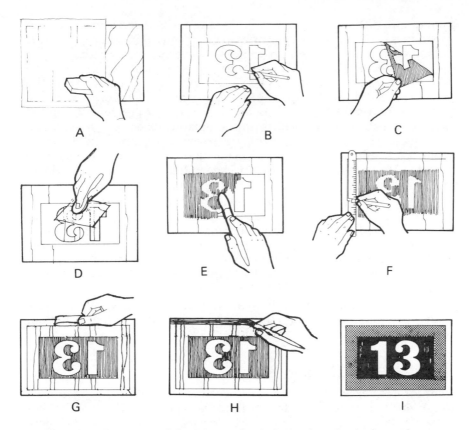

Fig. 10.7 Processes in foil cutting and painting a glass sign in three colours

the areas to be painted, and rubbing down the edges are exactly the same as described for acid etching, see fig. 10.7b-d. The glass areas can be wiped over with a damp sponge to remove any surplus gelatine, but if the size has been mixed to the weak proportions described above it will not cause any problems to the paint if it is not completely removed.

Painting
The most reliable paint to use with foil is signwriters colour, preferably the thinned form which has been thoroughly stirred. These are more brittle and break cleanly when the foil is removed. Enamels or gloss paints skin over and are much more flexible and tend to pull away from the glass when the foil is removed.

Large soft brushes should be used to apply an even, opaque coat, see fig. 10.7e and h. If two coats are necessary because the paint has poor opacity, the first coat can be stippled to reduce the risk of brushmarks showing. Although signwriters colours can be left until they are dry before lifting the foil it is more common to lift it as soon as the paint has set. If taken off too early the paint may still be liquid and could flow out over the cut edge.

If more than one colour is to be used on a glass panel the work should be planned so that only one application of foil is necessary. The sign shown in fig. 10.7i is a house number plate painted in three colours. A method of producing this sign could be: cover the entire glass panel with foil first, fig. 10.7a; secondly, cut, lift and paint the shaded area behind the numerals, fig. 10.7b-e; and third, cut, lift and paint the outside border, fig. 10.7f-h. The foil covering the numerals and the inner border would be lifted as soon as the two previously applied colours had set. When the paints had completely dried, which may take eight hours, the whole back of the glass would be painted in the third colour. Not only would this be easier than cutting in, it would be quicker, allow a more even coating to be applied, and would produce an acceptable backing in case the sign is to be viewed from behind.

If colours need to touch or be overpainted or be second coated it is essential that the first coats are completely dry. Lifting of the paint, patchiness or edges running together may result if too short a time is allowed and if these happen the only remedy is to completely strip the glass and start again.

Aluminium foil
Aluminium foil can be used instead of lead. It is cheaper and more readily available, but it is inclined to be more brittle and may not cut as easily or as cleanly as lead.

Screen printing glass
Identical glass signs can be screened. The process is no different to other printing except that signwriters colour is used. Outlining is often screen printed even if the design is to be repeated only two or three times. It does produce a very sharp, accurate line and can be more convenient on site work where access to the glass for signwriting is either difficult or inconvenient.

Glass Gilding

When gold is applied to the back of glass the effect from the front should be like a mirror. To achieve this the glass, tools, materials and surrounds must be kept spotlessly clean. Also the size must be mixed with care and the gold applied evenly. If a mirror-like effect is not obtained the work has not achieved the standard which makes glass gilding the magnificent decorative medium it should be.

Surface preparation
The same degree of care must be taken to clean the glass for gilding as described for glass painting. Any deficiency in the cleaning before painting may cause poor adhesion of paint. Any deficiency in cleaning glass before gilding will not only affect adhesion, it will spoil the finish of the gold. White acid etched glass cannot be gilded until it has been toned with dilute acid.

Glass can be gilded before or after painting. There are risks that the paint may be disturbed by the size getting underneath the film when the gilding is carried out as a last process, but it is common practice and every precaution must be taken to ensure that the paint has excellent adhesion and is thoroughly dry before gilding over it.

Cleaning glass surrounded by painted areas must be done with care. Methylated spirit may soften or penetrate the edge of the paint, whiting may scratch or break the paint edge, excess water may creep under the paint, therefore all these processes should be avoided. A clean chamois leather damped with warm water and wiped over the glass areas usually cleans the surface sufficiently. Water must wet the surface and not roll up into balls and this can be used as a test to ensure that the glass is not greasy.

Tools

In addition to the cushion, tip and knife, described for loose oil gilding in chapter 9 a gilders mop is required also for glass gilding.

A gilders mop is usually a flat brush with a squirrel hair filling about 25 mm to 50 mm wide, see fig. 10.8. A polishers mop can be used, either in a metal ferrule or quill and made from squirrel hair also.

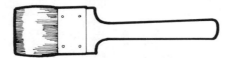

Fig. 10.8   A flat gilders mop

A clean glass jar is the best type of container for the size because glass is both easy to clean and readily shows when it is dirty. The clean condition of the size can be easily checked through the glass also. A stainless steel cup makes a good size container and is more practical on site and for carrying about.

Mixing the gelatine size

Glass gilding size must be sufficiently sticky to hold the gold to the glass but clear enough not to affect the burnish of the gold. A very dilute mixture of gelatine is the only size which will satisfy both these requirements.

Gelatine is the material obtained by boiling animal hoof, bone or skin. It is colourless and glutinous. Although the various forms of gelatine described earlier for adhering lead foil can be used for glass gilding only the capsules are of a sufficiently reliable quality to be suitable on every occasion.

The strength of the size is critical. If too weak it will not wet the glass and adhesion will not be sufficient when applying a second coat. If too strong it will form a film between the gold and the glass and reduce the burnish and leave marks on the gold. One gelatine capsule in 500 ml of water is suitable for gold leaf. For white gold or silver leaf which are thicker a slightly stronger size may be necessary and one and a half capsules should be used. On the rare occasions when aluminium leaf or Dutch metal are used on glass the size may need to have two capsules.

In certain areas of the country and at certain times of the year tap water can contain substances which although harmless when drunk can cause gelatine size to have a slight milky appearance. It is safer on all occasions to use distilled water to make gelatine size.

The method of mixing is as follows. Separate the two sections of the capsule and place them in a clean container and pour on a little distilled water so that they will absorb the water and start to soften. Heat 500 ml of distilled water, pour it on the soaked gelatine and stir until all traces of the gelatine have been dissolved. If the gelatine does not dissolve the mixture must be poured into a saucepan and simmered until the gelatine can no longer be seen. When cool strain the size through a nylon mesh tied over the top of a clean glass jar or stainless steel cup. The size is ready to use when it is lukewarm.

In a book published in 1870 the writer suggests that gilders size should contain spirits of wine which is indusrial alcohol. The method of mixing was to dissolve gelatine in half the quantity of boiled water and to make up the full amount with spirits of wine when the solution was cool. The original writer was insistent that no glass gilding would be successful without the spirits. Although a few gilders still use it, it is not a common practice today.

Gelatine size must be mixed fresh daily. Apart from collecting dirt and pieces of gold during use it putrefies and its clear glass-like transparency is reduced. When working in a warm atmosphere the putrefaction can be quick enough to require two or three fresh mixes to be made each day.

Glass Gilding Process

Gold can be applied directly to undecorated, or acid etched glass, or to the cut out shapes in lead foil, or to the plain glass areas left after the rest of the sign has been painted. In the last situation the areas left for gilding may have been either cut in with a sable brush, or foiled and painted over and the foil lifted.

Directly to Undecorated or Acid Etched Glass

This method takes the most time. It may be used where the decoration or lettering is entirely in gold without any painting involved at all.

Glass position
When gilding on site there is no control over the angle that the glass should be to obtain the best effect. When gilding in the workshop the glass should be either blocked up with a piece of wood about 50 mm thick so that it has a slight slope or is laid flat on the bench. Gilders work in either way depending on their preference. Some prefer the size to be running when the gold is laid on it, others prefer it to be still so that the gold floats out flat.

The size container with the mop in it or resting over the top should be placed as close as possible to the glass and on the side opposite to the hand which is holding the cushion.

The cushion, tip and knife are held in one hand and as close as possible to the glass so that the gold has to be carried the shortest distance on the tip. The book of gold is best kept in the cushion and leaves drawn out as required rather than laying it on the bench where it may be wetted by the size and become useless. Experienced gilders will tip a number of leaves onto the cushion and draw forward one leaf at a time.

Doors and windows must be closed to reduce draughts to a minimum otherwise the gold will be disturbed and may be impossible to control or lay flat. The gilder must move as little as possible throughout the process and then very slowly to avoid causing draughts which will disturb the gold.

Laying the gold
The gold leaf is layed to overlap completely the area to be gilded. If the glass is plain the drawing of the design or lettering is fixed to the face of the glass so that the gilded areas can be clearly seen. If the glass has been etched the gilded areas will be identified by the texture of the stippling or toning.

Size is taken up with the mop and flooded onto the glass so that the whole area to be gilded is wet with size, see fig. 10.9a. If the size cisses — does not wet the glass and rolls up into little balls — it is an indication that the glass is greasy and will need to be wiped over with a clean damp chamois leather until the size thoroughly wets the glass.

The gold has to be laid onto the sized glass in pieces as big as possible, without creases, and to overhang the extremities of the required gilded areas, see fig. 10.9b. If the area is big enough whole sheets can be laid. For smaller areas the leaf must be cut into convenient size pieces.

The leaf is cut and picked up with the tip in exactly the same way as described for tip and cushion gilding in chapter 9. The process is continued until the whole area is covered. The top of the glass should be gilded first so that size does not run over recently applied gold and mark it. Dry areas of gold can be protected from flowing size, which leaves streaks, by careful use of blotting paper or a chamois leather.

Although some creases flatten out as the size dries any very creased leaf should be wiped off and regilded, because they will be rubbed off when burnished leaving large bare places.

Once the gold has been snatched onto the size it cannot be touched again without damage. If a piece is considerably out of position it may be manoeuvred back by tipping the glass slightly so that the leaf floats into the place it should be.

At no time must the tip touch the size otherwise it will become so sticky that it will not release the gold. If this happens the tip needs to be rinsed in warm water and thoroughly dried.

Burnishing
When the entire area is gilded the surplus size needs to be removed so that the gold can dry. Large sheets of blotting paper laid carefully over the gold and gently rubbed with the hand is one method, see fig. 10.9c. Not only does this quickly absorb the size it pushes all the gold into

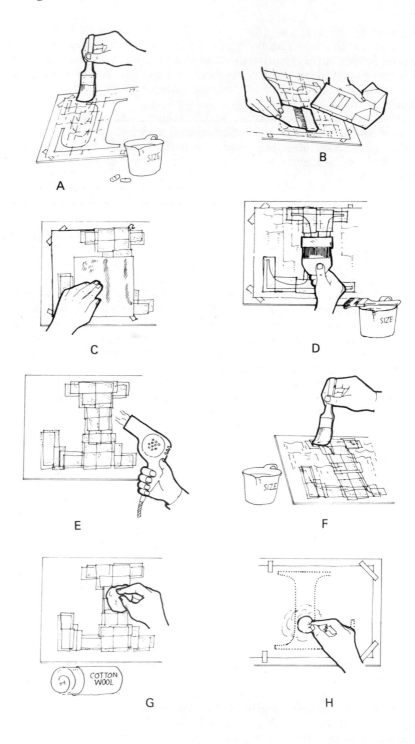

Fig. 10.9 Processes in glass gilding a letter without a painted outline

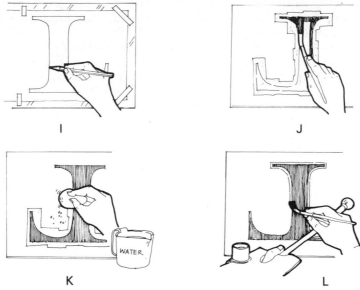

Fig. 10.9

tight contact with the glass. Another method is to dab over the gold with a pad of damp chamois leather.

If the dried glass is placed upright and a mild heat from a fan heater directed at it the gold will slowly take on a full sheen. When all the dullness has gone the gold should be dry enough to burnish. This is done with a soft pad of cotton wool lightly rubbed over the gold in a circular motion, see fig. 10.9g. Its first action will be to remove surplus pieces of gold which will float away, and as the process continues the joins between the pieces will disappear and the gold will become brighter.

During the burnishing small pieces of surplus gold may roll up into tiny fragments which could scratch the laid gold. To avoid this the cotton wool pad must be changed regularly.

Any bad areas of gilding show up at this stage and should be regilded. These are places where the gold has been laid so unevenly that most of it will be rubbed off when gilded. It is better to clean these areas with a damp piece of cotton wool before regilding. Although only small areas are to be gilded the whole area should be sized otherwise it will run over dry areas and leave streaks in the gold. If the glass cannot be laid flat the size should be laid in from the bottom up so that it does not run down and mark the dry gold.

After blotting, drying and burnishing the whole gilded area is coated with fresh warm size. The size should be laid in from the bottom in single, overlapping, horizontal strokes, then left to dry. Upon drying the gold will again return to its bright state.

Double gilding
Even after careful gilding and faulting the chance of small misses in

the gold is highly likely. Touching these in with small pieces of gold is not always successfull and a much better finish is achieved if the whole area is regilded or double gilded, see fig. 10.9d.

The process is carried out in the same way as the first coat except that the size should be applied with care so as not to disturb the first layer. Laying the glass flat at this stage prevents the size causing streaks as it runs. If *in situ* the size is best laid from the bottom up.

After the double gilding has been dried (see fig. 10.9e) and burnished to remove the surplus gold, it should be coated all over with warm size, see fig. 10.9f. This coat helps to bind the gold and allow the burnishing process to be carried out with considerable pressure without disturbing the gold.

Some gilders use a damp chamois leather to produce a high sheen after the size coat has been applied and allowed to dry. It is used either as a hard dabbing process or as a kind of whip to flog the gold.

Two or three coats of warm size can be applied, burnishing every time when the size is dry, until a very even brilliant burnish is obtained.

Scalding

This is a process of pouring very hot water over the gilded work as a very last process, which, when dry, leaves the gold very bright. It is more a process that is spoken about than carried out. Even in 1880 a writer on glass gilding condemned the process as being dangerous because making the glass hot could cause it to crack.

Before backing up the gold must be left to dry thoroughly. It is safer to leave it overnight.

Backing up and skewing off

After the gilding the gold will look lustrous from the front, but will not be in the shape required because of the way that the pieces of gold have been laid to overlap the design or lettering. To shape the gilded area the design or lettering has to be painted very precisely on the back of the gold and when dry the surplus gold around the shapes can be washed off. This is sometimes called skewing.

If the glass had been acid etched the shape of the design will be easily seen in the gold. When only the gold is on the glass it is necessary to remove the drawing from the front and transfer the design to the gold, see fig. 10.9i. This is most safely done by converting the drawing into a pounce (fig. 10.9h), see chapter 8. The shapes, now clearly marked on the gold, can be painted with a sable pencil using the normal signwriting technique, see fig. 10.9j.

The traditional material for backing up was Black Japan, mainly because it contained no oil which might have dulled the gold. This material is rarely used now and a signwriters tube colour, preferably in yellow or gold colour, is ideal for the job. If there are any tiny holes in the gold they are less likely to show up when backed with yellow. Gold sizes and bronze powder can be used but is not so easy to brush. The signwriting must be carried out with great care for the finished job will be as good only as the backing up.

When the backing is completely dry the surplus gold around can be removed with a piece of damp cotton wool, see fig. 10.9k. If the gelatine size is too strong the removal of the surplus gold will be very difficult. In these circumstances the rubbing must be done with great patience to avoid disturbing the backing or breaking the edge of the gold.

Pencil varnishing
If the glass behind the gold areas is not to be painted the gilded design or lettering needs a further coating to protect it from glass cleaners during its life. A clear oil varnish is applied all over the backing and onto the glass about 2 mm thick so that all gilded areas have a thin varnish halo around them, see fig. 10.9l. This varnish will not be seen when viewed from about 2 m distance.

Gilding with Lead Foil

A very common practice of glass gilding is to cut out the shapes to be gilded from lead foil in the same way as described earlier in this chapter. By using this method cutting in the backing is not necessary, and generally the cut line of the foil is sharper than the brushed line. In all other ways the gilding process follows exactly the method described before. It is essential that the foil is adhered with gelatine, not petroleum jelly. The backing should be signwriters colour and more reliable results are obtained when the foil is removed directly the backing colour has set.

Gilding between Painted Areas

When paint and gold are combined on a glass sign the commercial practice is to apply all the paint first, cutting in to the areas to be gilded so that plain glass sections are left when all the painting is finished, to which the gold is applied. When foil is used for glass painting the gilded areas can usually be left covered in foil until the painting is finished, when the foil can be lifted and the gaps gilded.

There is always a possibility that gelatine size will get behind the paint and lift it off. To keep this to a minimum the glass must be cleaned with infinite care and the signwriters colour mixed with gold size to give it maximum adhesive properties. The paint must be completely dry before gilding is started. This means leaving it for at least twelve hours in good drying conditions. Gilding by this method removes the need to cut in the backing coat.

If the sign shown in fig. 10.7 was to have gilded numerals with the background in black, the inner border in red, and the outer border in plain glass, a method of carrying it out would be:

Foil the whole area, cut out the shaded area behind the numerals, and paint in black. When the black is dry cut around the outer border and lift the inner one and paint over with red. There is no need to cut in the red. Once the red is dry the foil over the numerals can be lifted and the 13 gilded. The yellow backing for the gold can be applied over the entire back of the glass to produce an acceptable finish to the sign. When the outer border foil is lifted the sign is finished.

Gilding is often required between the painted outline of letters. If the background of the letters is to be plain glass the backing up must be cut in very carefully to the outline in the way described for gilding on plain glass. The letters also need pencil varnishing. An alternative method is to cut the outline from foil and paint in. When dry the letter centre can be lifted, gilded and backed up. The background foil is lifted when the backing has set.

Gilding with Other Metallic Leaves

White gold and silver leaf are commonly used on glass and both produce a lustrous effect, but rarely is it possible to completely remove the lines showing the joins between the pieces. With gold these are burnished out, but the harder silver does not respond in the same way to the polishing action. Backing for these metals should be signwriters white.

Aluminium leaf and Dutch metal also can be applied to glass and reasonable affects are obtained. The stronger size necessary to adhere them reduces the lustre and the joins will always show. Because they are available in larger sizes the leaves of these metals can be cut in bigger pieces and less joins may exist to spoil the effect.

Matt Gold

Anything painted or etched onto the glass between the gold and the viewer will destroy the burnish of the metal. The most common method of producing matt gold is to gild over acid etched stipple or toning. A cheaper method is to paint the area to be gilded with clear varnish or gold size first. When the coating has dried it can be gilded and the gold will be without a burnish on these areas. The varnish can be textured by scratching the film with the end of a brush handle when it has set. Careful texturing can produce a texture very similar to acid stipple.

Matt gold is most attractively used when it is contrasted with burnished gold. The sign shown in fig. 10.7 could be produced entirely in gold and still retain its legibility. If the 13 and the inner border were acid stippled or varnished and the whole sign gilded the numerals would show up as matt against a burnish background and the inner border would show matt between a burnish inner panel and outer border.

Tinted varnishes and translucent enamels also create interesting decorative treatments. They are often used to produce blended effects over gold and silver leaf. Burnt sienna oil colour mixed with varnish is a traditional colour for shading on gold. A greater range of colours can be used on silver or aluminium leaf particularly on decorative letters which have been blocked and shaded, similar to those traditionally used on fairground lettering.

Making a Silver Steel Cutter

Most glass decorators and many screen printers make their own cutters from silver steel rod, see fig. 10.3. The rod, which is high carbon steel, can be purchased from any metal suppliers. It is available in many diameters, but the most useful ones for making into cutters are 4.75 mm or 6.25 mm. The choice is personal and can be selected by rolling a piece of each rod around between the thumb and forefinger and choosing the most comfortable one. The length of the rod needs to be about 160 mm. It will be about the length and diameter of a pencil.

The first process is to make about 30–40 mm of one end red hot in a gas flame, see fig. 10.10a. The rest of the rod will get hot also so it must be held in a pair of pliers or an insulated glove. When cool the rod will be softer and can be ground down to a flat edge. The grinding can be done on a grinding wheel (see fig. 10.10b), on a coarse oil stone, or put in a vice and filed. The tapered shape should be about 15–20 mm long.

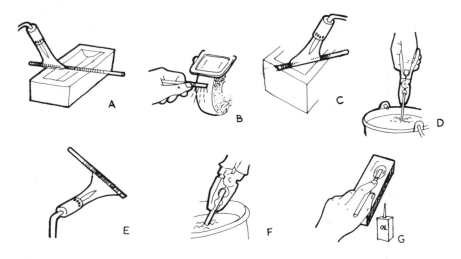

Fig. 10.10 Processes in the making of a silver steel cutter

The tapered end needs to be made red hot again (see fig. 10.10c) and plunged immediately into cold water (see fig. 10.10d) which will harden the metal again. It now needs to be tempered. This is done by holding the part of the rod just beyond the taper in a flame until that part gets red hot, see fig. 10.10e. Without moving the rod the heat will pass along the rod to the tip and as it travels it will change colour. When the cutter part is a rich straw colour it is plunged into cold water, see fig. 10.10f. The cutter is now ready to be sharpened to a fine edge on an oil stone, see fig. 10.10g. A coarse stone first followed by a fine stone is usually necessary.

The tempering process is very critical and may have to be redone a number of times before the right hardness is obtained. If the metal is too soft the fine edge will burr over when used to cut on glass and will need to be heated a little more at the tempering stage. If too hard it may scratch the glass or break off in which case it needs to be made red hot, cooled, and tempered for a little less time.

If the cutter is not comfortable tape can be rolled around it to make a thicker and more easily held grip.

Eleven
Screenprinting

Before the 1930s the only method of reproducing repeat signs quickly was by stencilling. This consisted of cutting letter shapes from card, paper or thin metal through which paint was brushed, sprayed or dabbed.

Stencilling had serious restrictions. Letters or logos had to be specially designed to include ties that both held letter centres in place and gave stability to the stencil plates, see fig. 11.1. Although careful techniques of applying the paint could be mastered to obtain reasonably clean edges, at no time could the finish of stencilled letters be favourably compared with printed or signwritten letters.

Fig. 11.1   Lettering designed with ties suitable for stencilling

Stencils are used where the finish of the sign is not important and where unskilled persons may be employed to produce them. Identifying crates when leaving factories or before shipment is a common use of stencilling.

When stencils are required they can be cut from card or oiled paper using a trimming knife or scalpel. Either entire signs are cut from one sheet or individual letters are cut and fixed together to form a text. Individual letters and numerals can be purchased cut from thin gauge zinc which are shaped so that they can be clipped together to form words.

Screenprinting
Since the 1950s screenprinting has become the most effective method of producing repeat signs of high quality.

This process has developed from stencilling and has overcome all the limitations of the original process. It reproduces signs very quickly, to a high degree of finish, and letters do not need ties.

Apart from printing signs the process has been adapted to printing posters, advertising placards, transfers, labels, wallpapers and fabrics. Under carefully controlled conditions screenprinting is sufficiently accurate for printed circuitry. Many signmakers have adpated the system to speed up the process of glasswriting and decorating. Letter outlines can be screened, intricate designs can be printed in resist before acid etching, and a special screen ink containing an acid can be applied to glass to produce a form of toning.

Many firms specialise in screenprinting. Some retain the simple hand operations printing at the rate of about 100 an hour, where others use automatic machines to print thousands of copies an hour. Regardless of the way that screenprinting has developed it remains basically a simple system that can be used by many small sign firms to produce repeat signs in one or two colours. Often it is more economic to print six or more identical signs than to signwrite them.

The Basic System and Equipment

Screenprinting requires a rigid wood or metal frame, tightly covered with a strong fine mesh material to which is attached a 'stencil'. Paint is squeezed through the open areas of the stencil to produce a clean and opaque sign.

Effective screenprinting can be carried out in a reasonably small space with the following simple equipment.

Printing Frames

Frames made from angle iron or extruded aluminium section are used by some of the large specialist screenprinters but the majority of printing is done with timber frames.

The essential qualities of a timber printing frame are that the wood is sufficiently thick not to bend, that the angles are jointed and not just nailed or screwed, and that it is truly square in each angle. Once made the printing frame can be used many, many times, therefore it is essential that it is made properly and of a size which can be adapted to most of the common size signs which may need to be printed. A convenient size may be 500×600 or 700 mm. This size frame will need to be made from 50×50 mm softwood with the angles mitred and dowelled or bridle jointed. A frame of this size will conveniently print any sign up to 400×500 or 600 mm. A simple frame can be made by cutting a square hole out of a piece of 15–20 mm thick plywood.

Support

The support is the material which is stretched across the printing frame and to which the stencil is adhered. This can be the most expensive item. A frame stretched with a quality material can be used for many stencils before it becomes too slack, or torn, or blocked and needs to be replaced.

Organdie
This is the cheapest and least effective support. It is rarely used commercially, except for short print runs of one colour which do not require a very precise finish. Organdie is a useful support for the beginner.

Organdies made from man-made fibres are very strong but can be difficult to fix some stencils to. The most convenient grade is cotton organdie and some suppliers offer a special grade for screenprinting. Some screenprinting suppliers do not stock organdie, but it can be obtained from most stores which sell curtain materials.

It is coarser than the other supports therefore it is not successful for producing fine detail or very clean printing. An organdie screen can be used for about fifty printings but after that it can become very slack or it may tear.

Silk or bolting cloth
Silk was the original material used as a support. Although the process is still widely referred to as silk screen printing, silk is rarely used now. Many suppliers do not stock silk.

Synthetic fabrics
The most common supports are nylon or polyester (Terylene). Of these two polyester is most favoured because it does not stretch so readily. It can be obtained as a monofilament where each thread of the material is of one piece, or multifilament in which each thread is made from a number of very fine strands twisted together. The monofilament is most commonly used for signwork because it is more easily cleaned.

The materials are available in three qualities and in a large range of mesh sizes. The heaviest quality is marked HD for heavy duty. T is a finer thread, and S is finer still. For screens which will be used and cleaned off many times an HD material should be used.

The mesh sizes refer to the number of threads per centimetre. The lower numbers have less threads and allow a lot of paint through. The higher numbers have more threads and let less paint through. It is essential to use the right grade of material for the job otherwise the quality of the printing will suffer.

For printing on fabrics a wide mesh is necessary and a mesh between 34 and 49 will be suitable. For the signmaker who is planning to use hand cut stencils only an HD fabric between 62 and 77 will give best results.

Photostencils are used when finer detail is involved and more precise printing is required and for this a higher numbered fabric is necessary. For the signmaker who intends to use photostencils a 90 fabric will give good results.

The materials are available in a range of widths between 1 m and 2 m.

Stainless steel mesh
Steel meshes are used principally for power driven printing and very rarely by the signmaker.

Stencil

The stencil blots out the areas of the support so that only the letters or logo are printed, see fig. 11.2.

Fig. 11.2 A screen stencil mounted ready for use

The earliest stencils were cut from paper and adhered to the support with glue or paint. Modern stencils are either duplex films for hand cutting, or photosensitive films or coatings for photostencils. Handcut stencils can be prepared in most workshops without the need of any special equipment, but photostencils need both equipment and preparation areas not normally found in a sign workshop.

Handcut
These are either duplex papers or coated films, which are available in sheets or rolls and sometimes referred to as Stemplex papers.

Duplex papers are thin coatings applied to a waxed transparent backing paper. The lettering or logo for the sign is cut from the coating and the backing paper holds it together until the coated side is adhered to the support when the backing is peeled off. There are two main types. Greenfilm is most suitable for synthetic fabrics. It can be used with all types of spirit thinned inks, but not for water based inks.

Amberfilm or profilm is most suitable for organdie or silk. It can be used on synthetic fabrics which have been used before or have been thoroughly prepared if new. They adhere best to multifilament fabrics. They can be used with all white spirit thinned inks but not with any ink that is thinned with methylated spirit. Amberfilm can be used for short runs of water thinned colour.

Coated films consist of a soluble plastic coating applied to a clear acetate film. They are more expensive than duplex papers but can be applied to any support and used with any type of ink.

Photostencils
These can be direct, indirect, or direct/indirect.

Direct stencils are coatings which are applied to the screen. Indirect are coated films which are applied to the screen. Direct/indirect combine both processes to produce well adhered stencils, mainly for long print runs.

The principle of the photostencil is similar to photographic printing. A photosensitive material is used which when exposed to light becomes insoluble in water whilst unexposed areas remain soluble. The direct coating and the indirect coating on the film are photosensitive material. The lettering which is to be made into a printing screen is painted onto a transparent film or paper and placed over the photosensitive material. When a strong light is directed at it the parts protected by the painted letter remain soluble but the rest of the coating becomes hard. After exposure the soluble part is dissolved with water leaving the lettering as a stencil and the background masked by the hardened emulsion.

Other equipment required for photostencilling
Photostencilling needs an ultra-violet lamp to produce the light source
to harden the photosensitive emulsion. Commercial lamps are available,
but can be very expensive. A small light box can be made using
minimum equipment and is suitable for making stencils for small and
simple signs, see fig. 11.3.

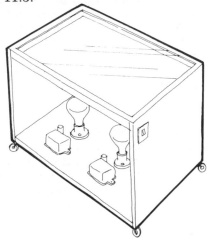

Fig. 11.3 A light box adapted with a glass top so that it doubles as a tracing table

Some means of washing screens after exposure is necessary for
photostencils. This can be done in a large sink using a rubber handheld
spray that can be pushed on to tap ends. Alternatively the screens can
be taken outside and hosed down with a fine spray.

Another problem with photostencil preparation is obtaining a good
contact between the artwork and the coated screen or film. If they are
not in very tight contact when exposed to the light some distortion may
occur.

For simple signs containing letters of 50 mm high or bigger a good
enough contact can be obtained by pressing the two materials between
two pieces of glass. This is a convenient method when using indirect
film, but is not so easy to adapt to direct coated screens.

Professional screenprinters use vacuum pumps to get good contact.
One of the common pieces of equipment for this holds the artwork and
screen beneath a rubber cover and sucks all the air out until they are
in very tight contact. The cover is situated over the light source and
when all the air is removed the light is switched on and the stencil is
exposed. These machines are very expensive and not a good investment
for the signmaker who will make photostencils occasionally. A cheaper
method is to use water pressure to create a vacuum. Screen suppliers
sell a special plastic bag in which the artwork and coated screen or
indirect film are placed. The bag is sealed and a connection is made
from a vacuum pump on top of the bag to a tap. When the tap is run the
water pressure operates the vacuum pump which sucks all the air out

of the bag and the artwork is drawn into tight contact with the photostencil. While still in the bag the stencil is exposed to the light. These vacuum pumps require a minimum water pressure to be effective and it is necessary to check the pressure of the available tap before investing in a vacuum bag.

Printing benches
Benches can be purchased upon which to mount screens and print the signs. They are available in many sizes and varying degrees of sophistication. They work on the common principle of a counterweighted hinged frame on a flat bench. The prepared screen is fitted into or onto the frame and the signs to be printed are laid on the bed. Some beds are perforated and have a vacuum pump beneath which, when operated, holds paper or card tight to the bench so that they are not picked up by the screen after printing. These benches are expensive, and are not essential to the occasional screen printer.

Any flat bench can be adapted for printing, see fig. 11.4. The screen needs to be hinged with 75 mm or 100 mm butts, and screwed to a stout batten bolted or clamped to the bench. If paper, card or thin hardboard signs are being printed small pieces of double-sided masking tape fixed on the bench approximately in the corner position of the signs will hold them in place when the screen is lifted after every pull. This is a cheaper method than investing in a vacuum bed.

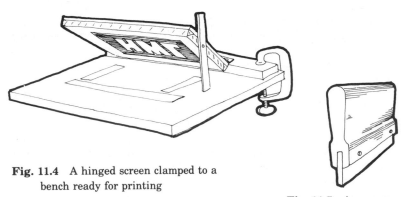

Fig. 11.4 A hinged screen clamped to a bench ready for printing

Fig. 11.5 A squeegee

Squeegee
The tool used to push the screen ink through the stencil is called a squeegee. It consists of a rubber or plastic strip about 12 mm thick and 50 mm wide. The strip is clamped into a wooden handle which can be any length providing it is shorter than the inside width of the screen. Squeegees can be purchased ready made or the rubber or plastic strip can be purchased and fitted between two pieces of wood which make the handle. A nail needs to be tapped into each end which will support the squeegee when it is not being used to stop it falling into the ink. See fig. 11.5.

Preparing a Screen

Expensive equipment is available which will stretch the material over a frame. Some use hydraulic pumps, others work on a simple screw basis which grip and pull the material. This type of equipment is essential for producing screens which are to be used for very precise printing, or are to be used many thousands of times, or in automatic printing machines. They are not essential for making screens to print simple signs. There are many firms which will stretch frames using mechanical equipment and fix the material to the top edge with resin so that no pins are used and the screen edges are free from material. These firms will also prepare a photostencil from supplied artwork and many screen printers find it more economical to subcontract this part of the work rather than purchase the stretching or exposing equipment.

The signmaker who needs to screenprint on the odd occasion will probably find that hand stretching is both effective and economical

To hand stretch a frame the following are required.

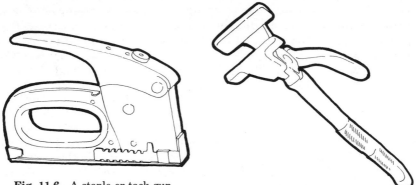

Fig. 11.6   A staple or tack gun

Fig. 11.7   Stretching pliers

(1) Either a staple gun (fig. 11.6) or stapler or a pin hammer and 10 mm tacks.
(2) Strips of card about 25 mm wide and as long as the sides of the frame.
(3) Stretching pliers, see fig. 11.7. These can be obtained from screen suppliers and are similar to engineers pliers but the jaws are about 50 mm wide and amply covered in plastic.

Before starting to fix the material the frame must be carefully rubbed over with a piece of glasspaper to remove any rough edges, splinters, or sharp arrises. Failure to do this could cause the material to tear or ladder as tension is applied.

Stretching man-made fabric
Lay the fabric on a bench, place the frame on top and cut the fabric about 50 mm bigger all round.

Stand the frame on end, double over one edge of the fabric, position it centrally along the top edge of the frame, place a strip of card on top and tack it in the centre. Pull the fabric to the end of the frame and tack along the length keeping the tension by pulling the material with the non-tacking hand. Complete the other half of the top edge so that the fabric has tacks about every 30 mm, which go through the card and a double thickness of fabric. See fig. 11.8.

Fig. 11.8   Stretching and tacking fabric to a screen

Stand the screen on the tacked end and doubling over the fabric stretch it to the opposite edge. Keeping the tension with one hand draw a pencil line on the fabric with the other hand about 50 mm away from the top edge. Grip the centre of the doubled thickness of fabric with the stretching pliers and using the top of the frame as a fulcrum stretch the fabric tightly. Keeping the tension and checking that the fabric threads are straight, place a card strip along the frame edge and put two or three tacks in the centre. Pull the fabric to one corner and stretch it with the pliers. Before tacking check that the material has been evenly stretched by comparing the distance of the pencil mark from the centre and the corner. When the mark is parallel with the edge tack along the edge, keeping the tension towards the corners as well as across the screen. Pull towards the other corner, stretch, compare pencil line, and tack.

The other two sides are marked, stretched and tacked in the same way.

When complete the screen should be drum tight, and the fabric threads running parallel with the frame sides. If there is undue slackness, or ripples in the fabric, two sides should be untacked and restretched.

An additional tightness can be obtained by pressing pieces of 3 mm or 4 mm thick wood lathes in the gap between the fabric and the top of the frame. The lathes must be very carefully glasspapered to make them absolutely smooth and the ends should be rounded off so that they do not tear the fabric.

At the corners where the fabric is inclined to bunch it can be trimmed off with scissors and the ends tacked down.

Organdie stretching
Organdie is not strong enough to withstand the tension created by the stretching pliers. When using organdie as a support only hand pressure can be safely used to obtain a taut cover. It may be necessary to insert thicker or more lathes to make organdie tight enough for reasonably accurate printing.

Degreasing stretched screens

Organdie and silk supports need no pretreatment before profilm stencils are applied.

Synthetic fabrics do not offer a good surface to apply hand cut or photostencils and must be thoroughly pretreated, otherwise the stencils will not adhere or will come off prematurely.

There are four pretreatments which can be used.

(1) Apply a weak solution of caustic soda made from 50 g of caustic soda crystals dissolved in 1 litre of hot water. A small amount of cold water paste thickens the solution and holds it on the screen. The screen needs to be coated on both sides and left for about 30 min. When the soda has been thoroughly rinsed off with running water, the screen needs to be scoured with pumice powder or household scouring powder to slightly roughen the fabric to help the stencil adhere. The powder must be thoroughly rinsed off.
Caustic soda is very corrosive and must be used with exceptional care. Hands must be protected with rubber gauntlets, eyes protected with goggles, and the rest of the body covered with a plastic apron and rubber boots.

(2) A proprietary cleaner based on caustic can be obtained from some screen material suppliers. It is used in the same way as described above and the same protective gear must be worn.

(3) A proprietary cleaner which does not contain caustic. This contains a degreasing agent and a slight abrasive. It is applied and allowed to soak for a period, then thoroughly scrubbed before being rinsed off.

(4) A proprietary cleanser based on emulsions which is available from screen material suppliers. The cleanser contains a degreaser which when left on the fabric for a period dissolves all the contaminants and can be washed off with water. Unlike the other three this cleanser can be safely used on silk.

Preparing Working Drawings and Artwork

A separate screen is required for each colour to be printed on the sign. Therefore for a two colour sign two screens are required, each one holding a stencil which will print its part of the sign. Whatever type of screen is being used a detailed working drawing must be prepared. If hand cut stencils are being used they can be produced from the working drawing regardless of the number of colours involved. For photostencils separate artwork must be prepared from the working drawing for each colour in the sign. The quality of the finished sign is dependent entirely upon the accuracy of the working drawing and the artwork.

Working drawing
The working drawing needs to be finished in outline only, and the suggestions on styles, spacing, layout and drawing described in earlier sections apply equally for screenprinting. They can be prepared on any good quality drawing paper.

Artwork
Whereas working drawings are full size precise line drawings, artwork is prepared in solid colour. It may be the letters or logo which are solid if they are the part of the design which is to be printed. If the letters or logo are to be left in the sign's original colour then the space around them will be made solid on the artwork. When the letters are solid it is called a positive artwork, and when the background is solid it is known as a negative.

Artwork for photostencils needs to be done on acetate sheet or a special tracing film prepared for this purpose and available from screen material suppliers. It has one slightly roughened face which allows for easier drawing and painting. Some tracing papers can be used but they should be tested before use. The inappropriate papers will wrinkle when painted on or they will not allow light to pass through them adequately.

Dry transfer letters can be used or the letters can be painted on using a water thinned opaque paint which can be obtained from most art shops. Drawing ink is not always successful. It is quite thin and light may pass through it.

When painting the letters the transparent film or paper needs to be fixed on top of the working drawing and the letters or background signwritten exactly to the sample beneath.

Dry transfer letters
Dry transfer letters can be purchased in a wide range of typefaces and each typeface is available in a number of height sizes. The letters are screened in reverse onto a clear plastic sheet and the backs coated with an adhesive. The sheets are manoeuvred until the letter needed is

Fig. 11.9   Applying dry transfer letters

exactly placed on the artwork film. When the plastic sheet is lightly rubbed with a hard smooth object the letter is transferred to the film, see fig. 11.9. One letter at a time is transferred and care must be taken to place the letters accurately to obtain good spacing as well as correct layout. If the working drawing is placed under the artwork film the position for each letter will be clearly seen. Wrongly placed letters can be removed by carefully scratching with a sharp knife or dabbing the letter with the sticky side of a piece of self adhesive tape.

When all the letters are laid correctly the transparent backing paper, which is supplied with each sheet of letters, is laid over them and rubbed with the same hard object used to transfer the letters. This ensures a tight bond.

Manufacturers of dry transfer letters supply a special stylus for rubbing down letters, but a ball point pen or a plastic tea spoon will perform as well.

Preparing Hand Cut Stencils

The working drawing needs to be stretched onto a hard flat bench, fixed securely with masking tape, and a horizontal and vertical centre line drawn through the sign layout. A piece of stencil paper is cut the same size as the screen, or, if the screen is much bigger than the sign, it must be at least 50 mm bigger all round the extremes of the layout. This is placed over the drawing with the coated side facing up, fixed with tape and the centre lines drawn in to match those on the drawing. These lines help to check that the film has not moved and aid the fixing of the stencil in the correct position on the screen.

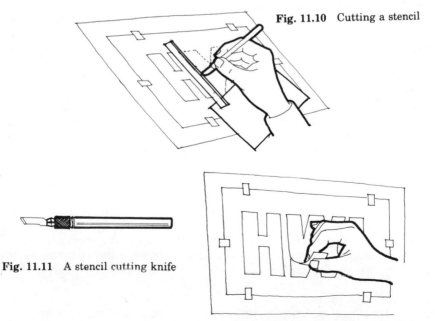

Fig. 11.10   Cutting a stencil

Fig. 11.11   A stencil cutting knife

Fig. 11.12   Peeling off cut stencil

Cutting the stencil

The knife for cutting stencils must be small and sharp. The knife made from steel rod described in chapter 10 is ideal, see fig. 11.10. Other pencil size cutters are available from art shops, see fig. 11.11. Compass cutters, rules, French curves and templates should be used wherever possible to produce a precise stencil. Slight errors in the stencil may not be noticeable until the stencil is printed. The heat and dampness of the hand may ruckle the stencil paper and to avoid this a piece of blotting or drawing paper should be placed below the cutting area upon which to rest the hand.

Sufficient pressure must be put on the knife to cut through the coloured coating film but not to cut the backing paper. If the knife is kept very sharp a light pressure only is necessary. No serious harm occurs if the backing paper is cut in a few places but if considerable cuts are made the stencil may disintegrate before it can be applied to the screen.

It is essential not to overcut at corners as these will print and spoil the precise appearance of the finished sign. Conversely it is important not to cut short of an angle so that the stencil has to be torn off leaving the corners of letters fuzzy.

When all the cutting has been completed the parts which are to be printed are lifted off. If the lettering is to be printed they are the shapes lifted out, see fig. 11.12. If the background is to be printed, then that is lifted off leaving the letters on the backing sheet. The cut parts lift off very easily once the point of the cutter is slid between the film and the backing paper.

Registering stencil and screen

Positioning the stencil accurately on the screen is important for precise printing. Generally it is easier to register a screen with the sign to be printed if the stencil is exactly central on the screen. The simplest way to ensure this is to draw horizontal and vertical centre lines on the screen with a soft pencil and line these up with the centre lines drawn on the stencil. Sometimes a large screen is used to print a small sign and a central position for the stencil can cause difficulties. In these circumstances the part in which the stencil is to be fitted should be marked on the screen and in this shape the two lines can be drawn.

The stencil is always fixed on the underside of the screen. If fixed inside where the squeegee operates it will be damaged.

A clean piece of hardboard about the same size as the screen provides a good bed to work on while mounting the stencil. The stencil cut side upwards should be fixed to this with tiny pieces of tape in each corner and the screen lowered on to it and moved around until the centre lines on the screen and those on the stencil match exactly, see fig. 11.13.

The method of adhering the stencil to the screen differs depending on the type of stencil being used.

Adhering Greenfilm

Greenfilm is water soluble, but manufacturers recommend a mixture of three parts methylated spirit and one part water to adhere it to the

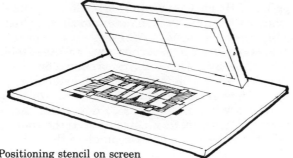

Fig. 11.13 Positioning stencil on screen

Fig. 11.14 Adhering Greenfilm

Fig. 11.15 Adhering Amberfilm

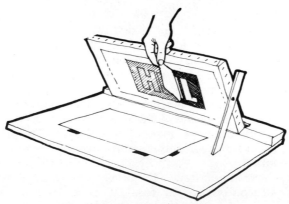

Fig. 11.16 Removing backing paper

screen. It is applied with a wad of cotton wool which has been soaked in the spirit and thoroughly squeezed out so that it is only damp. The pad is rubbed on the screen so that it penetrates through to the stencil. The work is best started in one corner and an area about 300 mm square should be done at a time. Extra pressure on the pad should release enough spirit to wet the screen and the stencil.

When the square has been treated a piece of brown packing paper should be laid over it with the shiny side down and the back of the paper ironed over with a domestic electric iron. If the thermostat is set to 'silk' the heat should be sufficient to complete the adhesion but not damage the fabric.

The colour of the film changes as it softens and adheres and when the first square has an even colour change the next section can be started and the process continued until the whole stencil is firmly adhered to the screen.

Adhering Amberfilm

Amberfilm is thermoplastic and needs the heat of the iron only to adhere it to the screen. The thermostat should be set to the same mark and a piece of brown paper needs to be used between the iron and the screen. Very little pressure is necessary and the iron needs to be kept moving. When the film has melted sufficiently it will appear much darker and when an even darker colour has been obtained over the whole stencil area the iron can be removed and the stencil left to cool. See fig. 11.5.

Adhering emulsion coated film

Coated films vary according to manufacture and it is essential to check the maker's instructions before using them. There are three common types. One needs to be sponged with water and blotted. Another requires a mixture of water and methylated spirit to be wiped over the screen and immediately dried off with a cloth. The other type is spirit soluble and has to be softened with a special solvent.

Once adhered the screens need to be dried with warm air for about 15 min.

Removing backing

When the stencilled screen is cool or dry it can be turned over and an edge of the backing sheet or film can be picked away from the stencil with a finger nail or very carefully with the point of a knife. See fig. 11.16. Once the layers are separated the backing will pull away easily leaving the coating on the screen. The backing must not be ripped off in one big motion otherwise if the stencil is not firmly adhered everywhere it will be torn. Move the backing a little at a time and if the stencil appears to move away from the screen, put back the backing, turn the frame over and treat the loose places again to make sure of good contact.

If the stencil has not adhered to the screen even after many attempts there are two alternative procedures.

(1) Tear off the loose pieces. If they are straight edges small pieces of film can be cut and used to patch up. They need to be placed with great care and ironed or dampened to get good adhesion. If the non-adhered spots are not straight edges but are small they can be touched up with water soluble screen filler. This is a heavy bodied paint which blocks out the texture of the fabric. The filler needs to be applied with a sable brush. It is only satisfactory if the areas are very small.

(2) If the non-adhering areas are extensive the entire stencil must be removed and a new one cut and adhered. Poor adhesion may be caused by inadequate preparation of the support. Therefore it is advisable to pretreat the material before refixing the stencil.

Removing stencils
Stencils may need to be removed if they have not adhered properly or are in the wrong place. They will always need to be removed after the job has been completed so that the screen is clean and ready for the next job. The method of removal depends upon the type of stencil used.

Greenfilm removal
Greenfilm is water soluble and will come away from the screen when soaked in hot water.

Amberfilm removal
Amberfilm is soluble in methylated spirit. If a large tray or dish is not available in which the screen can be immersed it is necessary to pad both sides of the screen with many thicknesses of paper or rags soaked in methylated spirit. The spirit may take half an hour to sufficiently soften the film so that it can be removed easily.

Emulsion film removal
The water soluble films come off with hot water in the same way that Greenfilm does. The spirit soluble films are softened with strong solvents such as cellulose thinners. If neither of these methods will remove the film a caustic soda solution should be tried or a special decorating material supplied by screen suppliers which generally has a caustic base. Both these materials must be used with the same precautions described when degreasing screens.

Preparing Photostencils

There are numerous types of photostencils available and each has its own characteristics. It is essential that the manufacturer's instructions are read carefully before work starts.

The basic differences between the three types of photostencils are described below.

Direct stencil
These are usually two pack materials which need to be mixed together in careful proportions before use. Once mixed they have a shelf life of

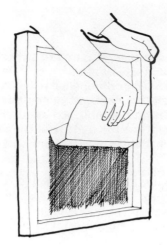

Fig. 11.17   Coating screen with trough applicator

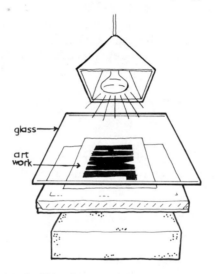

glass—

art
work—

Fig. 11.18   Exposing screen to mercury vapour light

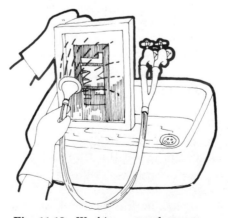

Fig. 11.19   Washing exposed screen

approximately two months providing they are tightly sealed in a light proof container. The two packs are a coloured emulsion and a sensitising material. In their mixed state they must be used in a 'safe light' only. A safe light is a weak tungsten light not exceeding 15 watt, a gold fluorescent tube, or natural light filtered through yellow lacquer or film applied to the windows. Strong blue or ultra-violet light must be avoided otherwise the material will harden or lose its light sensitivity.

The sensitised emulsion is applied to both sides of the screen and may need two or three coats. Manufacturers supply a special trough-like applicator which floods on an even coat, see fig. 11.17. Without this tool the emulsion can be applied with a squeegee or a piece of plastic or card. The screen needs to be stood in a tray with the emulsion in a wide container standing in front. The emulsion can be picked up on the squeegee and dragged up the screen. Even coats are necessary without runs or sags otherwise the thicker areas may not harden properly when exposed and will be washed off. The screen is properly coated when the mesh is filled.

When the screen is dry the artwork is placed in the exact position on the underside of the screen. Whichever method is used to ensure a tight contact between the artwork and screen is carried out at this stage. The screen is now exposed to carbon arc, mercury vapour or metal halogen light (fig. 11.18) for any time between 30 sec and 15 min depending on the type of stencil or light source, or the distance that the light is away from the screen. This information is available from the manufacturers or suppliers.

If exposure time information is not available a series of tests must be carried out to find the right time. The time is right when the exposed areas remain intact when washed and the unexposed areas wash off easily and cleanly.

After exposure the screen is washed by spraying with cold water until all the areas beneath the opaque artwork have been removed, see fig. 11.19. When it is all off the surplus water needs to be mopped up by dabbing with a chamois leather and the screen dried with warm air.

If the emulsion does not wash off it may be due to many causes. The sensitised emulsion may be too old, or been badly stored, or the coated screen exposed to daylight or bluelight during coating or storing, or the screen may have been exposed to the lamp too long.

The remedy is to remove the coating completely with a special screen cleaner obtained from the suppliers, and repeat the process with new emulsion, taking greater care to work in safe light only.

If too much emulsion washes off it may mean that it was incorrectly mixed, or that exposure was too short, or it was exposed to the wrong type of light. It may be caused also by the screen not being prepared properly before the emulsion was applied.

In these circumstances the entire emulsion must be removed, the screen degreased and the process repeated using correctly mixed sensitiser, and exposing it to the right light for the correct period.

Indirect stencil

These are films coated with a photographic emulsion. Most of them are sensitised and must be stored and used in 'safe light'. Others must be sensitised just before use, some when they are dry, others when they are wet. This type can be stored, taken out and cut in ordinary light.

The sensitising solution for the non-sensitised film can be purchased or made up by mixing three parts of a stock solution of ammonium dichromate with fifty parts of water. Just before use the mixture is doubled in volume with industrial spirit. The film can be coated by immersing it in the solution for 2 min or brushing it on with a soft brush. Details may vary with different types of films and it is essential to read manufacturer's instructions carefully before commencing any process.

Whatever type of indirect film is being used the procedure for exposing is similar, see fig. 11.20. A piece of film is cut about the size of the screen or the size of the sign if the screen is very much bigger. This is brought into tight contact with the artwork as described earlier and exposed to the light source for any period between 45 sec and 16 min depending on the type of film and the type of light. Precise instructions are supplied by the manufacturers.

After exposure the film is immersed in hardener which sets the exposed areas but leaves the unexposed areas water soluble, see fig. 11.21. The hardener can be obtained from the film suppliers or one may be made by mixing hydrogen peroxide with water. Best results are obtained if the hardener can be kept at 20°C. Immediately after hardening the film can be sprayed with 40°C water just long enough to remove the unexposed emulsion, see fig. 11.22. Excess washing may prevent good adhesion to the screen. The first process in fixing the stencil to the screen is to lay the film face down in the exact position on the underside of the screen and blot off surplus water. The screen and film is then turned over onto a piece of hardboard just a fraction smaller than the inside size of the frame. When weights are placed on the edge of the screen the film will be in close contact with the screen. The stencil adheres to the screen because of the gelatine content of the emulsion. To ensure good adhesion a piece of absorbent paper is laid on the screen and gently rolled with a rubber roller, see fig. 11.23. This both absorbs excess moisture and pulls the gelatine into the fabric. Finally the area needs to be dabbed dry with a moist clean wash leather.

The screen can be dried with a fan heater then the backing film can be gently peeled off, see fig. 11.24.

The advantage of indirect over direct stencil is that if the exposure is unsuccessful another piece of film can be used whereas a poor direct stencil will have to be stripped off. Indirect stencils can be removed more easily which is a great advantage if one screen has to be used a number of times.

Direct/indirect stencil

This requires the screen to be coated and then a film applied to it. It produces a thicker film, better definition and a longer lasting stencil for long runs. The extra cost and processes involved do not make this

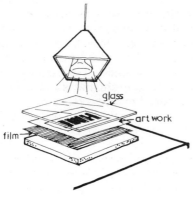

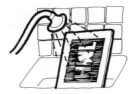

Fig. 11.21 Exposed film immersed in hardener

Fig. 11.20 Exposing film

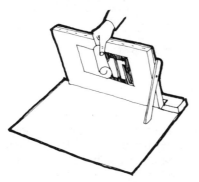

Fig. 11.22
Washing to remove unhardened emulsion

Fig. 11.23 Adhering screen to film

Fig. 11.24 Peeling off backing

Fig. 11.25 Applying screen filler around stencil

type of stencil an economic proposition for the small sign producer.

Masking Screens

After the stencil is mounted it is necessary to block out any open areas of screen outside the stencil so that paint only goes through open shapes in the stencil.

This is not necessary if the stencil is the full size of the screen. But if the screen is very much bigger than the sign this method can be expensive in stencil film. It is also difficult to get the stencil film to adhere tightly right up to the frame, particularly when using hand cut stencils.

The simplest method is to coat the screen with screen filler, see fig. 11.25. This can be obtained from screen suppliers. It is usually strongly coloured and water soluble. It is quite a viscous material and can be more easily applied with a squeegee or a piece of plastic with a straight, but not sharp, edge. The filler blocks up the holes in the fabric and any places in which this has not occured must be touched up. The stencil should be inspected carefully at the same time and if it contains any small holes these can be touched up with the filler. Small holes are more likely to occur with photostencils.

Another method is to cover the open screen with gummed paper strip. This is suitable for short runs and when very little of the screen needs covering. The paper must not be too close to the printing area otherwise the squeegee will ride on it and not make good contact with the fabric, resulting in a poor print.

Finally the gap between the frame and the fabric must be sealed. This can be done with wide masking tape or 50 mm or 75 mm wide gummed paper strip. A good contact must be made with the fabric all round with no gaps otherwise ink will squeeze through and mark the sign.

Printing

There is no standard way of screen printing. The right method is the one which prints each sign accurately and cleanly, and with the minimum of movement of screen, signs and personnel.

The method described below is one way which the occasional printer of small signs for short runs can adopt or adapt to the conditions in a workshop, providing that no special screen printing bench or unit is available.

Bench and screen

A flat topped, sturdy bench is necessary that is wider than the screen by at least 30 mm. To the back of the bench a stout block of wood should be screwed or clamped to which the screen is hinged. The block needs to be as wide as the screen and as high as the thickness of the screen, see fig. 11.4. If the signs to be printed are thicker than paper the block must be packed with the same material so that its top edge is flush with the screen resting on one of the signs.

When two 75 mm hinges are screwed into the top of the screen and the top of the block the screen will be easily raised to allow the signs to be placed beneath for printing. The hinges need to be of stout design and tightly fixed so that there is no lateral movement of the screen and it will drop into the same position after each raise.

A piece of wood lathe about 300 mm long can be fixed with one nail at one end into the left or right hand side of the screen so that it can be swivelled. This is used to support the screen in a raised position so that both hands are free to remove the printed sign and to place the next sign. When it is swivelled back the screen will be lowered back into its exact printing position.

Registering
The exact position for the signs to be placed under the screen must be marked so that every printing is in precisely the right place. This position can be most easily found by marking a horizontal and vertical line on one of the signs and sliding it under the screen until its lines exactly match those on the stencil. If the text is not to be precisely in the centre of the sign the horizontal line needs to be redrawn above the centre line by the amount that the bottom margin needs to be bigger than the top.

When the sign is in position, the screen can be raised and fixed by its support and masking tape fixed to the bench top around the outside of the sign. This will mark the spot within which all signs to be printed are to be placed. If the sign is very thick it may be advisable to fix two or three thicknesses of tape to make it easier to slip the sign into position. Small pieces of double sided tape can be fixed inside these register marks to hold paper or card signs so that they are not picked up when the screen is raised.

Distance pieces
The screen should not touch the sign when it is lowered ready for printing. There should be a gap of 2 mm or 3 mm between the fabric and the sign face. Then when the squeegee has been pulled across to push the fabric in contact with the sign and to deposit the colour the fabric will spring back into its original position away from the sign. If it remains in contact it will cause the sign to stick to the screen, and when pulled off the paint may smudge or have an uneven texture.

The gap can be achieved by stapling two or three thicknesses of card about 30 mm square to the underside of the front corners of the screen.

Preparing ink
If the sign to be pritned is either paper, card or emulsion painted the most suitable type of ink is one which is thinned with white spirit and dries to a matt film. For any other type of painted sign an enamel base ink is necessary. Whichever type is used they must be thoroughly stirred before they are placed on the screen.

The ink is either poured or applied with a palette knife inside the back edge of the screen, in a long thick puddle which is just wider than the stencil, but away from the stencil area.

Printing
A squeegee is required which is just a little wider than the stencil area. Because screen ink is quite viscous it is necessary to work it into a smooth and liquid state before printing by working the squeegee blade back and forwards in the paint a few times.

A couple of trial prints should be produced to make sure that the screen and ink are working properly. These can be done on paper which has been cut to the size of the signs and placed in the register marks.

The printing technique is to hold the squeegee in both hands with the fingers down the back and the thumbs to the front. The squeegee needs to be almost upright. A considerable amount of pressure needs to be put on the squeegee so that the fabric is pushed into tight contact with the sign and then it is pulled towards the front edge, see fig. 11.26. Equal pressure must be applied throughout the whole pull. When the squeegee has been returned to the back of the screen and rested on its nails protruding from both sides of the handle the screen can be lifted and secured on its stay. The print can then be inspected and adjustments made if there are faults.

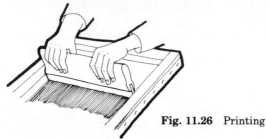

Fig. 11.26 Printing

If there are misses in the print it may be that the ink is too thick and needs to be slightly thinned, or that insufficient pressure has been applied to the squeegee. If paint is getting through the stencil in places where it is not supposed to, check for holes or loose stencil on the underside of the screen and touch them in with screen filler. If the print is not in the right place adjust the registration marks. If the screen does not immediately spring off the sign after printing increase the thickness of the distance pieces.

When corrections have been made a couple more trial prints should be made and if these are clean, even and correctly positioned the signs can be printed.

It may be necessary to do two pulls on each sign to obtain a truly opaque print. This can be done by pulling the squeegee for the first one and pushing it back for the second. A better print is usually obtained if two people stand either end of the screen and one pulls down and the other pulls back.

Fig. 11.27 A rack which takes many signs without taking up much floor space

Racking
Even when printing only a few signs the problem of placing them after printing so that they can dry without becoming damaged can cause

many difficulties. A close empty bench can be used but if the signs are about 500 mm wide a bench can be quickly filled. It is essential that facilities for storing the wet prints are organised before printing starts.

Production printers use racks which can hold up to 100 prints in a unit which takes up very little floor space, see fig. 11.27. These can prove too expensive for the signmaker who rarely has long runs.

Paper signs can be pegged on a line and hardboard signs can be leant against a wall but card signs usually need to be laid flat and are more of a problem. A simple method of racking is to pin thin wood lathes opposite each other on the inside of an old cupboard and suspend hardboard shelves between them. The shelves need only be 30 mm apart and many signs can be racked in a small cupboard. Another simple method is shown in fig. 11.28.

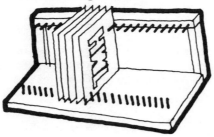

Fig. 11.28 A simple form of racking

During printing
Screens can block up during printing, particularly when using the quicker drying inks. There are methods and materials available which can reduce this problem. If the printing is maintained at a brisk pace, with only a few seconds delay between printings, there is less chance of blocking.

A method used by some experienced printers is to apply a heavy coating over the screen after it has been lifted. The thick film of ink is less likely to dry and when the screen is re-used after a few minutes the ink is picked up and absorbed into the next print. This method also returns the squeegee to the hinged end ready for the next print.

A more expensive but widely used method is to apply a special screen cleanser which can be obtained from screen material suppliers. It is available in aerosol containers and when sprayed onto a screen prevents the ink setting for any period up to about an hour. When the screen is used again a couple of pulls on the squeegee with some ink clears the screen. Some paper placed beneath the screen during the cleaning pulls keeps the area clean.

When a screen clogs and the cleaning spray is not available the screen must be washed with the thinners of the ink being used. This is effectively done by using a piece of saturated cloth in each hand and rubbing each side of the screen at one time. The screen must be free from all traces of spirit before printing recommences.

Cleaning screens
All surplus ink can be scraped up with a palette knife and replaced in

the container. Time spent on removing as much ink as possible by this method will make the remaining processes easier and less messy.

Without unhinging it a number of sheets of paper should be laid beneath the screen and the top thoroughly soaked with the inks solvent. A convenient method of applying the spirit is by squirting it from a plastic bottle with a restricted opening, similar to that used for washing up liquid. While it is wet with solvent the screen should be wiped with rags or absorbent paper to dissolve and absorb the ink. The process may need to be repeated two or three times until the screen is clean. The screen can then be raised up and the underside cleaned in the same way. Finally the fabric must be rubbed both sides with dry rag until a clear view is possible through the material.

Some inks require special thinners although the aerosol cleaners mentioned earlier can be used for all inks.

Many screen inks are reversible therefore if the same screen is to be used for two colours all traces of the first colour must be removed otherwise the second ink will dissolve the traces and change colour.

It is necessary to clean off the ink even if the stencil is to be removed because the methylated spirit or water required to soften the stencils will not penetrate the ink.

Twelve
Masking and Transfers

The fastest and most efficient method of producing a one off sign to a high standard of finish is by signwriting. Yet occasions do occur when the most practical method of producing a sign is to apply a low tack film, cut out the letter shapes from it, apply paint through the cut outs, and peel off the film to leave a finished sign.

It is a method used by persons whose cutting skill is better than their signwriting skill. This is a rare reason for masking because many types of signs and their situation make them very difficult to adapt for masking and cutting. The most important property of masking is that coatings can be used for the lettering which cannot be signwritten. Coatings such as cellulose paints, stoving enamels, vitreous enamels and some two pack polyurethane paints are of such a consistency or dry so rapidly that they can be spray applied only. It is a method also which can be more carefully controlled so that every job is precisely the same in shapes and finish. This applies where a company logo or livery has to be reproduced on a number of different signs or vehicles by various signworkers. Machine cut templates can be supplied which the sign contractors cut around and the client can be certain that a constant standard can be maintained.

Masking and cutting is a more expensive process than signwriting. The cost of the masking material must be added to the job and an expert cutter is rarely faster than an expert signwriter.

Many types of masking materials are used.

Lead Foil

This was probably the original material to be used for this purpose, but apart from its use by glass decorators it is rarely used in the sign industry now. It can be fixed with a thin film of petroleum jelly or soft soap or gelatine in the way described earlier. Ensuring a smooth film and making sure that the cut edges are rubbed down tight are the secrets of clean finishes. All traces of petroleum jelly must be removed with white spirit before any coating is applied. Soap and gelatine wash off more easily by a careful wipe with a damp wash leather usually removes all traces.

Lead foil can be applied without restriction to glass, metal and plastics. It can be applied to cellulose paints and stove enamelled surfaces providing care is taken not to cut through the paint system. With great care and using gelatine adhesive only foil can be used on hard, gloss painted surfaces.

Self Adhesive or Clinging Plastic Film

A great range of these is available, each of them having a lightly adhered backing paper which protects the tacky side until just before it is adhered. A few of them are marketed for the purpose of making signs but the bulk of them are made for other uses and have been adapted by many signmakers. Some are very tough with such a strong bond that they are not only difficult to remove but can pull off any dry coatings to which they have been applied. There are many that combine strength with low tack and these are ideal for signmaking. They are available as opaque films, as transparent films, or tinted films. The tinted types are easier to see when cutting, and the opaque ones can be marked out on.

Generally self adhesive films are expensive. They are not suitable for textured surfaces as they tend to bridge over peaks and paint penetrates through the gaps.

They can be used in two ways. The film can be applied to the surface, cut, sprayed and lifted, or the shapes can be cut out on a bench, applied individually to the surface, sprayed over and lifted, see figs 12.1–12.4.

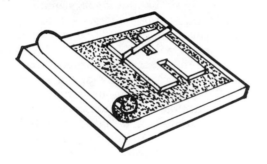

Fig. 12.1

Cutting a letter from self adhesive film using a board template

Fig. 12.2

Applying a self adhesive cut letter with a rag pad or squeegee

Fig. 12.3

Spraying over adhered letters

Fig. 12.4

Removing adhered letters after spraying

The first method can be used both as a negative (background removed to leave letters masking the surface) or as positive (the letters removed and the area round being masked). The second method invariably is used as negative.

The method of applying cut self adhesive letters is adopted by some airlines for painting the livery on aircraft. Cutting on the surface is not permitted because of the possibility that the aircraft fabric could be cut resulting in a dangerous weakness to the metal.

These films are effective only on clean and dry surfaces. They must be laid without creases. When applying large areas the film can be loosely wrapped around a cardboard roll and gradually unwrapped as the film is smoothed onto the surface to minimise the risk of creasing.

Some of the low tack films can be partially lifted as the painting is being carried out to inspect the finish and can be replaced again without affecting the seal.

Spray Coatings

These coatings were originally developed as sprayed plastic films for protecting components during shipment, or preserving equipment during long storage. They produced a tough waterproof film with very little adhesion so, when cut, they pulled off the surface cleanly and easily.

They are extensively used in the sign industry as a masking material. When the applied coating has dried to a tough film, letters or shapes can be cut from it and paint applied to the cut outs. Their greatest advantage over the adhesive films is their effectiveness on slightly textured surfaces. The fine relief surface of non-glare laminated plastics which are widely used for signs can be successfully masked with the sprayed coating.

Although advertised only as a spray coating it can be brushed on, but a thicker film is applied therefore it is less economical as a brush coating. When sprayed it can be applied with any suction, pressure or airless spray unit. With some suction feed guns the coating may need to be slightly thinned with water.

Surfaces to which the coating is to be applied should be clean and dry. Although the adhesion of the coating is not important, paint will eventually be applied through the cut outs and this will need a non-greasy surface for good adhesion. A damp surface may dilute the coating and make it too thin to be effective.

The effective film thickness is about 0.1 mm (100 μm) which is about four times thicker than a standard coat of paint. Manufacturers recommend application in one coat, but many signmakers prefer to apply two thin coats, allowing about two hours between coats for drying. This method reduces the risk of sagging.

The coating is water borne but not water soluble therefore once it is dry it cannot be dissolved in water. Spray guns should be washed out in water immediately after use otherwise they will need to be stripped down to remove the dry coating from the nozzle and material tubes. The dry film pulls off the gun quite easily but the stripping process is more time consuming than spraying water through the gun directly the job is completed.

Once applied the coating must be left until fully dry before cutting can start. It is specified as a two hour drying material but some signmakers prefer to leave it overnight because a better cutting film is produced after many hours. It is possible to mark out directly on the dry film using a wax pencil but the safest method is to transfer a full size drawing by chalking on the back and drawing over with a hard pencil or ball point pen as described in chapter 8.

There are many similarities between cutting hand cut screen stencils and sprayed coating. The type of knives used are similar and the technique of cutting the top film and not marking the substrate is an essential quality of the work. When the cutting is complete the shapes can be lifted and the exposed surface wiped over with a damp sponge or cloth. This final process is supposed to remove any static electricity which may develop when the plastic is peeled off.

If mistakes are made during cutting they can be repaired by sticking a piece of dry film over the error and recutting. The film will adhere to the surface without the need of any adhesive.

If cellulose paints or stoving enamels are used to spray through the cut film the paint can be left to dry completely before the film is lifted. Should oil paints be used the film should be peeled off as soon as the paint has set but before it has formed a skin. If left too long it is possible that the paint will not break cleanly at the edge of the film.

The sprayed coating mask can be applied to gloss painted or cellulose coated surfaces but great care must be taken when cutting not to sever the paint film and expose the substrate to corrosion. It is widely used on stove enamelled surfaces. The most common substrate upon which it is used is plastic, whether it is GRP, laminate sheets, or flat or vacuum formed acrylic. When used on clear or translucent plastics it is quite commonly applied to the back of the sign so that the exposed face of the sign retains the durable qualities of the plastic.

Transfers

Transfers can be small information signs of about 100 × 50 mm or they can be large enough to fill the side of a road tanker or large pantechnicon. As well as varying in size they are made from a variety of materials and are applied in many different ways.

The application of transfers has become a specialist job and one in which the small signmaker will rarely need to be involved.

Because of the variety of transfers available it is essential that the manufacturers instructions are carefully followed whenever a transfer job has to be done. The following are the most common types of transfers that are generally available. Most transfer manufacturers offer a technical service to potential customers and may design and devise a method of transfer that does not match any of these common forms.

Self adhesive vinyl transfers
These are often very large transfers which are used for vehicle sides.
They are pressed onto the surface after a protective backing film is
removed. Once applied the adhesive sets and the transfer cannot be
picked off. Some manufacturers guarantee their life for five years.

Self adhesive clear vinyl or polyester transfers
These are printed onto clear film and can be used on glass as well as
vehicle bodies or signs. The polyester films have a longer life.

Laminated vinyl transfers
These are printed onto vinyl, then laminated with a clear plastic by a
heat process. They are self adhesive usually, very tough and resistant
to chemicals, grease, solvents.

Solvent transfers
Tough, dry coatings which need to be treated with solvent before
applicaion. The solvent chemically bonds them to the coated sign or
vehicle. Once dry they are very tough and resistant films.

Waterslide transfers
A thin printed film fixed to a paper backing. When the backing is
soaked in water, the transfer can be slid from it onto the surface to
which it bonds.

Varnish adhered
Similar to waterslide, these are pressed to a previously applied coat of
varnish or gold size which has reached a sticky state. The backing
sheet is either peeled off or washed off when the varnish is completely
dry. Usually the transfer needs varnishing.

Thirteen

Cut Letters

The use of cut out letters for signs has been popular for many years. The letters have been cut from timber, plywood, hardboard, cork, and since the 1960s, acrylic sheet. They have been used on permanent signs both interior and exterior, as well as for less permanent signs such as those in exhibitions and on 'information' boards in public buildings. Most signmakers will be expected to make up signs from cut letters but very few signmakers purchase the equipment in order to cut the letters. There are many firms throughout the country who specialise in supplying cut letters in a great variety of styles, sizes and materials and signmakers generally find it cheaper to purchase the letters as they require them rather than purchase the rather expensive mechanical bandsaws, fretsaws or routers necessary to cut their own for what may prove to be a small percentage of their production.

As well as the capital outlay for power tools to cut letters there is also the problem of housing the machines and training personnel to use them efficiently and safely. Unless properly trained and qualified staff are available to use the equipment, small sign producers may find difficulty in obtaining comprehensive insurance to cover accidents to the machinery or to employees. It is a requirement of the Health and Safety at Work Act that such machinery must be installed, maintained and used in such a way that there are no hazards to the workers. If every precaution is not taken and an accident occurs the employer may be prosecuted.

The one area in which the small signmaker may purchase equipment is when cutting expanded polystyrene. Letters and logos cut from this extremely light foamed plastic are commonly used in exhibition and temporary displays in stores. The signmaker who works in these areas may find the comparatively low outlay to buy the cutters for this material to be a good investment. There is no danger in their use and the skill necessary to produce commercial standard shapes can be learnt reasonably quickly and without danger to the trainee. Although there are specialist firms who can supply expanded polystyrene letters to order, the production of a few specially designed letters or logos may be cut more quickly in the sign workshop particularly as speed is commonly the controlling factor for exhibition work.

Hot Wire Cutters

Expanded polystyrene is cut rapidly and accurately with a hot thin wire. Simple hand held tools which operate off a 2 V battery have been available as a childrens toy for many years and can be efficiently used for cutting an odd letter or logo. For more precise cutting, and production work, and cutting sheeting for any thickness up to 350 mm special hot wire cutting tables are available, see fig. 13.1. They are flat bed tables over which is suspended a metal arm. From the free end of the arm is stretched a thin wire attached to an electrical circuit. When the power is switched on the wire becomes hot and expanded polystyrene pushed against it melts along a fine controlled cut. Most of the cutters are thermostatically controlled so that the temperature of the wire can be set to suit the thickness or density of the sheeting to be cut.

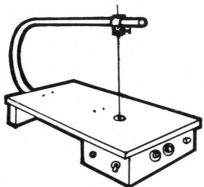

Fig. 13.1   A hot wire cutting table

Templates
Logos or letter shapes can be drawn directly onto the expanded polystyrene and fed freehand through the hot wire. Unless the operative is highly skilled or the job involves only a few odd letters or shapes this is not a very reliable method.

The most efficient method is to cut the letter shapes or logo from thin card first and use these templates as guides to run around the hot wire. Half or one millimetre thick card is most suitable and the drawing can be carried out directly on the card, using drawing instruments and any other aids to ensure that the final product is as perfect as possible. The card needs to be cut with care so that the edges are clean. A very sharp trimming knife, or scalpel, is best used for the cutting and a hard flat surface beneath, like glass, will ensure a more clean cut. If the edges feel slightly rough or fibrous they should be smoothed by rubbing with very fine glasspaper.

The template needs to be fixed to a piece of expanded polystyrene cut to a size about 30 mm wider and higher than the letter shape. A drawing pin pushed into each corner of the letter will hold it to the polystyrene, see fig. 13.2. If a number of the same shapes need to be cut the pieces can be fixed together by skewering them with long fine pins or fixing them along the edges with tape.

Cutting
The wire is the right temperature for cutting when it cuts cleanly with

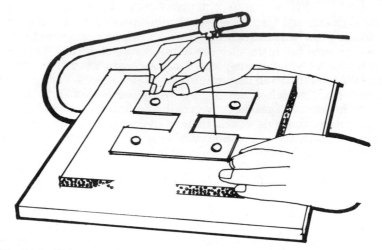

Fig. 13.2   Using a card template to cut a letter from expanded polystyrene

the minimum amount of pressure being placed behind the polystyrene. If a lot of pressure is required the wire is too cool and the excessive pressure may bend the wire resulting in an angled cut. If the wire is too hot it may melt the foam too rapidly leaving little indents along the cut when the movement of the foam has been slowed down. A few test runs on odd pieces of the material should be tried first to determine the right temperature.

When the wire is set the polystyrene is fed onto the wire until it reaches the templates, when it is directed along the edge (fig. 13.2). An edge must be cut in one movement and at a constant speed. If the polystyrene is stopped the wire melts the plastic either side of the cut resulting in an uneven line. If the pressure on the polystyrene is reduced the cut will be slightly corrugated. A too strong pressure will bend the wire and the return edge of the letter will slope.

When a corner is reached the cutter should be taken right through to the outside of the foam. The foam can then be turned and pushed in at right angles to the first cut. If the corner is turned it is unlikely that a true right angle will be achieved.

The letter or shape silhouette is cut first. Any inside shapes are carried out after. For example, if a capital letter O is being cut a disc is produced first by cutting around the outside circle. The wire is then cooled, unscrewed from the metal arm by loosening a butterfly screw, and pushed through the centre of the disc. When the wire is refixed and heated it can be pushed to the inside of the O template and directed around the shape to cut out the inside of the O.

The wire does not get red hot but it is hot enough to burn the fingers if touched while it is switched on. The wire cools in a few seconds.

With some cutters a straight edge and a circular cutting attachment are available. These can be most useful for more precise cutting when working on very large letters.

Setting Out and Fixing Cut Letters

The same degree of care is necessary when setting out cut letters as for any other form of signwork. Uneven, excessive or too small margins will spoil a sign made up with cut letters as much as they will influence a signwritten sign. Spacing, and space between words and lines must be carefully considered and adjusted until the most perfect arrangement is obtained.

Once the layout has been worked out letter height lines can be snapped in with a fine chalk line in the same manner described for signwriting. The letters can be carefully placed between the lines and moved backwards and forwards to obtain an even area of space between each letter. If the sign is *in situ* a small piece of double sided tape put on the back of each letter will hold them temporarily in place while adjustments are made. When the best arrangement is obtained a small vertical line should be placed to mark the left and right bottom extremes of each letter. This can be done with sharpened chalk or a wax pencil. This will ensure that the letters will go back in their exact position after they have been glued.

Fixing Letters

Timber, hardboard and cork letters
These can be pinned providing the sign is of a soft material. Pins are acceptable as a fixing for temporary signs only, such as on exhibitions. Usually the pin heads need to be touched up with paint to camouflage them.

For permanent signs, or fixing to hard surfaces, letters should be glued. A woodworking glue based on pva is one of the easiest to use and is most permanent. The glue can be obtained in small plastic containers with a long nozzle which allows a thin line of glue to be squeezed about 3 mm in all around the back of the letter. When put in position and pressure applied the glue should squeeze up to, but not beyond, the edge of the letter. The pva glue is milky white and water soluble when wet but sets to a clear film which is insoluble in water. It sets slowly so if used for fixing on signs *in situ* the letters may need to be pinned to hold them in position until the glue is hard. If the pins are not stuck right in they can be pulled out when the glue has set.

When fixing letters *in situ* where pins cannot be used because the background is not soft or the appearance of pins is unacceptable an impact adhesive can be used. This is a quick setting glue which holds to the surface immediately it is pressed in position. Many impact glues require both surfaces to be coated which makes them suitable for adhering small letters. Most of the double coated glues and some of the others are based on petroleum spirit which may soften paint and some plastics. These properties must be carefully checked before the glues are used or specified.

Expanded polystyrene letters
This material is dissolved by solvents and must not be adhered with solvent based adhesives. They must not be painted with solvent borne

paints for the same reason. Only emulsion paints are safe. The adhesive must be a water soluble one and the most effective is one based on pva. There are many types available made especially for adhering expanded polystyrene and they are usually thickened so that a good film can be applied to the letters to fill in the texture of the foam.

When being used *in situ* pins through the letters are essential to hold them in position while the glue sets. Expanded polystyrene letters are used for internal signs only and it is very rare that the signboard will be any other material than hardboard or timber. Very long thin pins should be used so that at least 10 mm will project in front of the letter which can be gripped with pliers and pulled out when the glue has set. Because of the spongey nature of expanded polystyrene the holes will not be noticeable once the pins have been removed.

If any glue does squeeze out during fixing it should be wiped off immediately with a damp cloth. It will not be soluble when dry.

Acrylic letters
Invariably these are fixed to acrylic signs and manufacturers of the acrylic sheet supply special adhesives for permanent fixing.

The glues are of many types and it is essential to read the technical information sheets supplied by the manufacturers before purchasing them. Some are single pack glues which are more convenient and less wasteful than the more common two pack glues. The two packs need to be mixed together just before use and if not used within a certain period harden to a non-reversible mass. Most of the glues are air setting but there are some which require heat or ultra-violet light to set them.

Whatever type of adhesive is selected the most convenient method of fixing is to apply a film to the back of the letter with a soft brush and press the letter onto the plastic sign. Once the adhesive touches the plastic it will be softened and become marked. If the letter is not in the exact position first time sufficient damage may have been caused to spoil the entire sign. When the adhesive has set the letters cannot be moved without severely damaging the substrate.

Strong solvents are commonly used for adhering acrylic letters although it is not recommended by the manufacturers. The solvents soften the plastic just sufficiently for the letters and the background to bond together. Solvents which are strong enough to do this are chloroform, dichloroethane, trichlorethylene, carbon tetrachloride, and dichloromethane. They are applied to the back of the letter with a soft brush and pushed onto the sign.

All these solvents present hazards to the user. All are highly volatile and the vapours can be obnoxious and anaesthetic, particularly chloroform. Although not flammable if the vapours are burnt by a naked flame they convert to a gas which can cause unconsciousness. There is evidence that some of these solvents may cause cancer. Advice from the manufacturers of the solvents should be obtained before any of them are used.

If gaps occur around the letters where they meet the background they can be filled by squirting adhesive or solvent from a hypodermic needle along the gap. Some fixers use this method to adhere the letters. Thin nozzle bottles similar to those used for woodworking pva glues can be used instead of a hypodermic needle but considerable care must be taken because if the letter should move only slightly as it is being held by one hand and squirted with the other the whole sign could be ruined.

Fourteen
Costing

A signmaker may obtain a contract or a commission in one of three ways.

(1) By direct contact with the client either by telephone, letter or personal visit.

These are usually small jobs and the method used by old customers or persons recommended by old customers. This method can represent the bulk of many small sign firms work. This type of transaction is usually informal and is based on mutual trust. Although occasionally the client may produce a very precise description of the sort of sign he will want, generally the instructions are very vague and the signmaker may be expected to suggest materials, sizes, layouts and even the text.

(2) Through a client's agent.

The agent may be an architect, a graphic designer, an advertising agency, or the contract's department of a local authority or government department. Larger jobs usually develop from this sort of contact but small, one-off signs can come through an agency. The liaison will be more formal and most often the work will be up for tender. This means that three or four signmakers will have been asked to submit their price for the job. It is very rare for local authorities or government offices to place a contract with any firm without first comparing estimates. Work through a clients agent invariably will be fully documented. There will be specifications describing the materials to be used for and on the signs and how they are to be fixed. Probably scale drawings or artwork will be provided also so that the signmakers job is to interpret the instruction precisely.

(3) From a main contractor.

This may be a builder who has to arrange for signs for a new or renovated building; or a signmaking company who does not employ specialist signwriters or printers or glass decorators; or a vehicle retailer or finisher who does not employ signwriters or liners; or a glazing contractor. This source of work will produce a variety of jobs, from a small one off sign to a sign system for a building or corporate identity scheme for a fleet of vans. The instructions can be equally varied. They may be a brief phone call asking for a sign to be completed the following morning or they can be detailed drawings and specification similar to that supplied by a client's agent.

The one common factor in all these forms of commissions is that the person requesting the work will want to know how much it will cost. The accuracy in preparing an estimate or quotation must be equal to that exercised when signwriting or printing. Inaccurate costing leads quickly to bankruptcy.

Equal care must be taken to price a simple one-off sign for a regular customer as for the big contract. The former may not be a competitive price but if it is too low the signmaker will loose money and if it is too high the customer may place his work elsewhere. Most work coming via an agent, and a large percentage of the subcontract work, will be competitive and the tendered price will be compared with quotations from other firms.

Accurate costing
The essence of accurate costing is careful consideration of all aspects of the job. Stating a price without seeing the site or reading the drawing or specification can cause considerable embarrassment when the cost is calculated at completion. Although a verbal estimate is not binding any considerable deviation from the original stated price may cause the signmaker to lose credibility and a good relationship with the client. It is good practice, even with the oldest customers, to note all the details of a proposed sign and either telephone or write an estimate when the entire job has been carefully considered.

Pricing by letter height
A number of standard books on pricing for building work are published annually. In each of them a small section is devoted to pricing for signwriting. Their purpose is to give guidance to builders estimators on how much to allow for minimal signwriting work which may be required on the construction or renovation of a building. The information published on signwriting costs are of very little value to the signwriter who is required to submit a firm price.

All the books base their prices on the number of letters which need to be signwritten. Some of them show extra costs for second coating, shading, outlining and gilding. They quote a figure in pence for each 25 mm height of letter. For example, if a figure of 60p is quoted for a 25 mm high letter, then 50 mm high letters would cost £1.20 each and 100 mm letters £2.40 each.

This is a very convenient method of pricing and sufficiently accurate for building estimators and quantity surveyors working on large contracts. It is a hopelessly inaccurate method for signwriters to use.

The letter height and number system assumes that all letters take the same time to paint and that 50 mm high letters take twice as long to paint as 25 mm letters. It also assumes that signwriting 100 mm high letters on a 3 m high fascia in a busy street will take no longer than the same height letters on a signboard in the workshop. If a sign estimator makes the same assumptions the price will be hopelessly wrong in most cases.

A slab serif letter will take longer to paint, draw or cut than a simple sans serif letter and this must be reflected in the cost. Some signwriters and stencil cutters specialise in small letters such as 25 mm or below, but most signmakers prefer and work faster when producing letters in excess of 50 mm high.

The time taken to erect, move and adjust to working on a scaffold can be as long as it takes to signwrite a sign in a comfortable workshop. These points must be understood by a sign estimator and carefully considered when preparing a price for a customer.

A Method of Costing

An accurate price is the result of careful calculation of at least three considerations:

(1)   The number of hours required to complete the job.
(2)   The cost of the materials.
(3)   The level of profit required.

Number of Hours

A job starts directly the order arrives from the client. Calculating hours must be based on the average time taken to complete each process. The processes must include negotiating with client, drawings, actual production time, delivery and site fixing where necessary. To these must be added time and costs involved in travelling to and from the site, as well as other non-productive time, such as delays on site caused by bad weather or difficult access; waiting for materials to set between processes; meal breaks; and other contingencies which cannot be anticipated but experience teaches a signmaker to expect.

When an estimated number of hours has been obtained the labour costs can be calculated. Calculating the hourly rate is critical.

Some estimators use an hourly rate that is the actual cost involved in employing a person, i.e. the amount paid to the signmaker plus the statutory payments for national insurance, redundancy and the various other schemes to which employers must subscribe. To this they add a percentage to cover overheads. These are the costs necessary to maintain the firm and supply equipment. Another method is to calculate the comprehensive hourly rate which includes wages, insurances and overheads. Both methods require very careful original consideration. The second method is often the simplest method to apply.

Every signmaker will have different commitments and no standard figure can be stated which will suit every situation. The following method of calculating a comprehensive hourly cost can be used by a one man business, and can be adapted to satisfy the slightly different requirements of other small firms.

Length of a working year
Possible number of hours to work   52 weeks at   2080 hrs
                                          40 hours
                                          per week

Less:
Number of non-working hours:

Holidays	5 × 40 hrs	200
Slack periods	4 × 40 hrs	160
Maintenance of equipment and workshop	20 hrs	20
		380

Working year expectation: 1700 hours

When this figure is divided into the salary which a signmaker considers necessary to maintain a living standard the actual wage rate per hour will be obtained, e.g. if £15 000 is considered to be a minimum annual salary the rate needed to be earned each hour is 15 000/1700 = £8.82.

To this must be added the following costs. These are sometimes referred to as overheads or establishment costs and can vary considerably from firm to firm and from individual to individual.

(1) Rent of workshop

(2) Rates to local authority

(3) Insurances:
       National Health and other statutory payments
       Public liability, to protect against damage to client's property or members of the public
       Personal security, in case of accident which prevents the signmaker working
       Fire
       Transport, either van or car used for business purposes

(4) Public utilities:
       Cost of heating and lighting
       Water rates

(5) Transport:
       Van or business car cost. The actual purchase price is not used for this purpose but the difference between the original cost and its present market value. This is called depreciation and is usually spread over three years.
       Maintenance of business vehicle
       Garaging where necessary
       Road tax
       Petrol may be added to individual jobs and included in travelling costs. If total petrol costs are spread over all jobs it could make the cost of local jobs too high

(6) Administration
       Stationery, i.e. paper, envelopes, ledgers, order books
       Printing, of paper and business cards
       Postage
       Telephone: a half yearly bill including rental and call charges

gives a reliable figure to use

Office equipment may only be a typewriter but filing cabinets, furniture and answering machine may be used and the depreciation of them over a three year period must be considered

Typing services

Advertising

(7) Bank:

Interest on loan or overdraft

Account charges

(8) Equipment:

Brushes are consumable and the full annual cost should be considered

Tools: mechanical tools will have a depreciation value but hand tools can be calculated as an annual outlay

Scaffold: like other equipment with a high capital investment a depreciation over three years is usually considered. If scaffold is hired, this cost will be added to the respective accounts

The annual cost for each of the above items needs to be calculated and a grand total obtained. When this is divided by the expected annual working hours (i.e. 1700) the figure produced must be earned every hour to pay for the establishment costs. This figure added to the earlier calculated labour cost will produce the actual hourly rate which needs to be charged to each job, e.g. if the total cost of the above items is £6000 then the amount required to be earned every hour will be 6000/1700 = £3.52. For this hypothetical signmaker the hourly rate which must be charged against every job will be £8.82 plus £3.52 = £12.34.

Cost of Materials

Costing of the materials required for each job is also a precise art. Unless all materials are included in an estimate their total cost over a year will reduce the profits earned.

The various costs to be considered are:

Cost of materials
Basing prices on charges made for earlier jobs can be most inaccurate. Current prices must be obtained from suppliers.

Cost to make a sign if subcontractors are used
A firm price from the sub-contractor is essential.

Cost of preparatory materials and paints
It is essential to itemise each process and to calculate the amount of materials precisely. For example, to prepare and paint a new timber sign 1.5 × 1.0 m the following materials are required:

Dry abrading — 4 sheets Garnett paper
Paint — total area of both sides of sign is 3 m² and the average

spreading rate of all coatings is 12 m^2 per litre
Primer: one coat = 0.25 litres
Undercoat: two coats = 0.5 litres
Gloss paint: two coats = 0.5 litres
Sundries: knotting, stopper and white spirit for cleaning brushes.

Cost of sign materials
The biggst costs for signwriting will be for gilding. For screen printing and glass decoration the cost of materials for completing the sign can be very high and needs to be calculated with considerable care.

Cost of fixing materials
When the signmaker is responsible for fixing the sign it is essential that the current cost of the materials required to attach the sign are obtained from the suppliers. Standard wall plugs are inexpensive but special fixings made from stainless steel or brass can be very expensive.

Profit Level

Whereas hourly rates and material costs can be calculated precisely, the level of profit to be added to an estimate has no such mathematical basis.

The profit level has two aspects. First, it is the return that a businessman wants for accepting the risks in signmaking. It can be the cost of the extra work involved in providing good customer relationships. These are the extra hours which cannot be costed and the intrusion into leisure time which most small businessmen accept. Secondly, it is the amount of money which must be invested in the firm to maintain standards or to expand. Although allowances are made for the depreciation on essential equipment money must be available when they need to be renewed or better models obtained. These costs are generally paid out of money charged under profits.

The simplest way to apply a profit level is by a percentage of the total hourly cost. This may vary from a nominal 10% with small firms to many hundreds percent for large companies.

Presenting a Quotation

When an estimate or quotation is sent to a client it is usual to state the final figure only. The detailed breakdown necessary to arrive at that figure is for the benefit of the estimator, and is not shown to the client. Sometimes a breakdown of the price is requested in which case a simplified version of the estimator's calculation may be sent. This may divide the work into: cost of supplying and finishing; cost of signwork; and cost of fixing. The three totals produce the estimated price.

A client will need to know what he is being offered for the submitted price. If drawings and/or specifications have been provided by the client it is necessary only to state that the quoted figure is for carrying out the work precisely to the client's instructions. When no precise instructions have been supplied it is necessary to explain quite clearly what the client can expect for the quoted price. Not only does this avoid unpleasantness or disagreements during or after the job, it also impresses the client with the professional and businesslike manner of the signmaker.

The usual method of describing the signs for which the price is quoted is by a specification and/or drawing.

Specification

This is a verbal description of the job. It is not a statement of how the signmaker will do the job, but a brief description of what will be done. It will name the material from which the signs will be made, and state the coating system which will be applied. It may state the style of letters to be used but this is more clearly shown on a drawing. The specification will state the method of producing the lettering or logo, i.e. by signwriting, or acid etching, or screenprinting. It will also describe the type of fixing which will be used.

A specification does not have to be a long document but it must be precisely worded.

Example specification
Proposed signboard for Hamwest Crafts

Sign   1.5 m × 1.0 m × 24 mm WBP standard plywood flush framed with 10 mm beech, pinned and glued with pva adhesive. Dry abraded and filled to smooth level surface. Front, back and edges:
1 coat leadless oil based wood primer
2 coats white oil based undercoat
2 coats white alkyd gloss finish.

Signwriting All letters to be Helvetica capitals and lower case, signwritten in azure blue enamel.

Fixing   4 brass keyhole plates recessed in back of sign. Fitted to 4 × No. 12 40 mm brass round head screws, fixed in wall by resin fibre wall plugs.

Drawings

Drawings show graphically what the finished job will look like and are more easily understood by most clients. Where drawings are submitted the specification can be written on them so that the detail can be related directly to the graphic reproduction and cuts the need for two documents.

The degree of detail put into a drawing will be influenced by the size of the job, the type of client, and the degree of competition. The one-off 'No Parking' sign to go outside the local doctor's house would not merit a specification or drawing, but the large information sign to be erected in the entrance to the new health clinic would need all the back up possible to impress the client sufficiently to obtain the contract.

Drawings may be prepared in one of three forms.

(1) Detailed scaled drawing showing the elevation of the sign which will include the layout and letter style. If it is for a new sign a section drawing will be provided showing the method of constructing the sign and the method by which it will be fixed. Although it is not often that signmakers will need to produce such a drawing they will receive drawings of this accuracy and detail from architects, local authorities and designers. Upon these they will have to prepare an estimate therefore it is essential that signmakers are familiar with this sort of presentation.

(2) Scale drawing of sign elevation only, showing layout and lettering style. It may show colours also. When a typeface is specified these drawings can be prepared by using dry transfer letters (see chapter 11). For convenience the size of the dry transfer letters available may determine the scale to which the drawing will be made and often it will not be one of the standard scales. Even so it is important that the sign is drawn to correct proportions. If great care is taken to prepare these drawings they can be enlarged by projection when a working drawing is required. Colour for these drawings can be supplied by coloured paper, poster colour or felt pens.

(3) Proportional sketches which show the shape of the sign accurately but not drawn to a scale. Their principal use is to show the layout and it is a method commonly used by signmakers. Notes and specification can be included and the use of coloured felt pens can produce very effective and clearly understood drawings. If the signs are to be fixed to an existing building it can be of considerable help to the client if a Polaroid picture of the building is submitted also with the position and size of the new signs sketched in with felt pens. If specifications or drawings are sent to clients it is a worthwhile precaution to keep photocopies in case a dispute should occur later.

Fifteen
Specialist Suppliers

If any of the specialist materials or equipment mentioned in this book cannot be obtained locally the following suppliers and/or manufacturers may be able to offer assistance.

E. PLOTON (SUNDRIES) LTD 273 Archway Road London N6 5AA	Gold and metallic leaf Metallic powders Gilders tools Gold size and gelatine capsules Signwriters brushes Signwriters equipment Tallow, beeswax, gum arabic
A.S. HANDOVER LTD Angel Yard Highgate High Street London N6 5JU	Signwriters brushes (full range)
GEORGE M. WHILEY LTD The Runway Station Approach South Ruislip Middlesex	Gold and metallic leaf Metallic powders Gilders tools Gold size Signwriters brushes and equipment
W. HABBERLEY MEADOWS LTD 5 Saxon Way Chelmsley Wood Birmingham B37 5AY	Gold leaf
JOHN T. KEEP & SONS LTD 15 Theobalds Road London WC1X 8SN	Gold leaf Metallic powders Gilders tools Gold size and gelatine capsules Signwriters brushes and equipment Signwriters colours and enamels Screen inks and equipment Brunswick black

WILLIAM WRIGHT & SONS LTD Grove Avenue Lymm Cheshire WA13 0HG	Signwriters brushes and equipment Gold size Gilders equipment Signwriters colours
GEORGE JOHNSON & CO (BIRMINGHAM) LTD Highlands Road Shirley Solihull West Midlands B90 4LP	Lead foil
DURHAM CHEMICAL DISTRIBUTORS (Wormesley Boome Division) Star Chemical Works Dovers Corner Rainham Essex	Hydrofluoric acid
E.T. MARLER LTD Deer Park Road London SW19 3UE	Screen printing equipment Screen inks
SERICOL GROUP LTD 24 Parsons Green Lane London SW6 4HS	Screen printing equipment Screen inks
SPRAYLAT LTD 7 High Street Ewell Surrey	Sprayed plastic film for masking
3M UNITED KINGDOM LTD 3M House Bracknell Berkshire RG12 1JU (Decorative Products Group)	Self adhesive masking film
EAGLE TRANSFER LTD Queens House Holly Road Twickenham Middlesex TW1 4EH	All types of transfers
A AND M CRAFT TOOLS 10 Wendell Road London W12 9RT	Hot wire cutters

GEORGE ELLIOTT & SONS LTD
Ajax House
Hertford Road
Barking
Essex LG11 8BA

Episcopes and graphic projectors

A. LUDWIG & SONS LTD
71 Parkway
London NW1 7QJ

Graphic projectors

JOSEPH MASON & CO LTD
Nottingham Road
Derby DE2 6AR

Signwriters enamels

Index